Indian Philosophy Today

Indian Philosophy Today

Edited by

N. K. DEVARAJA

First published 1975 *by*

THE MACMILLAN COMPANY OF INDIA LIMITED
Delhi   Bombay   Calcutta   Madras
Associated companies throughout the world.

SBN: 33390   085 5

Published by S. G. Wasani for The Macmillan Company of India
Limited and printed at Prabhat Press, Meerut.

Contents

Preface

This book is a collection of papers by scholars actively engaged in the pursuit and promotion of philosophy as teachers and researchers in various centres of learning in the Indian subcontinent. The volume may claim to be fairly representative of philosophical thinking in contemporary India. The editor would have been happy to include contributions by some more scholars, but, while a few eminent scholars expressed their inability to write papers for the volume, others were not approached for want of space.

India is a big country inhabited by the descendants of several racial stocks and by followers of several religions: it also has a long cultural history. It has only recently liberated itself from the political domination of a European power, whose cultural influence continues to be significant in its life. As a consequence of all these factors, Indian philosophy today does not represent any uniform mode of thought. The essays collected here reflect the many and varied influences—e.g., those of classical Indian philosophy, Anglo-American analytical and linguistic philosophy, and the phenomenological and existential philosophies of Germany and France—that shape the thinking of contemporary Indian philosophers.

The contributors were requested to discuss an aspect of philosophy that was of central concern to them, prefacing it, if possible, with remarks on philosophy and its method, the factors responsible for disagreement in philosophy, and the like. No restrictions as to problems and modes of approach were, of course, stipulated.

I undertook to edit this volume on behalf of the Centre of Advanced Study in Philosophy, Banaras Hindu University, in September 1972, at the behest of Dr. K.L. Shrimali, the scholarly and energetic Vice-Chancellor of the University who was also the Chairman of the Advisory Committee of the Centre. Shortly after, I was awarded a National Fellowship by the University Grants Commission which meant that I became involved with my own research project. However, invitations were issued to scholars to contribute to this volume towards the close of the year 1972. It took about a year-and-a-half to collect and edit the papers and another six months to settle terms with the publisher.

It is my pleasant duty to record my grateful thanks to the scholars who have contributed to this volume. My thanks are also due to Dr. K.L. Shrimali and the members of the Advisory Committee of the Centre functioning in 1972, who accepted my suggestion to bring out a volume of essays in contemporary Indian philosophy; to Professor Rajendra Prasad, one of the contributors to this volume, who suggested the title given to it; to Professor R.K. Tripathi, until recently Head of the Department of Philosophy, Banaras Hindu University; and Professor N.S.S. Raman, present Head of the Department, who were helpful in many ways in the preparation of the manuscript of the volume. I owe special thanks to Sri R.K. Tripathi, former U.G.C. Fellow at the Centre and now Lecturer in Kashi-Vidyapitha, Varanasi, who shared with me the burden of correspondence with the contributors in the earlier stages.

Varanasi   **N.K. Devaraja**
7 August 1975

Introduction

Indian philosophy today stands at the cross-roads of several traditions. Before independence, the best of Indian scholars were concerned with recovering and reinterpreting our past heritage, especially rich in religio-metaphysical thought, with a view, on the one hand, to inspire cultural self-confidence in the nation, and, on the other, mainly through reinterpretation, to imbue people with value attitudes compatible with the requirements of the modern age. The earlier spokesmen of the cultural awakening experienced by the Indian people during the nineteenth century— e.g., Rammohun Roy (1772–1833), Dayananda Saraswati (1824–1883), Sri Ramakrishna Parmahamsa (1836–1886) and Swami Vivekananda (1863–1902)—were all religious leaders. The tradition of reinterpretation started by them was later on continued by such illustrious personages as Bal Gangadhar Tilak (1856–1920), Rabindranath Tagore (1861–1941), Mahatma Gandhi (1869–1948) and Sri Aurobindo (1872–1950). It is noteworthy that the attainment of cultural self-confidence by the Indian people, particularly the Hindus, was due, to no mean extent, to the work of Western orientalists—German, British and French—who devoted their lives to the study and appreciative interpretation of the classics of Hindu religion and philosophy.

While Vivekananda, the foremost Indian interpreter of the Advaita Vedānta in the nineteenth century, lauded its merits as a religion, Western scholars like Max Müller and Paul Deussen stressed its significance as a system of metaphysics. It was also observed that the Vedānta of Śaṅkara had affinities with the world-view of the great German idealist, Immanuel Kant; later on it was discovered (or thought) that the Advaitic *Brahman* greatly resembled Bradley's Absolute. The vogue enjoyed by the German idealists and the neo-Hegelians in Europe during the last two decades of the nineteenth and the first two decades of the twentieth centuries greatly contributed to the prestige of the Advaita Vedānta which, thanks to the several influential writings of S. Radhakrishan —and, earlier, of Vivekananda—came to be looked upon as the representative system of Indian or Hindu thought. Gradually, however, and simultaneously with the decline of the idealistic modes of thought particularly in Great Britain, stress began to be laid on other traditions in Indian philosophical thought, e.g., the realistic systems of Nyāya-Vaiśeṣika and the Jainas, and the Great Buddhist Schools. In 1930, Th. Stcherbatsky published his monumental work on *Buddhist Logic*. The older and new works on Nyāya metaphysics and logic were also discovered. In the meanwhile, the comprehensive histories of Indian philosophy produced by S. Radhakrishnan and S.N. Dasgupta had done much to acquaint the scholarly world with the tremendous variety and range of ancient and medieval Indian philosophy.

II

In the history of thought two types of problems have exercised the minds of philosophers—those relating to nature, possibility, limits and validity of knowledge, and those concerning the conception of good or ideal life and the destiny of man. Indian philosophy is rich in the discussion of both these types of problems. In particular, philosophy and religion have been closely associated in India and we find a larger variety of conceptions in the field of religious philosophy or philosophy of religion here than perhaps in any other cultural tradition. This circumstance also accounts for the fact that philosophy in India never found it necessary to estrange or alienate itself from religion. In India, religion cheerfully accepted the guidance of philosophy. The cultural history of India does not record any instance of the burning alive of a philosopher like Bruno or the imprisonment of a heretic thinker or scientist like Galileo at the behest of a religious authority. Compared to the followers of Christianity or Islam, the Hindu mind has been much too metaphysical; it has, in fact, been as passionately attached to philosophy as to religion. If anything, the passion for religion in India has tended to strengthen the passion for philosophy under the conviction that the religious goal can be achieved only through knowledge born of deep metaphysical reflection. It is only recently that some of our younger scholars and philosophers, under the influence of Anglo-American analytical philosophy, have been pleading for a divorce between philosophy and religion.

Apart from having produced apologetic interpretations of the Christian tradition, Western thought does not seem to have made important gains in the field of religious philosophy during the last few centuries. This has led to the growth of scepticism and indifference in respect of religion on the one hand and to the feeling of increasing fascination for Eastern religions on the other. On the contrary, ever since the emergence of modern astronomy and physical science, Western philosophy has suffered a veritable revolution in the related fields of epistemology and logic. The varied and complex methodological problems raised and discussed in the fields of philosophy of science, philosophy of history, etc., have no worthy parallels in the histories of ancient and medieval philosophy either in India, Greece, China or in Western Europe.

III

Three traditions dominate the thinking of modern Indian philosophers: the classical Indian, including the new logic of the post-medieval Nyāya School, the Anglo-American analytical and linguistic philosophy, and the phenomenological and existential currents of thought prevailing mainly in Germany and France. So far as academic philosophers are concerned there does not appear to be any marked influence of Marxist philosophy on them. Standing at the confluence of these divergent currents of thought modern Indian philosophy seems to be struggling to attain a new identity.

It has been remarked, not without justification, by several observers that contemporary Indian thought, even after a quarter century of independence, suffers from a 'colonial' mentality with respect to Western thought or thinkers. Considering that the Western nations dominate the globe in economic and political fields, having as they do almost a monopoly of higher scientific knowledge, considering also their achievements and contributions to the human sciences, in political thought and organisation, even in art and literature, it is but natural that they should come to be looked upon as arbiters of taste and objects of emulation by dis-

discerning intellectuals the world over. Yet, there are other factors, economic and cultural, responsible for this state of affairs.

Intellectual work of the highest kind can flourish only in an environment where a sense of participation in a common endeavour prevails, and where both intelligent criticism and just appreciation are readily available. An intellectual worker not only expects due recognition from the experts in the field or appreciation from his peers, but also the assurance of intelligent fellow-citizens as to the importance and usefulness of his work. It is not an accident that a large number of logicians and philosophers of method in the West today are engaged in an intensive study and examination of the physical sciences; the propensity has a direct relation to the dominant role that the modern West assigns to those (and other) sciences. Comparative neglect of normative ethics, aesthetics, and philosophy of religion by the better known philosophers of the West is indicative of the same phenomenon. In general, philosophy (as conceived by the present writer) tends to occupy itself with the forms of cultural consciousness that are more conspicuously cherished by people. The Indian people today, being much too preoccupied with economic and political matters, are not, as a nation, cultivating any special form of cultural consciousness. Lured by the new craze for (or ideal of) better standards of living, they are becoming either indifferent to the claims of religion (and even morality) or they practise religion and morality as a matter of habit and routine, paying but little attention to the conflicting demands of tradition and modernity. Both science and democracy being commodities imported from the West, they have not yet succeeded in making our philosophers seriously involve themselves in their meaning and progress. Many a philosopher in India, like intellectuals in other fields no less than political leaders and people at large, continues to believe in both caste and democracy and to behave accordingly.

There can be no effective philosophising, either by an individual or by a people, without passionate involvement in some form of cultural life or the other, for philosophy is nothing but the inner, critical awareness of such life. Ancient and medieval Indians produced a variety of religious philosophies because they were passionately attached to religious values; and they created several significant systems of logic and epistemology because they considered valid knowledge to be of paramount importance for the attainment of the religious goal. Likewise, the dominance of the Christian world-view accounts for the special character of medieval European philosophy, even as the dominance of the scientific *zeitgeist* accounts for the special emphases in modern European thought. In addition, European thought from the Greeks onwards has been greatly interested in the freedom of the individual and the nature and form of the ideal state, which accounts for some of its impressive achievements in moral and political thought.

Viewed in this light the dominance of a particular style of philosophy among a people at a particular period in history reflects their important cultural concerns. This leads us to make another observation. The philosophical activity that evokes enthusiastic response in a people should have as its vehicle the language of the people themselves. Due partly to the lack of adequate demand for new types of philosophising in the regional languages, scholars of philosophy have been writing mostly in English. However, neither the professional philosophers nor the intelligentsia in the English-speaking countries have enough time or inclination to take detailed notice of what our scholars have been doing in different fields. At best they can extend a modicum of encouragement by publishing in their professional journals papers written by some of our scholars—provided that those papers are more or less in line with the philosophical activity being carried on in those journals. Occasionally, a reputed Western scholar or thinker may help an Indian writer by contributing a Foreword to, or by making a favourable comment upon, a work produced by the former. A Western university may also invite a scholar or two for a teaching assignment, or for delivering a talk or two. In general, Western universities and audiences are more interested in knowing about our classical heritage in philosophy and religion —Yoga, Vedānta and Buddhism for example—than in finding out about our present-day thinking. Only very recently, largely for political reasons, the governments in Europe and America have started evincing interest in modern Indian literature. One reason for this is that the better known and more influential writers of literature generally tend to use the several regional languages as the vehicles of self-expression. As for scientific and philosophical writing the absence of a well-developed national language which could constitute itself into a common medium for scholars and thinkers all over the counrty, is another factor hampering the progress of truly original thought. Taken singly, the regional languages do not have enough resources to foster and sustain such thought in the various scientific and philosophical disciplines.

In the present century, regional languages have been largely the vehicles of literary expression. Several of these have by now built up respectable traditions in creative literary writing comprising poetry, fiction and criticism. So far as philosophy is concerned while the post-Independence scholars and writers have, on the whole, been inclined to discard and go beyond the neo-Vedāntism that had been popular during the pre-War decades, they have not yet succeeded in creating or even consciously initiating a new tradition both Indian and modern at the same time. However, the awareness that our country needs new types of philosophy or new ways of philosophising is one important factor uniting the countributors to this volume.

IV

The essays collected here may be grouped in different ways, depending on the standpoint from which their contents are viewed. Most of the contributors have a measure of acquaintance with the indigenous philosophical tradition, almost all are familiar with the major trends in modern Western thought. They differ, of course, in the extent of their familiarity with one or other tradition, and the degree of sympathy they are able to extend to them taken severally. The essays may also be viewed as falling, in terms of their divergent approaches, styles and sympathies, predominantly within one or other of the three traditions mentioned earlier. I say 'predominantly' for, while a Sartre or a Gilbert Ryle may belong exclusively to one or other self-sufficient tradition in modern thought, the same can scarcely be true of an Indian scholar who is exposed to several traditions including his own. With this reservation it may be asserted that a scholar belongs mainly to the tradition wherein he tends to find his problems and his data.

The adoption of these criteria may enable us to roughly identify the contexts of at least some of our contributors. Thus Professors Sibajiban Bhattacharya and R.K. Tripathi, with their preoccupation with the problems of suffering and liberation, clearly belong to the indigenous tradition. Their vigorous restatement of the traditional problems serves to bring out, in a contagious manner, the significance and relevance of the tremendous issues involved and the proposed solutions. Stressing the importance of the teacher (*guru*) and revelation (*śruti*) Professor Tripathi retraces the steps by which ancient Indian philosophers were led to discover the essence of the Self. After examining several views of philosophy Professor S. Bhattacharya concludes that philosophy involves change in our consciousness or transformation of personality. After a penetrating analysis of two Indian theories, those of Nyāya and Advaita Vedānta, Professor Bhattacharya suggests his own view of self and the technique of self-realisation. Professors S.S. Barlingay, Kalidas Bhattacharya, G. Misra, Rajendra Prasad and R.R. Verma belong predominantly to the analytic tradition. Likewise Professors J.N. Mohanty and Ramakant Sinari seem to have leanings towards the existential approach which, in some respects, is nearer to our own tradition than the value-divorced analytical or linguistic approach to philosophical questions. An existential and religious orientation of thought is, indeed, discernible in almost all the scholars excepting those placed in the second group. While the religious motive dominates the thought of Professor Santosh Sengupta, Professor C.T.K. Chari, with his encyclopaedic range of information, dwells on the culture-bound character of man's entire thinking.

V

In the invitation issued to the contributors to this volume it had been stated that they could, if they so desired, preface their papers with remarks on their individual conceptions of philosophy and its method. Many years before, an important Indian philosopher, Prof. K.C. Bhattacharya, wrote: 'An explication of the concept of philosophy appears to me more important than the discussion of any specific problem of philosophy.'* Professor Bhattacharya considered the issue important because 'the possibility of philosophy as a body of knowledge distinct from science' was being called in question in those days. An additional and equally important reason why we should have a clearer conception of the nature and method of philosophy is that one's conception of philosophy tends to define both the nature of philosophical problems and the structure of philosophical arguments. Also, before one starts philosophising in right earnest, one should seek to arrive at some understanding of the phenomenon of chronic disagreement among philosophers and philosophical traditions, ancient and modern. One should also consider how to make sense of the radically divergent styles of philosophical thinking adopted by different individuals, ages and cultures. We shall return to this theme later.

It is interesting to note that quite a few contributors have been impelled to say something about philosophy and/or its method. Professor Kalidas Bhattacharya, reacting to the positivisitc attack on metaphysics, attempts to redefine the subject matter of that discipline. Metaphysics, according to him, is the study of several types of presupposition regarding science and common life. Having stated this he passes on to consider the (ontological) status of the objects of logic and of metaphysical thought. He seems to suggest that the objects of metaphysical thought (and logic) are transformations of features already present in the initial (empirical) situation. In calling these objects 'meanings', my own view permits them a sort of being which is not necessarily dependent on empirical objects. There can be *created* meanings or complexes of meanings also, as distinguished from abstracted meanings. Professors Mohanty and Sinari make extensive comments on the philosophical enterprise more or less within the framework of phenomenological and existential approaches. It is noteworthy that while Professor Mohanty is outspokenly critical of some traditional Indian conceptions of the function and method of philosophy, Professor Sinari is able to detect existential relevance in several doctrines in that tradition.

---

*'The Concept of Philosophy' in S. Radhakrishnan and I.H. Muirhead (eds.), *Contemporary Indian Philosophy*, London, George Allen and Unwin Ltd., 1936, p. 65.

Professor Chari is intensely conscious of culture relativism inherent in philosophical thought and views philosophy as the self-assessment of a culture. According to him all our cognitive enterprises, including not only social but also physical sciences and even mathematics, bear the mark of the culture that produces them. Dr. Chattopadhyaya, raising the question of the dependence of knowledge on human factors in a broader perspective and at a more sophisticated level, denies the plausibility of the conception of a manless world. Steering clear of the controversy between realism and idealism in its traditional form, he asks us to be content with a rationalism which is inevitably anthropological. Like Professor Chari, he is also constrained to deny that scientific knowledge is purely objective. To Chattopadhyaya, as to Mohanty and Sinari, the man-world, i.e., the world as viewed and responded to by man, is much more complicated than the one studied or constructed by the physical scientist.

Dr. Margaret Chatterjee characterises her view of philosophy as anthropological. She introduces the significant concepts of 'hinterland' and 'context' of thought which, together with language, determine, and should determine, the shape and direction of thought. She finds both analytical philosophy and phenomenology deficient as regards their responsiveness to the 'hinterland and context' of the concrete human problems. In laying stress on the human context of ethical, and even religious, problems Dr. Chatterjee comes quite close to my own conception of the tasks of philosophy. She has also interesting things to say about the method of metaphysics which deals with things that are objective without being perceptible. In this respect, too, her view has affinities with the view presented in my paper as also that of Professor Kalidas Bhattacharya.

Professor N.S.S. Raman's paper may be taken to be a continuation of the theme explored by Professor Chari, with special reference to the pursuit of Comparative Philosophy. Comparative studies in philosophy should make due allowance for linguistic barriers which are inseparably linked with cultural differences. Professor Raman rightly pleads for better acquaintance with modern linguistics on the part of students of comparative philosophy as of comparative culture. He also has some harsh but pertinent remarks for those Indian scholars who confuse the study of traditional Indian philosophy with the study of philosophy as such, the latter being concerned with the study of problems with contemporary relevance.

Professor Santosh Sengupta, having drawn a contrast between the Eastern or Indian view of philosophy as practical and the Western view of it as (predominantly) theoretical, elaborates the thesis that philosophy is theory with 'practice implications'. Characterising (more or less in the manner of Heidegger) the subject matter of philosophy as Being, Professor Sengupta contends that the approach of philosophy to the Being is mystical. However, he departs from traditional mystical doctrines in conceiving the mystical beyond as not necessarily spiritual and as plural. Interestingly, Professor Sengupta endorses the Heideggerian advocacy of 'withdrawal' from everydayness thereby lending support to the Indian ideal of detachment as characteristic of the man of poised understanding (*sthitaprajña*). In its practical implications philosophy involves change in the mode of willing, consisting in 'the attainment of the states of detachment and humility which are interrelated'.

Professor G. Misra examines the 'nature and relation of pure contemplation and pure action' in the context of the metaphysical controversy as to the nature (of) and relation between body and mind. Alive to the pernicious cultural consequences of the twofold dualism under reference, Professor Misra rejects both, incidentally rejecting, with Wittgenstein, the dogma of private language, and, with Ryle, that of a private mind.

The remaining three contributors, Professors S.S. Barlingay, Rajendra Prasad and R. R. Verma, deal with specific problems, avoiding any general statements about the nature and aim of philosophy. Professor Barlingay, indeed, prefaces his discussion of the main problem with brief remarks on the presuppositions and assumptions involved in philosophical reflection, but that is only incidental to his central purpose. The core of his paper is the way he uses his distinction between 'Distinguishables' and 'Separables' to demolish or settle certain age-old and respectable theories or controversies, e.g., those relating to space, time and universals. He ventures the remark that while science is concerned with understanding reality, philosophy aims at the explanation of it. One would have thought that the aims of the two were exactly reversible.

Both Professors Barlingay and Prasad, while arguing different positions, seem to move within the framework of ordinary language philosophy. Before discussing the possible relationship between God and morality, Prasad carefully defines the notions of logical dependence-independence, and logical oddity. He then appeals to common usage to show that the concepts of God and morality are logically independent. The appeal to common usage also includes appeals to prevailing notions about what is considered moral or immoral. For instance, he counts on the reader's support of the view that the killing of one's son (even with a view to pleasing God?) is an abominable sin. Having considered the question of the (moral) justification of single actions, Prasad passes on to the question of the justification of a system of morality. He discovers contradictions in the possible theistic justification in both cases.

In her paper 'Logic and Reality' Professor R.R. Verma tries to argue that logical laws are not analytic, thereby suggesting that 'there is some kind of connection between logic and reality'. In this connection, she proposes an important distinction, that between structural (formal) and epistemological analyticity. While structural or formal analyticity does not carry any truth-value, the latter type of analyticity, she argues, does not apply to the logical laws themselves. It follows that logical laws are synthetic and so have some connection with reality. Miss Verma does not consider the alternative that logical (and other types of non-physical) laws may be applicable not to empirical reality (the laws governing which are investigated by the physical sciences) but to realms of meanings which, though existentially dependent on the human mind, yet constitute objective orders of several kinds—the orders displaying the stubbornness of empirical reality to contemplating individuals. The acceptance of one or more realms of meanings does not necessarily amount to endorsing Platonism. According to the present writer the 'being' of these realms is bound up with man's use of symbols, linguistic and others. Thanks to man's capacity to make use of and react to symbols and numbers, propositions and arguments no less than theories of science and works of art enjoy a sort of objective being, disturbing, provoking and inspiring like-minded connoisseurs belonging to different times and places.

VI

The essays in this volume offer a rich and varied fare for the student of philosophy. How far, it may be asked, do they constitute or represent a developing tradition in contemporary Indian philosophy which may be entitled to be called both truly Indian and truly modern?

It is not easy to answer that question. Before Independence, as already observed, there undoubtedly existed a tradition of scholarship in philosophy aiming at exposition and reinterpretation of classical Indian thought, mainly the Advaita Vedānta. Among Indian thinkers, though K.C. Bhattacharya was outstanding both as a creative interpreter of ancient logico-metaphysical thought and as an analytical thinker, Sri Aurobindo alone successfully attempted to produce a full-fledged system of more or less speculative, religious metaphysics. For obvious reasons that system is not able to meet the demands of the modern minds.

I do not agree with those who discount the need for an Indian tradition in modern philosophy on the plea that philosophy as quest of knowledge is, like science, a universal cultural activity without a national stamp. It seems to me that philosophy, as the inner awareness of a country's culture, stands somewhere between science and literature and as such is a distinctive product of that culture. That is the reason why countries like England, Germany and France have, despite mutual borrowings and influences, a philosophical tradition of their own, as also a distinctive literary tradition. To put it differently, modern India should try not only to assimilate important elements from Western thought and culture but should also enrich world thought by its own distinctive contributions.

However, in a country with as variegated and weighty a heritage in philosophy as India, it is not easy to start new traditions in thought which would meet the needs of modern life and consciousness. If Europe was able to make significantly new departures from its medieval past it was largely due to the dawn of a new scientific consciousness in astronomy and physics. This revolutionary consciousness opened up entirely new vistas in logic and in theory of knowledge. At a later date, socio-political revolutions greatly affected the course of ethico-political philosophies. The new revolution in physics at the turn of the ncetury also gave a fresh impetus to methodological reflections.

As observed earlier a distinctive tradition in philosophy arises out of a people's special interest in the cultivation of particular forms of cultural consciousness. Such interest is determined, on the one hand, by that part of the heritage still valued by the people concerned, and, on the other, by the contemporary situation in their cultural history. The interaction of these two factors leads to new questionings on the part of the intellectual leaders of the people in question, which, in turn, leads to the formulation of new schemes of ideas in the relevant fields.

Traditionally, India has been the land of daring religious thought; the Indian mind has also been concerned with evolving philosophies of human happiness. Some of the philosophies of man's salvation or happiness concieved in India, e.g., Buddhism, have been both eminently rational and pronouncedly humanistic. In the present-day world these philosophies have to face the challenge of science as the sole or main architect of human happiness. The scientific challenge, be it noted, relates both to our notions concerning the meaning of knowledge or understanding, and its validity or validation; as also to the place of different types of understanding and aspiration in the economy of a meaningful life. A truly modern Indian philosophy, it seems to me, can make effective contributions to the logic and epistemology of man's value cognitions, including his apprehension of religious values. It appears to me that the scientific challenge cannot be met effectively by the religions prevailing in the West, with their unreserved commitment to the dogmas of creationism, supernaturalism, and divine revelation. Man, we believe, cannot live without religion as such, nor can modern man live without science. Unless philosophy can find a way to reconcile our value intuitions with the claims of scientific knowledge, man will be condemned to live forever with a split personality. A properly reoriented Indian philosophy, I believe, can help mankind in achieving a more adequate integration of its inner life.

Classical Indian philosophers, both Hindu and Buddhist, stressed the need for having the courage to know and face reality in its true nature (yathābhūtam), believing that such knowledge alone could lead us to true salvation. That spirit of courageous inquiry needs to be revived today.

The foregoing remarks should not be taken to mean either that I advocate chauvinistic exclusivism in the realm of knowlege or that I am insensitive to the need for the meeting and intermingling of diverse currents of thought—Eastern and Western. Thanks to science's abolition of distance and conquest of space such meeting and intermingling is now a fact of daily life. However, at subtler cultural levels, nations and societies still continue to display far-reaching differences, and the spiritual problems facing mankind are of such magnitude and complexity that every civilised society is not only welcome to contribute to their solution but is also expected to do so. Nor am I insensitive to the tremendous vitality displayed by Western thought in recent times not only in diverse scientific fields but also in philosophy, the social sciences and the humanities in general. I only wish that, for the benefit of humanity at large, this vitality could be mellowed with bits of traditional Eastern wisdom—the spirit of detachment that acts as a brake on destructive cunning and unrestrained arrogance.

However, Indian thought is not likely to make important contributions to the philosophy of science, or even to economic thought and political science, in the near future. In these fields, as in many other sciences, India has been learning and will continue to learn from the West for decades to come. But India cannot afford, in the manner of analytical and even existential philosophies, to neglect normative ethics and social philosophy. And this leads me to indicate another area in which Indian philosophers can do useful work. Modern Indian philosophy can revitalise itself by acquiring a revolutionary purposiveness in its approach to evils and institutions inconsistent with democracy and our new sense of values. Indian philosophers can have new problems to think of if, while advocating new principles of socio-political organisation consistent with the needs and the genius of the people, they are also careful to avoid what have proved to be mistaken enthusiasms in Western industrial societies. Our socio-political philosophers can profitably link their concepts with the insights of such teachers of the previous generation as Mahatma Gandhi and Rabindranath Tagore.

In his well-known monograph, *The Structure of Scientific Revolutions*, Prof. Thomas S. Kuhn has propounded the view that normal scientific research generally proceeds under the aegis of an accepted theoretical framework regarded as a paradigm.

The paradigm determines the sorts of problems that are attended to; it generally inclines researchers to ignore problems and puzzles that cannot be solved in terms made known by the paradigm. Much of current thinking in modern Indian philosophy is linked with paradigms not invented in modern India. Only a revolution in our way of thinking, brought about by a powerful modern genius, can reorient our thought to a new frame of reference, a new paradigm comprising new questionings and new modes of approach to problems of knowledge and valuation.

It seems to me that the more important revolutions in philosophy are bound up with changes in the conception of philosophy, its central problems and its overall aim and object. Such revolutions occur when the community, nation or age concerned suffers a sudden shift of interest from one area of cultural life to another; or when new problems in logic and epistemology, new doubts and certainties regarding knowledge and the norms of conduct, are thrust on the attention of the representative thinkers of an age or society. I believe such changes are occurring in modern India, which leads me to expect that new, powerful movements in philosophy, both truly Indian and truly modern, may emerge in this country in the near future.

1

Distinguishables and Separables

All our philosophical investigations presuppose some kind of initial philosophical position which is merely the conscious or unconscious product of our beliefs and the attitudes that we form in this world. I can, for example, believe that in this world there are many things existing in their own right and that these things have various kinds of characteristics which are dependent for their existence on other things. I can alternatively believe or suppose that Reality is one and indivisible. On the first set of beliefs I would be able to think of separation of things and the distinctions among them. On the second assumption, the question of either separation or distinguishing (amongst things) would not even arise. Thus, our philosophical concepts and hypotheses depend on our beliefs or rather on the set of initial beliefs which we take for granted without questioning their validity. Although, theoretically, there is nothing wrong in accepting one indivisible Reality, in our practical behaviour we start with a multiplicity of things and further believe or postulate that these things have certain characteristics, and that these things act on one another or are acted upon. Again this may further require us to presuppose concepts like Space and Time. For without Space and Time I might not be able to talk of things and their characteristics, and imagine how or where they act. Thus, if in my investigation I am analysing my experience, I must confess that I am already believing in, assuming a particular kind of picture of, Reality. This is a commonsense, pluralistic picture. In a way, I start my analysis of experience on the basis of this picture and so I am technically committing the fallacy of *petitio principii*. My only justification for this is that it is inevitable, for no investigation can start without some such assumption. Do we give the name presuppositions to such inevitable beliefs? I think we should make a distinction between initial beliefs and presuppositions. For example, that there is multiplicity in the universe should not be regarded as a presupposition. It is my belief only. But if such a belief logically requires Space and Time these should be regarded as the presuppositions. It should be necessary to point out that all our 'beliefs' and 'presuppositions' involved in our investigations are generic in nature unlike the beliefs in ghosts and vampires which are characterised by a certain specificness or particularity.

Let us see how the notion of plurality arises in our mind. If the phenomena that we experience were continuous and were not discrete or separated from one another, would we still treat them as many and independently existing? Suppose there is a person with two heads. Shall we regard this person as one or two? It is possible that if such a person has two different thinking or behaviour systems it would create a problem for us. In all likelihood each of such systems will be determined by some physical structure or pattern, and a certain physical structure and a certain behavioural system will form one nucleus. Thus, if there are two behavioural patterns we would somehow or the other demarcate the physical area of the behavioural pattern. The case of an earthworm with two mouths would be simpler. We do regard it as one being just as we regard a mirror, before it is broken into two, as one thing. If the earthworm is cut into two, then alone it would be regarded as two. It appears to me that actual separation or dividedness seems to be the basic notion by which plurality of objects is apprehended. From this basic datum the notion of divisibility would arise. A stone can be broken into two, a branch of a tree can be broken into two, although neither a stone nor a branch of a tree may actually be broken into two. So, from the actual separation or division we go to the possibility of separation or division. The things which are actually divided or which can be divided do give rise to the notion of distinctness which is, in fact, presupposed by a thing which is capable of being divided into different elements. Very soon, however, we find that we come across cases where there is definite distinctness but it is not possible to separate one distinct from another distinct. Such distinctness where the possibility of separating one thing from another is necessarily ruled out is distinguishability *qua* distinguishability. The colour and extension of a thing, for example, are distinct from each other, but one cannot be physically separated from the other. It should be clear that whereas separability gives rise to the notion of plurality, pure distinguishability may not give rise to any such notion. However, separability and distinguishability play a very important role in our systems of philosophical beliefs.

Traditionally, philosophy is primarily concerned with the explanation of reality. I believe the word explanation is very important in this context, for it is in relation to this word or the notion of explaining that one can distinguish philosophy from science which too, in some sense, is concerned with understanding reality. If we take a stone and divide it into parts, we understand that parts or particles of the stone can be separated, that the stone can be divided; we may also understand whether the stone is a graphite stone or iron ore or a diamond. But if we have to explain what we understand, we require an altogether different kind of activity, a different kind of technique. When we divide a stone, we are breaking it literally, when we are explaining (the nature of stone) we are not breaking the stone—we are only breaking, expressing the experience into language and concepts. This kind of 'breaking' is communicating, distinguishing, conceptualising. When we explain we re-arrange our experience in a linguistic form so that it may become meaningful or communicable.

But many a time philosophers have treated this process of explaining to be on par with a physical process. In a physical process just as one can break, divide something into parts, in the same way one can also join the parts. In philosophical analysis one can break the experience (into concepts). But the broken elements are not just physical units which can be reassembled. A flower is not made of fragrance, softness, a particular shape, a particular colour, etc., just as it is made of petals, stem, pollens, etc. The philosophically analysed 'units' are distinguishable. They cannot be physically separated, they are characteristics not things (or parts of a thing). And so they cannot be reunited in the way physical elements (e.g., mercury) can sometimes be reunited. Nevertheless, in their enthusiasm philosophers try to reconstruct or synthesise the world. Such an approach does not take into consideration the limitations of a philosopher. Moreover, in so doing the philosopher hypostatises, i.e., unconsciously regards the characteristics as things. Sometimes the characteristics are not even the objective characteristics (as, for example, when we say the flower is pleasant). Sometimes in our eagerness to reconstruct the reality, we speculate too, and this leads to some kind of anthropomorphism as, for example, when we say that the stone must be having pain, or when we say that God's form is like that of a man. Sometimes the different orders of the concepts are also confused, which leads to what Ryle calls category mistake or what Śankara would regard as *Adhyāsa*. However, my point is that all these errors arise out of the basic confusion of not distinguishing between pure distinguishables and separables. When I talk of two things or two parts of a thing, I talk of two separables. When I talk of two characteristics I talk of only distinguishables. It is possible that I might talk of two characteristics of two different things. In such a case, the characteristics may appear as separables. But it is not by virtue of their being characteristics that they are separables. It is by virtue of the separateness of things to which the characteristics belong that they are separables.

Let us follow the distinction between separability and distinguishability *qua* distinguishability more closely. When some things are not only distinguished as different but can also be separated or divided, I call them separables. When they are purely distinguished but cannot be divided or separated, I call them distinguishables. I believe this is a very fundamental distinction and ignoring it leads to several philosophical muddles. I believe this was the distinction which the Vaiśeṣikas first introduced when they made a distinction between *Samyoga* and *Samavāya*, although I am not sure whether the Vaiśeṣikas were aware of all the implications of this distinction. One can easily see that *separation* properly applies to things in the physical world. I can separate one thing from another thing; I can physically separate one table from another table or a chair, or I can separate one piece of furniture from another piece of furniture. I can cut a piece of stone, a piece of metal or a piece of wood or a thing similar to it and separate the two pieces. I can also separate one heap from another heap. But I cannot separate the colour of the table or the weight of the table from the table although I can distinguish the two. I cannot separate the mangoness of the mango tree from the treeness of the mango tree, although I can say that a class of mango trees is a proper subclass of trees and thus distinguish between the two. I can distinguish between emotions and expression of emotions but it is doubtful whether one can actually separate them. Similarly, I can distinguish between the earlier moments of time and the later moments of time or the past moments of time and the present or future moments of time. We can distinguish between these moments in the sense that they are different (or we know that they are different). But we cannot separate them. According to me even when two moments are not temporally contiguous they are not separate. In order to be separate there must be a possiblity of their existing together in their own right although at different positions in space. When we talk of moments of time this kind of divisibility is absent.[1] The two moments of time do not co-exist, although philosophers have talked of the divisibility or even infinite divisibility of time. The moments of time only succeed one another. When two things are separate, they can also be brought together, that is, they can exist in close proximity, they can touch each other, there can be contact between them. The space between them is logically reducible to no distance. In short, theoretically it should be possible to adjust the distance between two things which are separate. That is, it should be possible to say that such things are reversible.

But let us now come to 'objects' which are only distinguishable and not separable. Can there be any 'distance' between such 'objects'? Can each of such objects have an independent existence? What will be the relation between them? Can we adjust the distance between them? Can we say that they are reversible? The answers to these questions seem to be negative. In other words, where 'object' can be distinguished but not separated we cannot talk of them (the pure distinguishables) as existing by themselves. We can, for example, distinguish between a logical substance and quality. But it will be incorrect to say that a pure substance exists by itself or a pure quality exists by itself. The first such mistake was committed by Nyāya logicians who said that in the first instance of its existence (the produced) *Dravya* existed by itself without any quality.[2] The second mistake was committed by a few sensum philosophers who thought of sense data or qualities as existing by themselves. It merely means that both these types of philosophers regarded some of the pure distinguishables as separables. That is, the Nyāya logicians regarded the substance and some sensum philosophers regarded the sense data or qualities as things.

This was also the mistake of the Platonists who thought that universals were not only distinguishable from the particulars in which they existed, but they could also be separated from the particulars, that they had a separate, distinct existence. In regarding sense data, qualities and universals or even classes as separables, the philosophers were believing, or at least logically assuming, that qualities and universals and sense data and classes were existing in their own right. They thus thought that the qualities and substances or universals and particulars were related by the same kind of relations by which two things could be related. If two things were in some kind of physical space then qualities and substances and universals and particulars were in some kind of mental or logical space, and that they were related by the same kind of relations by which two separable objects could be related. In so doing it appears that they were committing two kinds of mistakes, though these two kinds could be intimately related to each other.

Two separables belong to the same 'category', and this category is the category of things (or, loosely, the substance). Two distinguishables which cannot be separated may belong to the same or different categories. But even if two distinguishables belong to one category there is some uniqueness about each distinguishable. It cannot be thought of as having a separate or independent existence. So, in treating pure distinguishables as separables we are (1) either mistaking objects belonging to different categories as belonging to the same category; or (2) we are treating distinguishables as things, i.e., we are hypostatising the distinguishables.

Amongst the distinguishables there appear different types. Thus, the concept of the distinguishable *qua* distinguishable seems to be applicable even in the situation of knowledge. The knower and the known in the strict sense are only distinguishable, but are not separable as knower and known. I am aware that this statement of mine will be disputed, for certainly the particular object that is known and the particular knower that knows the object exist as independent objects. But to exist as an independent object is quite a different thing from remaining unrelated (or related) in knowledge situation. The same objects may play two different roles, one in ontology and the other in epistemology. In fact, my point is that we should distinguish between the absolute terms and the relational terms. The relational terms are only distinguishable as relational terms, although their denotation may exist independently and, therefore, may be separable. Someone, say X, may be a mother and some other, say Y, may be a son. The role of a mother and a son is different from the role of a woman and a boy. If these two roles are confused one is likely to regard either (1) the relational terms as the absolute terms; or (2) the absolute terms as the relational terms. Śaṅkara, for example, has used the terms *Viṣaya* and *Viṣayī*. These are relational terms. They are related to each other and one cannot properly call someone as *Viṣayī* or something as *Viṣaya*, unless they refer to one common context. So, even if in ontology there is a possibility of a person corresponding to *Viṣayī* and a thing corresponding to *Viṣaya* existing independently, in the realm of knowledge they are only distinguishables. Of course, distinguishables in respect of knowledge situation and distinguishables on account of abstraction of a thing should not be regarded on par.

A common phenomenon that we see is about the distinction between things and beings. Beings are distinguished from things on account of the fact that beings have characteristics like automatic movement, feelings, willing, reasoning, etc. In short, beings are supposed to be 'conscious' as against things which are regarded as 'unconscious'. And even if someone regards things 'as having consciousness', my basic distinction is not affected as the consciousness of things will have to be distinguished from the consciousness of beings. Again, some beings are not only conscious but they are self-conscious. However, beings have not only the characteristics pointed out by consciousness, but also the characteristics of things which are indicated by their bodies. So, the principle of division would not be whether the substance has extension or is extensionless.[3] Of course, one can certainly distinguish a spatial characteristic like extension from a characteristic like consciousness. But, can one separate consciousness from the body? The usual argument is that there is a time when the body exists and consciousness does not. From this people conclude that body and consciousness are separables. Even the Vaiśeṣikas, who were the pioneers in making the distinction between

separables and distinguishables *qua* distinguishables, regarded
consciousness as a separable object and called it *Ātman*. If our
argument is properly understood then it would follow that there is no
time when consciousness and 'body' exist separately. It may be that
consciousness and 'body' co-exist for some duration and after
a certain point the consciousness simply ceases to exist. So when
they exist together they are inseparable and after that only one
exists and the other does not exist. From these facts it should
never be concluded that both of them have a separate existence,
even after one of them has ceased to exist. The situation is very
similar to a thing with a particular colour, e.g., a green leaf. If
the greenness of the leaf is taken away by some chemical, does
that mean that greenness and the leaf exist separately? The separate
existence argument is the result of confusing distinguishability
qua distinguishability for separability. When the body is with
consciousness the 'body' is different from things like stones. It
is only a distinguishable. When consciousness is extinct the
'body' behaves differently, only like a thing (although in a very
crude sense of the term).

I have argued above that when a person dies, the consciousness
simply ceases to exist. Had it been separable, one would have to
think of consciousness and its material counterpart, generally
called body, to co-exist separately. Now one may say that their
separate existence cannot be disproved. That is true. But let us
try to understand the problem in a larger context. Let us take the
case of a tree. As an organic thing its status is different from that
of inorganic ones. If the tree dies, that is becomes dry, we
will of course say that it is no more living. Shall we say that the
consciousness or the 'soul' of the tree and its material counterpart
co-exist although separately? And what happens if one branch
of the tree dies? Does it mean that the consciousness of the
tree has withdrawn from one part of the tree and is concentrating
on the remaining part, or does it mean that the part of the
'consciousness' alone exists separately from the tree? If we
accept the first alternative that consciousness can cease to exist
from one part alone then it is possible that it ceases to exist from
all parts. This means that consciousness and body are simply
distinguishables and not separables. On the other hand, if we
say that the dead part exists separately from the 'conscious' part,
then we will have to think that consciousness is separable into

parts, such that one part lives independently and in its own right and the other part lives along with the remaining tree. Or we will have to think that although consciousness itself cannot be completely separated a part of the consciousness, although continuous with the total consciousness, can exist independently of the tree. I think some kind of absurdity is involved in these positions. A more legitimate hypothesis, though speculative, would be to regard consciousness as only distinguishable and not separable from the 'body'.

We have seen that two separables as well as two distinguishables are different from each other. But in the case of distinguishables the difference is either because of the difference in quality or because of a category difference. For example, a particular colour may be distinguished from another quality say, smoothness, or it may be distinguished from the thing which has that colour. Such is not the case when we talk of separables. The separables must primarily belong to the same category and further we believe that this category must be 'substance' which, we again presuppose, is capable of existing by itself. It is our belief that only things have this capacity, i.e., the capacity of existing by themselves, although in the philosophical language we do say that the category of substance exists by itself and that all other categories depend on the category of substance. It must, however, be said that the category of substance is as much an abstraction as any other category. And if we say that the category of substance exists by itself we are equating substance with a thing, i.e., although we talk of a substance we really mean by it a thing as we understand in our ordinary language. So we ought to have really distinguished between substance as a thing and substance as a category.[4] It is not an abstract substance which is separable from another abstract substance. It is a concrete thing which is separable from another concrete thing. Such a belief about a thing presupposes a certain nature of the thing. One cannot say that the above description of a thing would fit a geometrical point for example. It appears to me that such a description of a thing primarily presupposes the spatial characteristics of a thing. It is by virtue of these spatial characteristics that we are able to separate one thing from another. It is true that we do extend the use of the term thing to non-spatial objects too; for example, we do talk of two societies or two minds. But when we extend our use of things to minds or societies—if we carefully look to our use of the words—we would find that in our use of the words we are actually presupposing some kind of metaphorical space. This is so even when we talk of separability in time. As Bergson would put it, unless we talk of time in some spatial way, it would not be possible for us to talk of separability in time. In fact, even the problem of infinite divisibility of time requires us to think of time as a length, even to think of non-existing future time as existing simultaneously with the present time.

But this raises two kinds of problems: (1) How are we to decide that such and such is the meaning of existence (and a thing)? For the kind of a thing that we have taken for granted in the above discussion is the macroscopic thing. How are we to suppose that by a thing we mean something like a table and not a molecule or an atom or an electron? How are we to apply the criterion of spatial characteristics at the microscopic level; and (2) how are we to decide about the spatial characteristics of a thing? Does this mean that the concept of separability applies strictly to macrophysical objects? Do we think of the microscopic world of atoms, or electrons and protons, as non-spatial? This is a mistake committed by many. But, again, the question may arise: How do you distinguish between a thing that is actually in space and a thing that is merely imagined? Is not an imagined thing imagined with spatial properties? Is it not the case that whenever you imagine a thing you imagine it in space, in the same physical space? Here strictly we do not have any criterion by which we can distinguish space in imagination from the physical space. But we believe and presuppose that physical space is prior to imagined space and it is only on the basis of this belief that we work out our theory of space.

But now imagine that the characteristics which are true of separables alone are applied to pure distinguishables. If this is done we would immediately think that the 'things' which belong to different categories belong to only one category; that although the distinguishables as such do not exist, on account of our mistaking them for separables we would require them to have thingness and spatial characteristics. We would regard pure abstractions as reals. We would regard qualities, actions, classes and universals as things and even non-existence would be thought of as having existence. We would begin to think that these distinguishables are in space, that they can be related to each other (externally) by the relation of physical contact. In short, we would be creating a pluralistic universe of pseudo-existents. One category would be mistaken for another category, an element in knowing situation would also be mistaken for a being situation.[5] In other words, as soon as we mistake distinguishables for separables we would reduce all categories to things (or 'substances') and this would be a fallacy, for we would regard a real thing and a pseudo-thing on par.

Can we in our analysis ignore the factor of time altogether and restrict our analysis only to spatial characteristics? I should confess that this will not be possible. All our experience is characterised by spatio-temporal characteristics. In human life too, as elsewhere, both these characteristics, the characteristic of space and the characteristic of time, are present. One cannot isolate spatial characteristics alone from the temporal ones. Space and time are distinguishables only, not separables. Let us understand the peculiarities of temporal characteristics. To begin with, we may say that time is concerned with the basic concept of duration or persistence. Where, in experience, do we find this duration? Where can this duration be verified? As regards the answer to the first question one may not be certain. For it is very often said that things endure in time. But without doubt persistence is verified on the basis of human existence alone. The duration of things is verified only by contrasting it, measuring it against human existence or human life. Awareness of duration in human beings is itself the source of the concept of duration. 'Persistence' and 'life' thus overlap and the end of life also becomes the end of persistence. If there is X length of life one cannot break this length into two parts, say A and B. The 'first' break itself signifies the end of life and durations.[6] In this respect, life or existence in time is to be contrasted with existence in space. The existence in space consists of extension and parts and even if the existence is negated, the parts, as parts, continue to be there. Thus, a thing in space can be destroyed by breaking it.[7] A temporal existence, as I have suggested above, cannot be broken into two temporal segments. The end of temporal existence is signified by the end itself. No part of temporal existence remains beyond this end moment. I, therefore, think that finally the basic concept of measurement of time is supplied by man's own life or experience. The clocks and the movement of the earth and the sun, etc., are finally measured in terms of human life or experience. It is the human life or experience which gives the awareness of duration. You must measure duration by duration and unless there is awareness of duration, duration could not be measured. I, therefore, venture to say that the *concept* of time—not time itself—arises from human life. Life and time are inseparable, one of the important distinctions between them being that life is finite, it comes to an end sometime. But although one particular life ceases, another life is continuing. This gives rise to infinite temporal continuity. And that is time.

Time and space are distinguishable. But they are not separable. In our experience we do not come across any pure temporal or pure spatial existence. This can be either on account of the fact that it is impossible for space and time to exist independently or it may be on account of the fact that the medium of all our experience is inseparable from human beings and the temporal nature of human beings modifies the nature of experience. Whatever it may be, whenever we think of a thing we always conceive of it as having spatio-temporal properties. Space and time, so to say, are the scaffolding or frame in which we put all our perceptible experience. Space and time supply the forms of things.

It is indeed true that we conceive of space and time in relation to things. This is how they are called forms of intuition by Kant. They do not appear to be things in the sense in which things are regarded as things. But how are we to conceive of empty space and empty time? I believe that the limited notions of space and time carry us beyond the limitedness and we begin to think of unlimited space and unlimited time in which the 'limited space' and 'limited time' of our primary experience are 'parts' or constituents. We believe that it is all one space and one time (which can be divided). If something is supposed to have parts, the next step would lead us to the belief that it is a thing or rather a composite thing having parts. Perhaps for some such reason the Vaiśeṣikas thought of space and time as independent things or substances. I, however, want to argue that isolated space or isolated time cannot be regarded as things, even as the form of things. For, ultimately, the thing is mingled with spatio-temporal properties. Space, Time and Thing permeate one another. Simple space or simple time would give us distinguishables but not separables. Even space and time jointly or separately cannot give us separability. For, it is only the thing in space and time which can be separated, neither space nor time. It is because space or time cannot be separated but only distinguished as different spaces or times in relation to things that things can be separated in space and time. Thus, although we presuppose space and time, they are not separable from things. Space and time are only distinguishable from things.

Ever since the days of Plato in the West and the Vaiśeṣikas in the East, people have been thinking of universals. Universals are supposed to be some common element possessed by (all) particulars. But I think this is an oversimplification. The problem of universals cannot be understood in this way. Let us take the case of an animal, say a cow. On account of certain similar properties found in different cows we may distinguish a universal cow from particular cows. But in this search for universality we may distinguish two different kinds. We may, for example, talk of cowness as some common characteristic possessed by all cows. This characteristic evidently does not have parts like legs, head, etc. But when I know something as a cow but do not remember whether it is my cow or somebody else's, I am not talking of cowness. I am talking very much of a concrete animal cow although I am not talking of this cow or that cow. It means that when I talk of cowness I am not talking of a thing, but when I talk of a cow I am talking of a thing having spatio-temporal characteristics. What I am eliminating are the specific qualities which go with a particular cow. Thus, to regard cowness and a cow on par should not be justified. Although one is likely to say that in both these cases abstraction or universalisation is involved, I think the two operations are significantly different. When one talks of a cow (though not a particular cow) one is generalising, when one talks of cowness one is abstracting. For example, it would be possible for us to count different cows without recognising each cow. It would not be possible for us to count cownesses. The Nyāya philosophers of India have distinguished between special (Viśeṣa guṇa) and general qualities (Sāmānya guṇa). When you know something with Sāmānya guṇa alone, you would, for example, get a general cow. The distinction between a general cow and cowness is very similar to the grammatical distinction between a common noun and an abstract noun. A common

noun may have a bearer of the common name in space and time.
The abstract noun does not have any bearer. It appears to me
that this distinction was at least vaguely present in the mind of
Aristotle who distinguished between Form and Idea. Similarly,
the early Nyāya philosophers distinguished between *Jāti* and
Ākṛti, Jāti corresponding to abstract characteristic or abstraction
and *Ākṛti* corresponding to a general thing. If we apply our
distinction of separability and distinguishability to phenomena
it should be clear that the possibility of separability arises properly
in the context of *Ākṛti*. It is only the *Ākṛti* which gives the thing
the potentiality for separation. *Jātis* can only be distinguished but
not separated. I think it was this distinction operating in the
process of universalising and abstracting, that was overlooked by
G.E. Moore when he thought that there are some concepts which
are complex and others which are simple and further thought
that horse was a complex concept and good or yellow was a
simple one.

But I think universals can be distinguished in yet different
ways. For example, while seeing some cows, just as we distinguish
some common characteristic cowness, similarly, we also know
the oneness of each cow. To say that we distinguish oneness and
cowness in exactly the same way does not seem to be correct. For,
then, we are likely to discover *oneness* in the search for cowness
and vice versa. Again, in the presence of many cows I do not
simply distinguish *oneness* common to all cows. We are also
able to add different cows. We are, for example, able to say that
the cows are ten in number. Ten is also regarded as a universal.
But the concept of ten is not formed in the same way as the concept
of one is formed. The concept of ten is formed by adding different
ones. Again, we can talk of cows as a group. When I am talking
of ten I am not talking of a collectivity. I am rather talking of
some discrete number. It is by virtue of this discrete character
of numbers that I am able to count the cows. On the other hand,
when I talk of cows it is merely grouping the cows. Now, when
I abstract 'one' from a cow it is certainly an abstraction. But it
is a different kind of abstraction from the one when we talk of cowness and abstract it from a cow. All these different kinds of
universals are distinguishables. To put them under one category
without further distinguishing would be as much a fallacy as to
regard distinguishables as separables.

There is yet another kind of the so called universal represented by values like beautiful and good. Do we get these values in the same way we get other universals? When one says that something is beautiful or something is good, are we discovering some common property shared by different things which are either beautiful or good? Are we abstracting goodness and beauty the way we abstract either cowness or the number one? It appears to me that we do not do any of these things. (Again, there is likely to be a difference between the way we get *good* and the way we get *beautiful*.) To say the least, when we say that something is beautiful[8] we are passing a *judgement* on something. This cannot be done unless the thing and the one who judges somehow come together. So, if good and beautiful are regarded as universals, it will be incorrect to say that all universals are of the same kind. In that case, to say that something is beautiful will be to say that 'beautiful' and the thing that is judged as beautiful are inseparable. But this, too, would not be a correct statement. The strangest thing is that beautiful and the things that are beautiful are not even distinguishable like the colour of a thing and the thing. 'Beautiful' is a characteristic of a certain situation in which a thing and the observer are constituents and the opinion or the judgement of the one who judges is somehow superimposed on the thing.

One of the problems connected with our previous discussion is whether values exist. I think this problem is purely a linguistic one. We begin to think that values exist because we are able to say significantly that there *are* values. But the proposition that there are values and the proposition that the values exist are not synonymous. The proposition that there are values is like the propositions: there is society, there is a technique, this is socialism, etc. We have also seen that in the primary sense we cannot say something exists unless the thing has spatial characteristics. Let us contrast values with something which either exists or which we think exists. When I try to bring before my mind's eye the concepts of 'value' or 'beautiful', I do not succeed, as also in the case of 'nothing', in getting anything spatial before me at least directly. I cannot imagine any spatial picture of these notions. Let us see what happens when we think of ghosts and souls. Do we have a mental picture of a soul or a ghost? Do we think of them the way we think of tables and chairs? Let us see how we use these words. It appears to me that although we say that ghosts and souls do not have spatial properties we do not think of them in any other way except in spatial terms. The soul[9] is smaller than the smallest thing in the world or is bigger than the biggest thing in the world. It is plain that in this context the smallest and the biggest are spatial terms. Similarly, when we say the ghost is coming through the wall, although we do not attribute to the ghost a body like ours, we do attribute to it some body, may be a skeleton body of geometrical length, when we think of its transmission. So, whether ghosts and souls exist or not when we attribute existence to them we think of them only in spatial terms. Descartes failed here.[10] Descartes' concept of extensionless substance has limitations. Although it is true that we cannot measure mind or soul with something that is spatial, the spatial nucleus of mind or soul is not altogether negated. This is not the case in regard to values.

So far we have based our analysis on the presupposition that whereas two things (*qua* things) can be distinguished and separated, two categories can only be distinguished but not separated. But theoretically this distinction does not seem to be absolute. If two things had infinite magnitude would this distinction apply? Our analysis is true only in the context of things which have finite spatio-temporal characteristics. By any chance if we begin to presuppose that there are some things which are all pervading, say, for example, the all pervading God, the notion of separability would be simply inoperative. The notion of separability would also be inoperative if you somehow believe that space and time, which cannot in any sense be regarded as finite, are *things*. If we start with the presupposition that there are things with infinite magnitude, then the criterion of separability (and with it the criterion of spatiality) simply fails. The criterion of distinguishability alone remains. But on this criterion one cannot distinguish between things and categories. Either the things are likely to be mistaken for categories or the categories for things. At least in its rudimentary form we owe the distinction of distinguishability and separability to the Vaiśeṣikas. But, unfortunately, they are also responsible for its doom. Since they forgot to make a proper distinction between substance as a category and substance as thing, their substances were usually mistaken for things. And amongst such things they included Space, Time, *Ākāśa* and *Ātman*. Space, Time and *Ākāśa* are non-separable, distinguishable and all-pervasive. All-pervasive things can be distinguished but not separated. So it is easy, though not correct, to regard a thing which is non-separable but distinguishable as all-pervasive. Once *Ātman* was given the status of a thing it was thought necessary to regard it as all-pervasive. One cannot separate Space, Time, *Ākāśa* and *Ātman* from one another by actual division (although conceptually division or distinction of space may be possible).

So once our logic proceeds in the above way, at some stage the separability criterion for their being things is given up, e.g., by the Vaiśeṣikas, and with it the clear line of demarcation between categories and things is also lost. We have seen that the notion of thing and the notion of separability go together. But when this itself is given up, the edifice of philosophical presuppositions tumbles down. Once the presuppositions vanish, what remains is only the 'anarchy of beliefs', and even if one tries to reunite the 'forces of beliefs' in the absence of proper or consistent presuppositions one is surely rolled down the valley of fallacies. For, our initial philosophical position, which is formed on account of our practical attitudes, is then cracked and difficult to repair.

Notes

1. This should also explain that two events cannot properly be separated although they may occupy two different positions in time. I think the idea of separability is intimately connected with that of reversibility.
2. In fact it is very clear that when the Nyāya philosophers made a distinction between *Dravya* and *Guṇa*, they did not regard it as purely a logical distinction. They did not regard *Dravya* as abstract. Like Aristotle they also regarded it as substratum. But they forgot that the pure substratum could not be regarded as existing by itself as it was not a thing.
3. Perhaps the principle on which beings and things can be divided is that whereas a being procreates a thing does not.
4. In fact, it will be interesting to point out that amongst the distinguishables also we are unfortunately inclined to give greater existential weightage to some constituents. We have a tendency to thihk that substance is more important than the qualities and thus think that the qualities inhere in substance. Here we treat the substances as things and unconsciously postulate that they are capable of existing by themselves. I think it is this kind of prejudice which has made the very pregnant notion of Samavāya of the Vaiśeṣikas insignificant Samavāya should have suggested inseparability where we are able to

distinguish. But very soon the notion of pure distinguishability was replaced by that of the substratum-superstratum relation. It goes without saying that we are unconsciously treating a substance as a thing.

5. For example, a known-situation is merely a special case of an is-situation. The is-situation is converted and distinguished into a knower-known situation. As stated earlier, these are simply relational terms. But now we would start thinking that the knower—the logical knower itself—is an existing object and thus convert a subject into an object. It need not be added that the concept that the knower has existence is formed in this way. (In the same way it is possible to mistake something which really exists as an idea.)

6. Of course, on the hypothesis that there is rebirth, several such breaks are allowed!

7. Spatial objects can be divided. But such a division signifies the destruction or death of the objects.

8. The case of good is still different.

9. *Aṇoraṇīyan Mahato Mahīyān.*

10. His division of substances was based on the principle of whether something is spatial or non-spatial. But if spatiality is common to all substances, the division would not be exclusive.

2

Metaphysics—A Genuine Cognitive Pursuit

KALIDAS BHATTACHARYYA

Anti-metaphysicians have done a good service to metaphysics. They have compelled the metaphysician to re-state his case, keeping in view the objections raised against his vocation. He could re-state his case in various ways, at least one of which is as follows: 'Metaphysics is a sort of analytical study of some particular types of presuppositions of science and common life, the distinction between science and common life being only of degree of clarity, precision and order (systematicness).' Note the words 'a sort of analytical study' and 'particular types of presuppositions'. What is suggested by the first word is that analytical study in metaphysics is different in nature from that in science, and what the second word suggests is that the presuppositions which metaphysics studies are not like other presuppositions of science. It is taken for granted here that everybody knows what science is.

The presuppositions of a study X are those which, though used by X, are not studied by it, X leaving that study to another discipline Y, from which it may or may not take lessons and in which it may or may not get interested. Such presuppositions are normally of four different kinds—postulates, axioms, heuristic principles and those material truths of another science Y which X might profitably heed, but usually does not, because of a convenient and generally accepted division of labour. Postulates are those principles which, without further ado, are assumed and used as necessary instruments when a particular science is to be conceptually constructed; they are neither deducible from, nor analysable into, more elementary assumptions (including themselves). Axioms too are some such assumptions and are used that way, but as principles—like, 'A cannot be *not-A*', 'whatever is true of a class taken distributively is true of every member of that class' and 'if $A = B$ and $B = C$, then $A = C$'—they are assumed and used by *every* science (in fact, by every cognitive discipline). What is more characteristic of them is that once we are conscious of them they show themselves as self-evident, their efficacy not being, thus, exhausted in the construction of that particular science or that group of sciences. Many of these axioms have, indeed, been sought to be deduced from other propositions supposed to be more primary. But that does not make them, or those other propositions, postulates for that reason. They are, even then, axioms in the sense indicated, unless, of course, one is determined from the beginning to prefer a parsimonious conceptual scheme to the total disregard of unresolvable intuitive certainty. Intuitive certainty may not always be dependable. But whether it is dependable or not is determined solely by whether it has proved unfaithful and that happens only in definite particular cases or groups of such cases. One should not generalise such unfaithfulness, unless, of course, as just said, one just chooses to abide *only* by conceptual schemes. In that case, assuredly, there would be no distinction between postulates and axioms. But even in that case our main thesis on the nature of metaphysics would remain unaffected.

Heuristic principles—like, 'the things of the world are ordered or form a system', 'knowledge proper is a search for such order', and 'there should be as much generalisation as possible, particulars being placed under classes, those under wider classes, and so on'—are presuppositions of another kind. Although assumed, they are perpetually under test, even though we are equally assured that no empirical test worth the name (called verification) is ever adequate, or even necessary, because these principles concern a never exhaustible whole. In their case there is also no question of verification like that of the empirical laws of science. None of them are deducible from other propositions, and they cannot also be taken as statistical laws. Not the latter, because statistical computation itself presupposes these heuristic principles. They are ideals which every cognitive pursuit has to start with. And yet they are neither postulates nor axioms. Not postulates, because they are not confined to a particular science or a particular group of sciences; and not axioms, because they do not show themselves as self-evident: like postulates they are only assumed and used for the construction of other systems.

All these three kinds of presuppositions are such that the science *X* which presupposes them is not itself interested in their study. These presuppositions are studied in another discipline which, relatively to *X*, may be called *meta-X*, such that this *meta-X* can in no sence be considered to be either an extension of *X* or supplementing it in any manner, *X* having a self-contained subject-matter of its own so that if *X* could be actively interested in it, this would only be at the cost of the growth of its own subject-matter. This is the relation, say, of physics or economics with mathematics (logic). There is no intrinsic integration of *X* and *meta-X*. They belong to two different levels of study. It may even happen, as in the case of science *vs* metaphysics, that *X* cannot significantly study the problems of *Y*, their methods—or, better, the languages they use—being incommensurate with each other.

There is, however, a fourth kind of presupposition which, though studied by another discipline *Y*, does not belong to a new *level* of consideration. In such cases, *Y* is not a *meta* study. *Y* is here a study coordinate with *X*, and, except for a convenient division of labour, it is always desirable to integrate *X* and *Y* into a wider study. Economics, anthropology and psychology are such coordinate studies.

We now add to these four kinds of presuppositions a fifth one which would go a long way to explain the attitude of the metaphysician.[1] Metaphysics studies concepts like *space, time, substance, matter, cause, being, non-being, self* and the like, which are all presuppositions of the sciences *X, X′, X″*, etc., such that their study can in no way be incorporated in *X, X′, X″*, etc., these latter being not necessarily interested in that study, and yet the study in question is not like one of axioms and postulates. While in the study of axioms and postulates we find only their enumeration, analysis and interrelation, and at most the study as to how they were *used* in *X, X′, X″*, etc., in metaphysics we find the question of the 'validity' of the presuppositions it studies raised and answered, whatever the word 'validity' means in this connexion. Logic and mathematics which study axioms and postulates of science do not raise such questions of validity: taking, from the beginning, the axioms and postulates as unchallenged, they can at best point out that some pseudo-principles are not axioms or postulates at all. They only analyse (in a rough and ready manner) these axioms and postulates, enumerate them, find their interrelations and show how they are used in X, X', X'', etc. Serious consideration of the validity of presuppositions is the *sine qua non* of the metaphysical attitude.

The sciences themselves have, indeed, in recent days turned toward the examination of the validity of the concepts of space, time, etc., and even the concept of self, say in psychology. But such concepts, which the sciences themselves are examining in modern times, are not the ones which metaphysics has been studying traditionally. What modern scientists are doing is only to show that these traditional metaphysical concepts do not fit in with their sciences as adequate, or just adequate, postulates. They simply ignore metaphysical concepts and replace them by adequate, or just adequate, postulates. If they appear to criticise traditional metaphysical concepts, this is avowedly to impress that these are not the legitimate *postulates* of science, and this leaves open the possibility that metaphysical concepts are of another sort, having a different purpose altogether.

Metaphysical concepts are not the axioms and postulates of the sciences. Like the presuppositions of the fourth kind, they, in metaphysics, form a subject-matter *sui generis*, and yet, undeniably, their study does not supplement the sciences which use them without study. True, modern science does not profess to use them. But, first, what it all means is that modern science has proposed to ignore them altogether, replacing them with newer postulates, and replacement here is no form of correction. Replacement here is drastic and amounts to supersession. Correction means that the basic structure remaining the same, there is only alteration of details. But when the structure itself is altered what happens is supersession which is as good as revolutionary.

Metaphysical concepts, though ignored by modern science, still hold their own, not indeed as postulates any longer but as presuppositions of a new kind in the context of classical science. Space, time, self, etc., as presuppositions of classical science, are taken from the beginning—whether in metaphysics which studies them or in the sciences which use them—as proposed realities out there as referents of corresponding propositions. What metaphysics does specifically is to analyse and enumerate these

presuppositions, taken as much by themselves as in their interrelations, and also examine whether or how far they are real;
and if enumeration is considered a part of analysis, the task of
metaphysics would only be their analysis and the examination of
their reality. If the word 'concept' is used in its restricted sense as
a form of thought, the 'reality of a concept' should be taken to
mean the possibility of an autonomous referent of the proposition
into which the concept may be expanded.

A distinctive feature of the analysis done by a metaphysician is
that, unlike what is done by a scientist, it is neither wholly nor
even predominantly conceptual. 'Scientific' analysis has so much
of a conceptual character that some modern philosophers of
science have been led to regard a scientific attitude itself as purely
operationalistic, as though science has nothing to do with what is
over there as real. Even those who are not so drastically
operationalistic have held that the reference of scientific propositions to those reals which should correspond to them remains always
presumed. It never enters into, i.e., affects, the conceptual
analysis.[2] In metaphysics, on the other hand, all analysis is
inextricably the analysis of referents, so much so that the
conceptual (in modern terms, linguistic) part of the analysis is
determined throughout by that analysis of referents. Per definition, the referent, though referred to by thought=concept
=proposition=language, is over there in its own right. Unlike
science, metaphysics directly analyses such referents, and the
propositions it uses are only expressions of such analyses. The
concept or thought that accompanies any such analysis is,
therefore, coloured from the beginning. On concentration, the
referents themselves get unfolded in various aspects and in inter-
relation. This is a kind of non-logical perceptual analysis, a type
not far different from what we meet within our common daily
life where greater and greater concentration reveals more and
more features that were not noticed before. The difference
between such reflective perception in our daily life and that in
metaphysics will be discussed later. The point to note here is that
metaphysical analysis is predominantly non-logical, i.e., perceptual (intuitive).

Logical analysis relates to a content that is either already known
(somehow) as over there or wholly a (logical) construction. In
case the content is already known as over there as the referent

of a proposition, what logical analysis does is to speak *about* it in different ways, not speak *of* it directly as intuitive analysis spoken out does, and in case the content is wholly a (logical) construction it only speaks that very construction out. In neither case has logical analysis any direct dealing with the referent, which, however, is the exact business of what we have called intuitive analysis.

Logic and Reference[3]

Logicians have never been at ease with autonomous referents. Every proposition refers, at least initially, to something *over there in its own right* and logicians have failed to bring it within the domain of logic. The maximum they have done is to replace it by some intrinsic function of logic (=thought=language), treating it either (to quote a term used generally by phenomenologists) as an *intention* of logic or (as has more often been done) as a construction. Intention and construction, be it noted, are in two different dimensions: while construction constitutes the breadth of the logical domain, intention constitutes its width. In either case, however, the referent as such escapes untouched, for whenever a proposition refers to something it refers to that-in-its-autonomous-standing.

Some logicians have indeed postulated ultimate non-logical data as what one is just acquainted with and which form the base for all logic. But that only means that they have proved false to the logic with which they started as an overpowering attitude. It is good that they have done their best to maintain their loyalty to logic as far as it was possible for them, but then the problem of reference remains. Some have even proposed to strip the data further and prefer to stop with mere *this-now*s under the comforting notion that 'this' and 'now' are after all also conceptual. But how can they get rid of the fact that these are, equally, non-logical?[4] This type of see-saw we find in mathematics too, particularly in that branch of mathematics which is called topology where 'space' is sought to be understood as some function of 'distance', or even of 'neighbourhood' (with, of course, the help of certain other mathematical notions), as though distance or neighbourhood is all conceptual. The problem remains: how to connect logic with non-logical presentations?

Initial definitions in a particular axiomatic system have often been taken as just conventions in the field with which that axiomatic system is concerned. It is enough, we admit, that for that particular conceptual scheme they are taken as conventions. But this does not warrant them to be treated as merely some conventions. They could be so taken if, and only if, there were other beliefs in the field under consideration clashing with these, or if from out of just those beliefs as initial definitions another parallel self-contained conceptual scheme could be constructed, the schemes being in either case adequate descriptions, on the whole, of most of the behaviours in that field. But even this does not warrant the assumption that these beliefs are mere conventions. They might all have ontological import, though some of them might well be wrong ontologically. All beliefs are meant to be ontologically valid, though some of them may not actually be so. Even when with a particular set of beliefs a fully adequate account is constructed, the beliefs need not be mere conventions, except as an abstract requirement of that conceptual scheme.

This tussle between logic and the non-logical is a long-drawn story in the history of Western philosophy. In India, on the other hand, except in the case of some Buddhist systems, there has never been such a problem—why we shall see later. In India, except with these Buddhists, the non-logical presentation (the given) was never understood as 'what is left over after all that is logic is abstracted away'. The given was never understood as merely the sense-data or, alternatively, what James called 'blooming and buzzing' experience. Chairs, tables, fields and seas, indeed everything that could be perceived as integrally one and over there, were taken as given and so far non-logical. Not that these things do not involve logic. To quote an old term, the (direct) awareness of these things is, of course, *judgemental*, but the experience here is not 'perceptual judgement'. It is, rather, 'judgemental perception', meaning that the total thing is in each case directly contacted (intuited). So long as the thing is intuited, the logic that is involved does not stand distinguished: it stands as undistinguishedly fused in the total presentation, which means that at that stage of intuition there is no question of logic. It is only at a later stage, where logic comes to be distinguished in itself and understood as autonomously manipulable for building a whole study called formal logic, that it could be said to have been involved. It is not true also that since as a matter of fact logic has now stood as so distinguished it must have been there *as logic* even at the lower stage. Assuredly, it was there, for it was not created at the next stage; yet there is some snag somewhere. For, were it there in the way a thing unnoticed could be in a perceived heap, it has to be described as what came to be added to certain definite things that were already there. But in the case under consideration one cannot speak that way. Nobody knows definitely what was there before logic came to be added. There is no experience of any datum that could be spoken of as bereft of all logic—neither a sense-datum nor what is called 'blooming and buzzing' experience. Such datum cannot be postulated without any further evidence, for then such postulation would be entirely *ad hoc.* The only legitimate way of describing the situation would be to say that though logic in its freedom can be dissociated from the given, the converse is not true. There is only a one-sided independence: logic is independent of the given, but not vice versa.

To understand (interpret) the given in terms of logic—in other words, to offer a complete description of the given—is thus an impossible task. If philosophers in the West have tried that, it is because they have been systematically deluded by a false dignity regarding logic. Logic can, indeed, be dissociated from the given and developed on its own account, but it is *valid* just in so far as—how, nobody knows—it can remain involved in the given in the sense of having been undistinguishedly fused with it. This is exactly the way memory and thought remain in perception, or forms (taken in the widest sense) remain in a given complex (where these forms have not been distinguished), rendering thereby the base, in either case, completely indefinite (indescribable), except negatively as just *what they are not,* when they are dissociated. When dissociated, logic shows a variety of forms in an infinite number of possible permutations and combinations, and the only criteria for choice from among them are consistency (non-contradiction), generality, and parsimony (adequacy). But these are no considerations for the *validity* of logic. Validity can be established only with reference to the given from which it was dissociated or with reference to a givable, understood in terms of one or more such 'givens' with the help of that logic. Western philosophers, called rationalists (or, sometimes, intellectuals, in a pejorative sense of the term), have not noticed this need for validity and, in spite of Kant's definite pointers, have, since the days of Hegel, tried in different manners to extol its dignity beyond all bounds. They have declared, so to say, a sort of revolution by proposing to do away with the non-logical given (referent) altogether. But have they succeeded?

Supposing they have succeeded, what much they have done is to replace the given by logical construction. But the crucial question remains: What do they mean by 'construction'—constructing or constructs-which-are-already-there? If 'constructing' is at all distinct from 'construct', it is a psychological process in time, something that is not extra-logical, and they cannot be meaning that. If, on the other hand, they mean 'construct', what is it, after all, but non-psychological and non-temporal? In what way does it differ, if at all, from the much maligned entities called metaphysical? What it all comes to is that when a logician 'constructs' something logically, this act of constructing (God only knows what the expression stands for if it is not nakedly psychological and temporal, for otherwise it is little different from 'construct') 'recovers' a construct that is eternally there. The only thing that the logician has gained is that the construct is not sense-perceived but logical. But how does it differ from the metaphysical which is also not sense-perceived and yet eternally (better, non-temporally) over there? Worse than that, if the logician-philosopher's construct is from out of empiricals, they are not non-sense-perceivable, i.e., non-observable, unless, of course, they have persuaded themselves that they have successfully liquidated 'datum of observation' by the so-called concept 'this-now'.

Another way of escape has sometimes been proposed by modern linguistic analysts. It is to treat logic as only the rule (or a set of rules) for the use of language. Whether there can or cannot be an unalterable set of rules for all languages is not the question here. Whatever will be said here will be true as much of an unalterable set as of a contingent one. What these analysts intend is that no rule be existent on its own right, no matter whether one applies it or not. 'Apply it' here does not mean

that it is first there like a surgeon's scalpel and then it is used.
What is intended is that its entire status be exhausted in just
being used, quite as much as is the case with moral rules. When
certain (given) data are woven logically into a construct what
actually happens is that these data are linguistically used in a
certain way, and not that something else has happened or is discovered or referred to.

But this too will not save the situation. A moral rule, in so far
as it is unused, has, in a sense, no ontological status. It is primarily
formulable only as 'Do this' and 'Do not do this' and not as
'Something there is such and such', except in a formal mode of
speech. But once used and embodied in an action or a state of
affairs, does it not acquire some ontological status? The action,
or the state of affairs, once resulting, is a fact over there—a
fact among other facts of the world—and the rule in question
is there too, though not as embodied (realised) quite as much, but
in just the reverse direction, as logic was shown earlier to have
already been 'in the given' before it was distinguished out. There is
a difference between logic as an ontological affair and as a moral
rule, and the difference consists of when exactly each is spoken of
as involved in a given situation. That difference is there, but,
quite as much as logic, moral rules are found involved in states
of affairs standing 'over there'. As so involved, they too are
'over there' with as much ontological status as those states of
affairs. If moral rules, considered only as 'to be used', have yet,
in this sense, an ontological status, one ought not to make an
exception for logic. Logic too, when realised, i.e., having woven
a construct from out of observable data, may well be said to be
ontologically there. Even if a logical rule may not as such be
'over there' with any ontological status, this does not guarantee
that what is constructed by means of such rules is not 'over there'
ontologically.

Other Wrong Ways of Solving the Problem of Reference

A most popular way of handling the problem is to hold that the
very nature of logic=thought=language is such that it cannot
move without referring to something which is extra-logical
=extar-thought (called also *real*)=extra-linguistic (and some have

further held that even this something which is referred to is of such a nature that it has to be referred to, that its very being, not merely its objectivity, consists in being referred to by thought).[5] It follows that at the formal level of speech too, a proposition 'S is P', with definite values put for the variables, has to be talked of as one that refers to a particular empirical situation, and 'S is P', without such values put, as referring to *any* empirical situation.

This could be a simple and elegant solution if only logic had not, as we have already seen, claimed a sort of transcendence. If logic can transcend the given, and it does as a matter of fact transcend it as when different formal logics are built, can one hold so easily that logic has to express itself in a proposition that necessarily refers to something which is extra-logical? Further, is it not because logic=thought is capable of such transcendence that we are faced at all with the problem of validity of a proposition apart from its logical consistency?

This popular way of solving the problem of relation between logic and reference is as naive and *ad hoc* as the old theory of pre-established harmony, designed to solve the old problem of the relation between thought (consciousness) and extension (reality). There, too, the very problem could be occasioned only because thought was understood as autonomous, i.e., capable of transcending the real, and it is only because thought could be invalidated that there arose the problem of its validity. Otherwise, neither this theory nor any of its ilk could explain why there should be invalid thought after all.

There have been several other attempts to solve the problem. Some have held that thought (logic) constitutes reality (referent). This, undoubtedly, is a better account than the naive one just disposed of. But all depends on how this fact of constituting is understood. If it means that thought belongs to one region— subjective or logical—and reality to another, viz., objective or extra-logical, nothing would be gained thereby. For, the question would recur: how exactly is the other region to be understood as constituted by thought, assuming that this other region is not nothing but thought? And it is not nothing but thought. Were it so, the world of our daily life would be purely formal, with no material content whatsoever. Material content could, no doubt, be reduced to subjective ideas, but even then the distinction between form and content would remain, and our original problem would only get translated to: how are form and content related to one another?

It cannot be said, again, that the extra-logical is after all content plus form and that the form side of the extra-logical is but thought. This would presuppose that there is a content side, i.e., mere content—a mere datum that is either an atomic sense-datum (or many such) or what James called the 'blooming and buzzing' experience. But we have already seen that such mere data cannot be admitted, except on an illegitimate *ad hoc* basis.

Also, the content cannot be reduced without remainder to mere form, as a third dimension of this form, either as its self-negation, i.e., as just *not*-form, *not*-ing being only a logical function, or as some purely *a priori* anticipation, often called intention. The self-negation in question does not explain the empirical variety of content. There are, of course, some *logical* varieties of contents, which could be understood as logical modes of self-negation of thought. But the central problem is not about the relation of thought to these logical varieties. It concerns, rather, the relation of thought to empirical varieties of content. Neither Kant nor Hegel, nor Advāita Vedānta, nor even the phenomenologists, have tackled this problem. Bracketing nature is a laudable procedure, but that does not solve our problem. Kant, it may be remembered in this connexion, has not answered Hume, and Hegel's idea of abstract reason concretising itself into concrete reason is, without further ado, only a piece of rhetoric. Advāita Vedānta, though not concerned immediately with the problem of thought *vs* empirical contents, struggled hard with a similar problem, viz., pure consciousness *vs* empirical contents, and wisely left it as insoluble—why we shall soon see.

Nor, again, can it be said that it is no problem at all because thought, according to those who hold this view, is nothing *sui generis* but only movements of the same experience that gives us empirical data. First, because, as we have already seen, data bereft of these movements, quite as much as bereft of thought, are all postulated *ad hoc;* and, secondly, because these movements also, quite as much as those of thought, have a transcendence of their own. The same charges could be levelled against those who consider these movements as those of language.

Equally abortive would be the attempt of some modern analysts who, in the line of axiomatics, propose that first-level propositions that refer to something non-logical should be treated as initial, not-further-to-be-analysed and universally accepted propositions that form a base along with some other primitive propositions for a new axiomatic system which should be called 'logic proper'. They hold that unless such harmless primitive propositions are started with as a base, this logic proper cannot be built.   But are such primitive propositions really necessary? If the whole purpose of the new logic is to determine whether when the proposition 'S is P' is *true* or *false* another proposition—whether a function of 'S is P' or not—is true or false (or neither), such primitive propositions would, indeed, be needed.   But should the new logic be necessarily truth-functional? May not the whole purpose of the new logic be more primary: just to determine whether if 'S is P'[6] is 'yes'ed or 'no'ed, another proposition is 'yes'ed or 'no'ed (or neither), 'yes' or 'no' not meaning 'true or false'?   The problem as to whether a proposition is true or false presupposes that propositions, in general, are either true or false. But how propositions could be true or false is precisely our central question here.   It is no use bypassing the question.   Even '*if* true' and '*if* false' presuppose that there is at least one case of 'is true' and 'is false', why should such a case of 'is' be presupposed by logic which proposes to be most primary, i.e., strictly formal? Truth-functional logic may well be understood as the first grade of *applied* logic which is evidently more concrete than the logic which is to be strictly formal.

To take this strictly formal logic and the applied logic of the first grade in one sweep would, indeed, be a sort of generalisation yielding a generalised system perfectly in keeping with the relational logic supposed to supersede the ancient Aristotelian logic of syllogism. But that does not necessarily make relational logic more primary than the Aristotelian.   The Aristotelian logic can be shown to be more primary than the relational one, and while the more primary is necessarily more general, in one sense the reverse is not true in that sense. So also is the case with what we call 'strictly formal logic' *vis-à-vis* logic that is truth-functional. Let us explain.

The Aristotelian logic of syllogism as more abstract has for its informing principle the axiom: 'If P is predicated of M and M of S, then P is predicated of S.' As more abstract, it is in no need of considering the *modus operandi* of either of the predications, viz., how exactly P is predicated of M and how exactly M of S (whether P is to the north of or greater than M and whether M is to the east of or greater than S). What is intended by the principle of syllogism is that if P is predicated of M in a certain manner, and M of S in a certain manner, then P has to be predicated of S in a manner that has to be computed out of these two manners. That computation may be empirical or non-empirical. In case it is empirical it is either a case of the application of the Aristotelian principle or just an empirical convention; and in case it is not empirical, it is, again, either an application of the Aristotelian principle or a pure conceptual convention. In either case, it is either a post-'Aristotelian principle' or a convention. One can build up a system of computation—a theoretical calculus—so far as these applications and conventions are concerned and call it logic, but that would be more complex and, therefore, less abstract and, in that sense, less general than the traditional Aristotelian logic. Similarly with the truth-functional logic *vis-à-vis* what we have called strictly formal logic. Truth-claim (whether S being P is true or false) and truth-game (if S being P is true or false) are extra considerations that would only add complications to a pure-propositional formal logic. Sometimes, again, as in cases of strictly empirical specification, these additional considerations may not have a logic (system of computation) of their own. Conceivably, however, they may have one in special cases. But then this would be a complex or applied logic, though more formal than other grosser systems of computation.

There are three points which require to be clarified in this connexion. Our more general logic, viz., the Aristotelian, is evidently of a narrower range than the relational logic which we have called comparatively less general. Relational logic covers more cases than the Aristotelian logic of syllogism, not merely because intuitively the range is wider but more because the Aristotelian logic could be shown to be only a case of relational logic— a case where the relation studied is one of substance and attribute. This is the first point to be seriously considered. The second point, not unconnected with it, is as follows: The so-called axiom 'if P is predicated of M and if M is predicated of S, then P is predicated of S' may not really be an axiom at all. It may not even be a postulate or a primitive proposition just going unchallenged in a system of axiomatics. Some set-theorists have claimed they have deduced it from propositions which are more primitive, and which, on that account, are precisely those on which the new logic of relations is based.

The third point for consideration is of quite another sort and more relevant to our main issue. It is that even what we have called strictly formal logic may not help being truth-functional, and that on the following grounds: A propositional form is rendered into an actual proposition immediately as the variables are replaced by definite values. Obviously, these replacing values, being definite, cannot be wholly conceptual, because by definition they are constants, and nothing is a constant in the truest sense of the term if it is not either a definite empirical or one that is conceptually constructed out of some such definite empiricals, in which latter case too its constancy derives directly from a definite empirical. It follows that wherever there is an actual proposition, as distinct from propositional form, variables are replaced by empiricals. These empiricals, again, are exactly those on account of which the proposition in question is true or false. If, therefore, propositional forms which alone constitute the subject-matter of the strictly formal logic have to contain variables, they cannot but be considered as having some generalised reference to the empirical and, therefore, as having some relation with truth such that it shows itself at least as a truth-game. (A propositional form has no truth-claim; only an actual proposition can have it.)

The three points listed above have now to be examined. Let us take up the first point.

In the Aristotelian logic 'S is P' should not be understood as S is a substance to which P stands related as an attribute. The relation is much simpler and wider than that. It is the *subject-predicate* relation, the presumption being that anything whatsoever— an attribute, mode, a relation, etc.; or even in some cases a substance—may be predicated of S. This subject-predicate relation covers all other relations, and covers them precisely in the way language covers extra-linguistic things said to be spoken of. When language speaks of things it speaks of them as related among themselves. Language represents them as related and yet this act of representation is itself, in whatever way, a sort of relation to the things represented, and, therefore, a relation of quite another type belonging to a different level altogether. It covers all those relations and does not seek to represent itself along with them.

Language only shows and does not state itself, except in a formal mode of speech. What are ordinarily called relations are all stated, or statable, in the material mode of speech. They are all 'over there'. But not so the subject-predicate relation which is never genuinely 'over there.'[7] If in the formal mode of speech it appears to be spoken of as over there, this is immediately followed by the implicit speech, at the same formal level, that it is not really over there, but only the subject-predicate relation as just spoken out, not spoken of. Confusion of the two levels would only lead to the fallacy known as category confusion.

Ordinarily, when C is taken as more general than a, C is understood as covering that a and some other element or elements. Ordinarily, the whole situation is understood extensionally, as though C, a and those other elements are all equally over there and, to that extent, on par. Thanks to the famous Russellian puzzle, we have not only to distinguish between levels (in Russell's language, types), we have also to admit that all classes may not be understood extensionally. Most classes can indeed be treated that way, but in some cases, particularly where the Russellian puzzle emerges, the classes in question may be understood differently—one may say, intentionally, i.e., conceptually; and as there is no bar against treating the other cases too from this point of view all classes whatsoever may be understood that way, though treating those which do not generate the puzzle extensionally may be more convenient.

It follows that a consistent way of defining 'more general' is to say that C, taken as a concept, i.e., as what is only shown and not statable in the material mode of speech, covers $a, b, m, n, o,$ etc. That would also corroborate the common view that the abstract is more general than the corresponding concretes. It is in this sense that the Aristotelian logic of syllogism is more general than the logic of relations.

This explains away the second objection raised on page 32 above. If predication is no relation on par with what are ordinarily called relations that are statable as over there, it would be illogical to deduce the Aristotelian principle of syllogism—'if P is predicated of M and M of S, then P is predicated of S'—from more primitive propositions in the way the proposition, 'if x is greater than y, and y greater than z, then x is greater than z', is sought to be deduced. Nor, if the latter cannot be shown to be a theorem deducible from more primitive assumptions but has to be taken as itself a postulate, should the Aristotelian principle of syllogism be treated otherwise.

What we have shown so far is that the Aristotelian logic is more general, more abstract and, therefore, more primary than the new logic of relations, called symbolic logic. Our main purpose was to show that exactly in this way genuine formal logic is more general, more abstract and, therefore, more primary than logic which is truth-functional. With this we come to consider the third objection raised on page 33.

Admitted that propositional forms use variables and admitted also that these variables can be replaced by constant values which, in the present case, are always empiricals, should this necessarily mean that variables cannot be understood except as what have to be so replaced? A theoretical study may well be turned into an applied one, but this does not mean that to apply to a definite concrete field constitutes its central motive, its very life. When it goes on developing itself it is rarely worried about whether it can apply and, if so, how; and this is particularly true of symbolic logic. Symbolic logic is intended to be the most primary, most theoretical, system of axiomatics and, so, should not bother about whether it could also be empirically true.

A concrete science of empiricals need not, one may argue, stand to the corresponding system of axiomatics as an applied science like engineering stands to the corresponding theoretical one. It may just be the empirical concretisation of the corresponding axiomatic discipline, as concrete physics is of physics as an axiomatic discipline, this latter again, of geometry, that geometry, in its turn, of axiomatic arithmetic and that last too of logic as an axiomatic system. In none of these cases, one may contend, does the presupposed study stand to the presupposing as a theoretical (in the ordinary sense) science to the corresponding applied (in the ordinary sense) science.

But even this amendment would not entitle one to claim that the ultimate axiomatised logic cannot develop itself except as so presupposed. True, in order to determine the consistency of some axiomatics we may have to use a correspondingly more concrete axiomatic system as a model, and truth-functional logic might, by some, be considered as such a model for the more primary axiomatised logic. But, unfortunately, the so-called model here does not in any way differ, so far as axiomatisation is concerned, from the logic which is more primitive except that the 'yes' and 'no' of the propositions of the latter are translated into 'truth' and 'falsity'. Truth-functional logic cannot be considered a model for a more primitive logic. As for multivalued logic, which is sometimes understood as more primitive (because it is more general) than the truth-functional one, it must not be forgotten that the only value which, in multivalued logic, has been added to truth and falsity is probability which, unfortunately, ought not to be taken as other than truth and falsity but only as lesser truth and lesser falsity, quantity of truth or falsity being assumed as measurable. A proper 'neither true nor false' should not be taken as less true or less false. If it has got any meaning, that should be beyond truth and falsity, which is either the 'yes' or 'no' in 'if S being P, 'yes'ed or 'no'ed, then S' being P' 'yes'ed or 'no'ed, or some transcendental metaphysical status, with which, however, we are not immediately concerned here. We are thus forced back to the mere 'yes' and 'no' of formal logic.[8] Mere assent and mere dissent are different from positive and negative *assertion*. Assent is just entertainment: 'Suppose "S is P" is not "if 'S is P'" is true.' Mere assent and mere dissent belong to a level which is more primitive than assertion and denial (denial=negative assertion).

Logic as a Complete Substitute for Referent Examined

The relation of logic to the referent is thus a problem not yet accounted for. For a reasonable solution there are only two other ways left—either to regard logic, i.e., proposition, as a complete substitute for the referent, or vice versa. Present-day rationalists— call them logicians, intellectuals or by whatever other names— are for the former alternative, and metaphysicians, whether of the old type or modern,[9] are for the latter.

From what has been said earlier it is evident by now that if one *stars with* logic, whether as self-evident or as axiomatically developed, there is no intelligible (logical) passage to the extra-logical. The entire system of logic has, therefore, to be understood as distinguished out from common life and concrete sciences in which it had remained from the beginning as undistinguishedly fused.[10] The most primitive axiomatics, usually called logic proper, could be constructed at all if, and only if, the constituent propositions, whether as undefined and undemonstrated ultimates or as defined and demonstrated (which latter two are, incidentally, the same, i.e., logical deduction), were phenomenologically distinguished from out of common life and concrete sciences. There is no gainsaying the fact that the undefined and undemonstrated propositions are so distinguished out. How, otherwise, could the logicians get at them at all? They could abstract these simply because they had a long training in the process of abstraction. As for propositions which are *deduced*, one may legitimately ask: how could they know the *principles* of deduction, principles which they had to apply to deduce those secondary propositions? Further, is it not true that in their very axiomatics many of the deduced propositions are themselves the principles of deduction? How can these logicians escape the charge of *petitio principii*? The only way of escape would be to hold that when logic itself deduces certain propositions what it really does is just to unfold itself through stages, and logic is not, in this respect, different from phenomenology.

If logic as the most primitive axiomatics is non-different from metalogic it is difficult to see how the acceptability of the rules with which it demonstrates logical theorems could be guaranteed. Their acceptability does not consist in their consistency (their not clashing with one another) and completeness, nor in their conventionality (added to these merits). Not this latter, because whereas the conventional has always some contingency about it the rules that logic employs are *ex hypothesi* not capable of being otherwise. Not that this 'not capable of being otherwise' is known intuitively in the ordinary sense of the term; it is not capable of being otherwise only because there is no going beyond this logic=metalogic to another meta study. It is a factual limitation, because any attempt to go beyond brings back the explorer to the field of that logic, thus generating an inevitable *petitio principii*. The rules in question are factual ultimates, which means that they are in no way extrinsic to the axiomatics called logic=metalogic. We may add, too, that one or more theorems of some logical axiomatics could well be used as rules for *deducing* som rule or rules of another alternative logical axiomatics, so that some rules can always be shown to be theorems and some theorems rules, which means that rules and theorems in the field of logic are only phenomenological self-exposures of logic, some of which are relatively simple and some more complex.

Phenomenologically speaking, as logic is sought to be distinguished from out of common life and science, certain logical propositions first unfold themselves, then certain others that had till then stood undistinguishedly fused with these and, therefore, more deeply involved that way in common life and concrete sciences started with, then still others at the next higher level, and so on. In this process of stage-wise self-unfoldment, there is no question of *deducing* any proposition from others. But once the whole field in its details is thus mapped out level-wise, one can *from outside* re-arrange the whole thing mechanically by choosing to start from any set of these unfoldments and deducing others from them. Basically, however, the whole story is one of stage-wise self-unfoldment, followed phenomenologically and, so far, intuitively.

Intuition can indeed go wrong. But so may a conceptual scheme— no human endeavour can claim absolute certainty. There is no point in condemning intuition *a priori*. One can condemn intuition only when in the face of unresolved contradictions a particular system of unfoldments is dogmatically adhered to.[11] When in such systems contradictions arise, what is demanded is that one first tries one's best to resolve them, keeping oneself committed to that system and, secondly, in case this turns out impossible, to see if the whole thing cannot be re-intuited from the beginning in another way. If this is the normal procedure in our common life, it need not be different in other cases.

Whether logic is developed phenomenologically (intuitively) or by way of axiomatisation, the central attitude of the modern-day logician is that when one has known the logic of the world he has known its essence and need not turn to lesser details, i.e., to the referents, whether by themselves (if that is possible) or in whatever other structural relations. The final essence is the final structure which is logic par excellence. Different concrete sciences are interested in different lesser structures, and these sciences can themselves be arranged in a hierarchy of precedence, mathematics being next to logic (if the two are distinguished at all) and physics next to mathematics. Physics, no doubt, as more concrete than mathematics, is concerned more pronouncedly with empirical referents, but even there its main (one may say, sole) concern is with their structural relations, called laws, which, though phenomenologically distinguished from out of sciences lower in the hierarchy—the structural relations in these lower sciences being similarly distinguished from out of still lower sciences and ultimately from common life—may be axiomatised from an outside 'angelic' point of view. Whichever way one chooses to proceed, it is somehow believed that when the structure as the essence is known, everything worth knowing is known. Laws (logical structures) are thus sought to replace the referents, whether phenomenologically or from the point of view of axiomatics. This is the modern revolution in all cognitive pursuit.

This, however, was not the story in earlier days except in the field of metaphysics. Sciences in earlier days were principally concerned with empirical details and whatever law was discovered was understood inevitably in the context of its application. Sciences were understood as accounts of the empirical world—as a concrete story of it and, one might say, as its history. There is, of course, one difference: in contrast with history, predictions in these sciences were progressively more precise and more confirmable (verifiable). But this was possible, only because the structures (laws) concerned were better known—known or precisely and more thoroughly; and that too was possible because mathematics and logic, which contained the most comprehensive laws, came to be used. In other words, these sciences came to be more and more conscious of mathematical and logical laws (structures).

This is what we meant by 'replacement of referents by logic'. Attention was focussed more and more on laws, and ultimately on logic (and mathematics), which became more and more autonomous. Phenomenologically, the laws—whether logical or more concrete ones—were understood sometimes as over there, as though they were referents of a Platonic order, transcending all that is empirical and yet over there; sometimes, again, as just modes of subjective thinking. In either case, however, in course of time, these philosophers were faced with difficulties. Doubts crept in regarding whether there could be any Platonic entity at all: were there such ghostly entities, they would be incommensurate with whatever is unquestionably over there, viz., empiricals. Naturally, in this new attitude, logicians resorted to a simple logical device, viz., the rule of parsimony, which, they held, ought to be applied whenever there was any serious doubt about the independent existence of a thing.[12] Applying this device they found that Platonic entities could be reduced to modes of subjective thinking. But sooner, again, they found that even this alternative was not free from all difficulty. Subjective thinking, as it is normally experienced, is private, but about the modes of thinking that are in question here there is always a consensus. This led some logician-philosophers to talk of *universal* subjective thinking. But that too was not found easily acceptable, involving, as it did, a large number of psychological and other irregularities. The whole thing looked like an *ad hoc* hypothesis.

Because of these difficulties on either side some were driven to hold that logical entities were neutral—neither subjective nor objective. As against the possible objection that no real could be neither subjective nor objective, they held that these were, therefore, not existent at all, though not, for that reason, non-existent either. According to them, these entities could have no ontological status at all. But, even then, all difficulties were not over. If they had no ontological status, could they be anything more than mere usages—uses *qua* use? Any use of a thing is, of course, an event in time and, so far, existent, but a usage, i.e., a use 'as use', is *exhypothesi* a non-event. It is not even a generalisation, in any proper context, of use-events of a particular type. It is just use, use *qua* use, and that, precisely, constitutes its logical character. Modern linguistic analysts understand logic in this sense. They speak of logic as the use of language. (When, in the interest of greater precision, they speak of it as the rule of the use of language, by 'use' in that case they mean use as an event, and by 'rule' precisely the use as use, i.e., as a non-event.)

But even this last account of the status of logic is defective, if only because it is largely negative. What it claims is, negatively, that logic is neither any empirical event like the actual use of subjective thinking or, alternatively, like an event over there as an object, nor even anything of the Platonic order. The only positive thesis it offers is that logic is usage, but even there we come across a qualifying clause which is negative, viz., that no usage is to be understood as an event. About what it positively is we are left in the dark.

Metaphysics Proper

The entire difficulty originated from a wrong approach to our central problem. The correct approach, as we saw it long back, is as follows: Whatever is phenomenologically distinguished, as over there, from out of a starting situation is inevitably understood as what was (and, therefore, also is) in that situation, though as undistinguishedly fused in it, but now standing as distinguished. i.e., by itself, in its proper shape. As it is impossible to find it in this proper shape in that initial situation,[13] we have to take it as over there, i.e., real, only at a higher level. In all such cases there is, first, the epistemic higher level of *consideration*—higher, because the new consideration is more reflective—and, second, what is thus distinguished is not apprehended as what was not there. Were it apprehended as what was not there, and if it is anything more than the initial situation, what the episteme at the higher level would appear to refer to would have to be taken as created by reflection. But when distinguished it is not apprehended as created for the first time. Inevitably, it is apprehended as what was there already, though not in the shape in which it is now discovered. It is apprehended now as discovered in its proper shape, for that is the verdict of all reflective discovery: whatever shape in which a thing is discovered in reflection is its proper shape. If, then, it appears in its proper shape and corresponds to (not 'is created by') a higher level of epistemic consideration, there is no way out but to admit that the proper shape (or the thing in that proper shape) belongs to a higher level of *reality*.

If the logician-philosophers, discussed in the preceding section, could not recognise this higher level of reality, this was because of their prejudice that whatever is real has to be empirical. They were prepared to admit epistemological (logical) types (levels) of *consideration* (vide their theory of types), but their empiricistic prejudice stood in the way of their recognising types of reality. Little did they see that types of reality have to correspond to the types (in their sense) of consideration. A type of consideration always reveals some particular feature of the content not noted before. Normally such features are found unambiguously to have been in the initial situation in exactly the same shapes in which they are discovered in the new type of consideration. But the case is otherwise when (1) a feature is discovered in a new shape which yet (2) is believed to have been present somehow in the initial situation. Obviously, it could not have been there in that shape. Hence, it must have been there in another shape and, as that another shape cannot now be defined in terms of the new shape in which it appears to reflect (except circuitously as 'the new shape was *somehow* present at the earlier stage'), it was quite indefinite there. This is what we meant by the expression 'undistinguished fusion'.

If types of reality are not admitted, even Carnap's distinction between formal and material modes of speech would be of little significant help. For, whatever is *significantly* spoken of in the formal mode of speech is exactly what, Wittgenstein says, is *shown*[14] by a proposition, and what is shown at a stage without being capable of being stated at that stage is exactly what is called logical, the status of which is here under consideration.

There is indeed a formal mode of speech which has nothing to do with the content of the corresponding objective speech. This happens when from a higher level we just speak about a sentence we spoke at the lower level of material speech, as when we say that 'This table is brown' is an English sentence or that it is one in the indicative mood. But this is meta-language of a new sort altogether, having nothing to do with what this sentence was about. What we are considering here is, on the other hand, how the referent of the lower level speech stands to the speech at the higher level.

Logic thus is real of a higher, trans-empirical, level. But so understood, how does it differ, one may ask, from metaphysics so far as their status is concerned? Viewed that way, logic is only a part of metaphysics. Metaphysics, it will be shown in the next section, contains a lot of other propositions besides what are strictly called 'logical'. It will also be shown that logic as the system of these logical propositions belongs only to one particular metaphysical level, and that, too, as forming a horizontal dimension of that level which, along with other metaphysical levels (of reality), stands in a vertical hierarchy. We shall further show that (1) some metaphysicians, primarily interested in the vertical hierarchy, may not turn at all to the study of logic which, like anything in the horizontal dimension of any other plane on the vertical line, may only be of secondary importance to the metaphysician, and (2) while Indian transcendentalists belong mostly to this group of metaphysicians their Western counterparts have preferred logic and sought, rather, to metaphysicise it.

If logicians have attempted to replace referents by logic, in a way the same thing has been done by metaphysicians in practically the same spirit. When metaphysicians, through their typical reflection just discussed, discover different levels of reality, each such level is taken directly as the essence of the level that is immediately transcended and indirectly of others that had been transcended before. And, exactly as the logician-philosophers have done, they presume that once an essence is known there is knowledge of all that is worth knowing in that field. Logician-philosophers, in line with modern revolutionaries called scientists, have held that it is unworthy of a wise man to get interested in details except as structured through that essence, i.e., in terms of corresponding laws. As we have already seen, this is the way they have sought to reduce referents to logic. Our metaphysicians too have done the same thing. They have sought to discover purer and purer essences at higher and higher levels of metaphysical reflection and on this score, therefore, they cannot be taken to task by the logician-philosopher. The only difference—and that is a vital one—is that the metaphysician has started with the world as it is empirically presented, not with logic as more or less an accomplished system of abstractions. This is why we said earlier that the metaphysician has rather completely replaced logic by the referent; and keeping in view what has been said so far in this section, viz., that logic emerges out of the given, one may not consider it unjustified.

Metaphysical entities (essences) at different levels of reflection have been sought to be distinguished broadly in two ways—objective and subjective. What is attempted in the objective attitude is the distinguishing of space, time, self-identity, difference, negation, other logico-metaphysical relations, matter (if that is distinguishable at all), etc., and with regard to human situations, the distinguishing of sensing, life, remembering, judging, willing, consciousness, self, etc.—all, however, considered as objects, i.e., somehow other than the corresponding epistemic distinguishing; and these acts of epistemic distinguishing are not, in that attitude and in that context, distinguished as objects. They cannot be distinguished as objects, if only because in that case there would be vicious indefinite regress or *petitio principii*. As subjective they are indeed there as presupposed, but neither as stated nor even as shown. Things could be stated or even shown if, and only if, we were consciously, interested in them. But when we distinguish metaphysical entities objectively, what we are consciously interested in are only these objects (by themselves or in relation to those from which they are distinguished), not the corresponding epistemic acts of distinguishing.

As soon as we turn to these acts of distinguishing, however, the whole attitude changes and we find them as merely shown and not statable except in a formal mode of speech. The attitude in which we feel interested in something as just shown may be called subjective attitude.

Sometime back when, in connexion with the Wittgensteinian concept of 'shown', we argued that the shown is the same thing as the logical, we meant by 'logical' one that is part of the metaphysical, and by 'metaphysical' what is discovered in the subjective attitude. The metaphysical which is discovered in the objective attitude is not even shown beforehand. It is what comes to be discovered, for the first time, as having been involved, though as undistinguishedly fused, in the initial situation started with, and that too without having given any prior indication. This proves that one need not be an objective metaphysician at all: one may remain a positivist all one's life. It is only in case one happens to have the type of reflection which unfolds a factor that is clearly apprehended as not capable of having been in the initial situation, in the shape in which it is now discovered, that one turns into a metaphysician with an objective attitude. As for turning into a metaphysician with a subjective attitude, it is a *must* for those who have consciously attended to the Wittgensteinian 'showns' and more so, as will be presently seen, for those who have once become metaphysicians with an objective attitude.

Objective metaphysical entities are all statable in the form of literal propositions, though of a higher order than ordinary natural propositions. There is either the statement of (objective) metaphysical propositions or no occasion whatsoever for these— objectively, one is either a (an objective) metaphysician or a wholehearted positivist: no one can be neither, objectively. Subjective metaphysics is in a new attitude altogether. It is a sort of novel development—in an altogether new direction—of what are shown as fringes of literal propositions, natural or metaphysical.

The showns, just so far as they are fringes of literal propositions, need not occupy our whole attention. They may pass off half noticed as mere fringes. But once we turn to them the whole atmosphere alters. It is never enough, and in no case authentic, to stop with speaking of them in the mere 'formal mode of speech'. They demand to be followed authentically in their details of development. The moment, however, we begin following them that way we find ourselves in a completely new attitude—we call it a subjective attitude—where it is evident that we are no longer interested in the objects, whether natural or metaphysical, in their independent objective status. Whatever interest we then have in these objects is only in so far as we have violently turned away from them and so no longer consider them as over there on their own right, involving the showns or not. This is in sharp contrast with what happens when we metaphysicise objectively. In objective metaphysicising, when starting from the empirical world, called Nature, we first distinguish certain metaphysical objects, say, space and time, the Nature from which we are supposed to turn away is not understood as not there, although it is understood as involving the metaphysical objects now distinguished; and similarly at every higher metaphysical stage with regard to the relation between what is distinguished and what is distinguished from. In Aristotelian language, far from a form-as-distinguished negating that from out of which it has been distinguished, the latter continues to be taken as real, though involving that form at the same time. Aristotle, of course, denies that the form as such can remain in an abstract metaphysical region independently of what it is distinguished from, but that is another question with which we are not concerned here. There is no denying the fact that with Aristotle, form has a status different from that of Nature, though, assuredly with him, it remains forever in Nature. This is why he holds that though ultimately a pure form can be distinguished (of course, in Nature, not away from it) there is no pure Matter so definitely distinguishable. As much as with Plato, he holds that matter as such is indefinite. Whether a form could remain Platonically away from Nature is, as just said, quite another consideration. Our point here is that when forms, i.e., metaphysical objects, are distinguished, Nature is not thereby negated. Those philosophers who, like Plato, have gone to this extreme length have, we contend, confused objective metaphysical distinguishing with its subjective counterpart.

In subjective metaphysical distinguishing, the metaphysical entities which, primarily shown as fringes, are next attended to self-consciously, could not be so attended to if in that very act the initial situation from out of which they are distinguished and which yet involve them was not explicitly negated as over there. In the objective attitude, when we turn from an object *a* to another *b* which remains involved in *a*, our attention is not wholly removed from that *a*: some tail-end of our attention still touches *a*, if only because it continues to be felt that *b* itself, in whatever shape, is still present in *a*. But this does not hold good when *a* shown, as attended to, is in that attention distinguished out. This may be illustrated by the relation between one's body and self.

The Concept of Subjective Attitude Clarified

Although the (my) body, which shows an *I* as not statable along with it, involves that *I* as much before this *I* is attached to as after it, for otherwise it could not be *my* body (and, assuredly, the *I* under consideration is not connected directly with any other body)— although from the point of view of the body *I* is thus apprehended as involved, the case is completely different when this *I* looks at the whole situation from its own point of view. When *I* that has hitherto been at the best *shown* comes to be attended to it refuses to have any truck with the body, however much that body had been, and is even now, showing it and that way claiming to be *my body*. *I*, in so far as it is attended to—in the language we have been using till now, *distinguished*—refuses to be spatial, temporal or have any empirical feature of that body. In so far as it is distinguished from my body it is not experienced as having any length, breadth or thickness, or as born or to die at a specific time. That way it refuses equally to incorporate even mental features which are temporal, like having committed a folly three years back or having a particular feeling now or knowing a certain state of affairs at a particular time. The shown *I*, just in so far as it is attended to, claims to transcend these quite as much as bodily features and events. This is testified to by the incontrovertible fact that they are taken as *mine* or as having occurred *in* me. *I*, as attended to, transcends the whole system of these features, called mind, which may, so far, be understood as some form of body (*sūkṣma-śarīra*).

From the point of view of the body, *I* is understood as involved in that body, and is only thought to be attended to, i.e., pseudo-distinguished, and in that process there is no further development or further unfoldment of the secrets of *I*. Such further unfoldment is possible only when it is followed up in the subjective attitude, where, as just shown, there is a refusal to incorporate all that can be grossly or subtly called bodily.

Even in the subjective attitude, at every step of distinguishing the subject proper there are two stages—one of demand and the other of actual distinguishing. What is felt at the stage of demand is the necessity that the subject proper (*I* so far as it is actually distinguished at whatever step) *ought* to be—better, has to be—distinguished. The stage of actual distinguishing is that where this demand has realised itself. This explains why in our attempt to distinguish *I* from what is bodily (gross or subtle) it does not sometimes refuse to incorporate the latter. At the semi-reflective stage of demand, *I* is even felt (not merely thought as felt) as bodily and spoken out in propositions like 'I was born on such and such date', 'I shall die one day', 'I am black' and 'I am happy'. But this only means that *I* has not been actually distinguished; there is only the demand that it has to be actually distinguished such that it would eventually refuse to incorporate all that is bodily. Through such propositions, once we are in the semi-reflective (semi-subjective) attitude, there peers the demand in question, viz., that all that is bodily be refused acceptance, i.e., negated. This semi-reflective, semi-subjective, attitude is different from what we have earlier called 'thought of *I* as distinct' which is pseudo-distinguishing. A semi-subjective attitude occurs just at the point we turn from the objective to the subjective attitude.

At whatever step, when *I* is distinguished, there is nothing left over, although it is equally true that *I* was distinguished from my body. As *I* distinguished has no business whatsoever with my body this latter is completely negated. Presently, however, it will be shown that the distinguished *I* is not the only thing occupying the field at that stage; even at that stage[15] it carries a substitute for my-body, a sort of reference *sui generis*, which is an intrinsic dynamic moment of *I* not yet discussed.

As *I* transcending my body negates it, even though, from the point of view of the body, this latter continues to involve *I*, the relation between the two is, so far, very unlike that between a metaphysical *object* which transcends Nature and that Nature, or between two metaphysical *objects* one of which transcends the other—similarly in every case of a shown metaphysical entity attended to in the subjective attitude. The shown entity is, no doubt, in the context of something apprehended in the objective attitude as over there, whether that something is natural or metaphysical. But attended to as shown, and, therefore, as subjective, it immediately negates that object, though that object has no business either to negate or even to assert the shown. Yet, even from the point of view of the shown-as-attended-to, i.e., in the subjective attitude of distinguishing, the object which is negated has somehow to be spoken of, if only as what has been transcended, as what is not over there (even as what was not over there, for what is negated not only is not but also could not have been over there). Such negative characterisation of the object spoken of is not, however, enough. As spoken of, it cannot be merely that which is negated, for then we really do not know what it is that is being spoken of and so are not really speaking of it. As spoken of, it has to be something definite and positive. As, however, nothing definite and positive that is yet entitatively other than what is distinguished can be spoken of as what is, or even could be there once we, in the subjective attitude, are aware of the distinguished as it is in itself, the only positive way to speak of it legitimately would be to describe it as what is projected or created by the subjective that is now distinguished. To describe it in that way is obviously also to admit that it is and also was so.

This is the basic point of distinction between objective and subjective distinguishing. It may be noted now that the distinguishing of a subjective of this sort is no other than the subjective itself. Distinguishing here is of the shown, which means that the shown has distinguished itself. What is shown and not statable is precisely what is subjective in the proper sense of the term—the subjective which is somehow evident and yet not an object. Metaphysical objects never stand shown that way. What is shown at a level, more particularly at the primary unreflective level (the level of the material mode of speech) is, *qua* shown, only at the fringe of that level—an overtone, a half-elusive (according to some, 'systematically elusive') halo, so to say, of the content at that level. None, however, of the metaphysical objects that, otherwise like metaphysical subjectives, posit themselves only as being distinguished from out of lower-level contents, primarily from out of Nature, could ever be apprehended before they were distinguished out as fringy that way. Space, time, substance, etc., were, before they were distinguished, understood somehow as constitutive, though not recognised in their proper shapes. And for that, as wholly constitutive, they never, even as parts, tended to stand over against natural empirical objects as fringes or overtones. From the point of view of Nature, there is no empty space, nor empty time, and, obviously, there could not be empty substance, empty cause—indeed, any empty metaphysical object, except, of course, the characters which are *logical* in the strict sense of the term. But they, as will soon be seen, are no metaphysical objects but belong only to a dimension of some metaphysical subjectivity at a certain level.

At whichever stage, then, the subjective in its proper shape (proper for that stage) is discovered, this is possible only as one negates the object, (the whole gamut of objects) at that stage. It turns away from it in an opposite direction. There is no rule, however, as to when such turn will occur. One may, for example, in search of *I*, suddenly turn from Nature—maybe through an experience of some basic paradox of Nature (as the Advaitins sometimes propose) or otherwise. One may, again, go a long way, first in search of objective metaphysical entities and then, failing further progress, turn to the subjective. It is possible, again, to turn to the subjective at any stage of objective distinguishing, by simply turning to what is 'shown' at that stage and trying to follow it up further.

But what is common to these approaches is that some shown fringe is sought to be followed up, and in every such approach what much is subjectively discovered is only what is just then 'shown'. In none of these approaches, and at none of these stages except at the highest, is the entire storehouse of the subjective laid bare all at once. For discovering further subjectives one has to deepen the subjective attitude and explore stages after stages.

At any of these stages of exploration what is transcended may appear as object relatively to what is transcendent. But there is a significant distinction never to be lost sight of. When Nature itself is transcended there is a total turn away in a contrary direction, no tail-end remaining in touch with Nature or any object there. Nature, in that case, is completely replaced by the shown now apprehended as a transcendent subjectivity. This replacement, please note, is possible only because the natural objects which are transcended could not be apprehended, at the pretranscendence level, without the transcendent having been, from the point of view of those objects, apprehended somehow in another shape, mostly as their adjectival feature, as when with regard to *I* the body is from the beginning apprehended as *mine*. What actually happens in subjective transcendence is that this adjectival feature, like the mine-ness, distinguishes itself and in that act spurns the natural objects transcended and, along with that, all objects of Nature in a lump. Replacement means occupying the whole field of consideration.

The relation is different, however, in other cases of transcendence. Consider, for example, the case where one turns from a metaphysical object to the corresponding subjective. What is distinctive of the subjective transcendence here, is that the metaphysical object that is transcended had nothing to do, before this transcendence was effected, with what was just shown at that stage. This is either by way of asserting or negating it or by way of paying any attention to it, it being remembered that it is the shown which, when attended to, i.e., subjectively distinguished, reveals itself as transcendent subjectivity. It follows that this transcendent subjectivity does not occupy the whole field that was previously considered. It occupies quite another field, and so there is no question of replacement. No doubt, as already said, it negates the metaphysical object in question. But it does not seek to replace that. What is true of this relation of the subjective transcendent to the metaphysical object transcended is true equally of the relation it bears to Nature which it sometimes transcends directly without there being any discovery of intermediate metaphysical objects.

But how could, then, the transcendent subjectivity refer at all to (or speak of) metaphysical objects, and, therefore, of Nature too, at least as what is transcended? To elaborate what we have already said on this point: if the transcendent subjectivity cannot itself refer to them, something else is required to bridge the gulf, and that something must yet belong to the field of subjectivity. In the same process by which the shown came to be apprehended as transcendent subjectivity, it is also apprehended as referring to those objects in the form of projecting or creating them out of itself, and this projecting or creating is apprehended as its intrinsic act (power).

For a clearer picture two points need be noted here. One is that this act does not descend down either to Nature or to metaphysical objects, as though these are still there (they have been replaced); and the second point is that although the transcendent subjectivity has that power of projection (creation) the power as such is undefined, definiteness of content coming only from some object, viz., that which, in the objective metaphysical field, has just transcended Nature or the metaphysical object said to be referred to, as the case may be. No doubt, transcendent subjectivity negates whatever is an object, whether natural or metaphysical, which it transcends in its own way; but, unlike what happens when it is a question of transcending Nature, it does not negate the field itself of metaphysical objects. As both transcendent objects and transcendent subjectivity are metaphysical, the tail-end of the latter always remains in touch with the *field* of the former. What we mean is that the act of referring as an intrinsic power of transcendent subjectivity is but positing the whole metaphysical field anew, quite in the same way, though in an opposite direction, in which the subjective attitude started with the denial of the whole field of Nature. This is exactly what Kant means by 'object-in-general' which, according to him, is as much object as the most general thinking act. When the phenomenologists speak of 'intention' they too probably mean this, though one cannot be too sure of that. Hegel is only half right when he takes it as an act of self-negation by abstract thought (in our language, 'subjective thinking'). He ought to have seen that nothing positive can come out of mere negation, even though that negating act works in the bosom of 'abstract thought'. Dialectical synthesis is possible if only the negation in question is additionally positive, not merely because it is in the bosom of the positive which wields that act of negation. When Fichte postulated his 'dark background' or Schopenhauer his 'blind will' they hinted, no doubt, at the truth but did not make the situation clear.

Even Kant proceeded only half-way. The most general act of thinking (thinking=distinguished subjectivity that is cognitive, i.e., referring) is, according to him, also *object*-in-general and he holds that it concretises itself into different types of objects only as the act in question uses space and/or time which had been distinguished out at lower stages of transcendence. But this is concretisation of a sort not under our consideration; Kant did it only with a view to align pure thought (in our language, metaphysical subjectivity) once again with Nature from out of which subjective transcendence began. He, in short, practised transcendence to a limited extent, always tending to return to Nature, though armed with the transcendental wealth earned, and this was wholly in the interest of 'science'. On the other hand, the type of metaphysics we are considering here practises transcendence for its own sake—to unearth all the possibilities that remain hidden there. Kant stopped midway. Not that there is no return from transcendence to Nature, but that is another question with which we are not concerned.

The problem we are tackling here is pronouncedly that of Indian transcendentalists like Sāṅkhyists, Yoga philosophers, Vedāntists of different schools, Śaivists and Śāktists and, also in another way, of many Buddhists. Once transcendence began all of them did not choose to shut out Nature for all time to come. But, assuredly, all of them were determined to follow up to the end the process of distinguishing and unearthing hidden treasures as far as possible.

Notes

1. The study of heuristic principles may also constitute an important part of metaphysics understood in another sense. (The study of the nature of metaphysics is meta-metaphysics, called epistemology.)
2. Conceptual analysis is a broad affair equal to description, including inference and construction.
3. The relevance of the following discussion need not be questioned. Here we have analysed in detail the reasons which have led logician-philosophers to deny all metaphysical analysis and have also refuted their theses. These philosophers have intended to replace metaphysics by mere conceptual schemes. What we have tried to show in the ensuing sections is that such replacement is grievously inadequate.

4. *This* and *now*, as concepts, are not on a par with concepts of superlatives like 'the best'. The concepts of I, you, etc., again, belong to a third order.

5. With this latter thesis, however, we are not concerned here.

6. The copula in '*S* is *P*' is here understood as a characterising tie, not as an assertive tie.

7. *Naiyāyikas*, however, take it as genuinely over there, although here, as in the case of *svarūpa sambandha*, they admit some paradox involved. Their idea is that although, methodologically, paradoxes have always to be removed one may yet stop with a paradox if it is *given* as ultimate. One should, in other words, struggle as much as possible to remove paradoxes but should not fight shy of admitting one if in spite of best efforts it cannot be removed. The justification is that it is after all *given*, though given as a paradox.

8. It may be noted that in pure formal logic there is no going beyond *yes* or *no*.

9. Excluding, of course, modern *descriptive metaphysicians*.

10. This is not, however, the traditional approach of the empiricist logician. For traditional empiricism, logical forms and principles are empirical abstractions, either on a par with inductive generalisations or mere verbal abstractions hypostatised through words. In the former case the empiricist's logical forms and principles lack the *necessity* which is characteristically theirs, and in the latter case they miss the autonomy or transcendence which equally they ought to have. The type of abstractions which we are speaking of have both these characteristics. This will be clear as we proceed.

11. A particular system of unfoldments, as such, need not necessarily be conceptual, though it may be represented conceptually.

12. These logicians, however, have often used this device indiscriminately. They have used it even when the independent existence of a thing has not been seriously doubted. Inordinate love of reduction has made them intellectuals of the extreme type.

13. That initial situation, be it noted, continues even after the distinguishing is effected, for such distinguishing is neither partitioning nor any form of reduction.

14. Wittgenstein's characterisation of 'shown', as distinct from 'stated', is of momentous significance for philosophy. In the present section and the succeeding ones we have frequently used these terms assuming that the readers are conversant with them.

15. Earlier we distinguished between step and stage in connexion with actual distinguishing and corresponding demand. As that point is now over we shall be using the two terms indiscriminately, except where that distinction comes up again for consideration.

3

Philosophy as Self-realisation

SIBAJIBAN BHATTACHARYA

Philosophy has been conceived differently by different philosophers and it is difficult to find anything common to all these conceptions. We analyse here a few views about philosophy in order to find out their essential features.

Philosophy is the art of living a tranquil and serene life—it is a skill to be acquired by prolonged training and rigorous practice. There may be a theory behind this art, as there is one behind every art, and that theory too may be called philosophy but only in a derivative sense. Too much concern with theory may be an impediment to attaining the practical goal in philosophy as elsewhere. So, theorising is discouraged and the emphasis is on practice. Patañjali, for example, in his celebrated theory of the eightfold method for attaining Samādhi, which consists in arresting the movement of the mind, includes moral practices (like non-violence, truthfulness, honesty, abstinence, cleanliness, contentment, etc.), physical exercises (like physical postures, breath-control, etc.), and exercises of attention (like concentration, meditation, etc.). As a result of these practices, one attains a practical result. Patañjali, of course, asserts that these practices remove *Avidyā* which is the root of all *Kleśas*, and ultimately leads to self-realisation, but this self-realisation is automatically achieved without any intellectual or cognitive activity. As soon as all movements of the mind are arrested, the self remains in its pure state and this staying in its pure state is what is meant by self-realisation. The point to be noted here is that although self-realisation is really a state of pure self-consciousness, yet in order to achieve this no specifically cognitive activity is needed. As a matter of fact, according to Patañjali even knowledge about empirical objects can be attained without any cognitive activity. Thus, in giving details of the results of the various exercises, Patañjali mentions that by meditation on the sun we attain knowledge about the world, by meditating on the navel we attain direct knowledge of the state of the body, by concentrating on the heart we attain direct knowledge of the mind — of our own as well as of others. But the results of all types of concentration are not cognitive; for example, by concentrating on the throat, we get rid of thirst and hunger, but do not attain any knowledge of objects, empirical or non-empirical. Thus, concentration sometimes yields knowledge, sometimes non-cognitive powers. The knowledge attained through concentration on specified parts of the body or on special objects, although empirical, is still extraordinary in the sense that ordinary people do not have this type of knowledge. This type of knowledge is empirical, not in the sense of being derived from sense-experience, but in the sense of being about spatio-temporal objects.

The Hegelians conceive philosophy as a form of knowledge, indeed, as the highest form of knowledge, a sort of superscience which is superior to science, just as science is superior to common sense. This highest knowledge is at once immediate and rational, all-comprehensive and concrete. Now, Reason has two aspects— a theoretical and a practical one. Kant, although admitting the unity of Reason, still made a distinction between pure theoretical Reason and pure practical Reason. A cognitive act, according to Kant, is an act of theoretical Reason and cannot be identified with a moral action which is the function of the practical Reason. But according to the Hegelians this distinction is not ultimately valid. For, anyone who attains philosophical knowledge also attains moral perfection. Now, it is not clear whether this identification is achieved only at the highest level or is present at lower levels too. For, apparently being moral, i.e., performing moral actions and moral actions only, is not a way of knowing. It is not clear how at the highest stage morality and knowledge become identical. Reason, which is the synthesis of sense and understanding in the sphere of knowledge, seems to effect a harmony in the moral life of a person so that a philosopher necessarily leads a morally perfect life. This relation between theoretical knowledge and moral perfection needs to be explained; we may ask, for example: Is every morally perfect man a philosopher, i.e., does he possess the supreme knowledge of the Absolute which is the unity of sub-ject and object, matter and mind, which is, indeed, the highest synthesis?; or: Is philosophising a way of becoming moral?

The linguistic analysts deny that philosophy is knowledge. They identify philosophy with a particular method of thinking. To 'do philosophy' is to practice analysis which dissolves, rather than solves, the philosophical puzzles. The goal of analysis is thus a practical goal—getting rid of the philosophical puzzles which trouble the mind. Philosophical analysis is claimed to have a therapeutical value comparable to that of psychoanalysis. (Indian philosophers in general go a step further and claim that philosophy not merely rids the mind of puzzles, but puts an end to all types of worries, indeed, to all suffering.) The problem is: How can analysis achieve this practical result? The analysts say that the puzzles arise only when the rules of language are violated; and if we realise this by practising analysis of philosophical problems, then we shall cease to ask these questions. That is, the mere knowledge that the puzzles are due to a mistaken use of language suffices to put an end to all philo-sophical questioning. The reason for this is that we cannot be genuinely puzzled by knowingly misusing language. No further explanation seems to be necessary; yet as we shall see, much clarification and even theorising will be necessary to explain this point.

The phenomenologists, too, identify philosophy with the phenomenological method, rather than with any particular result. The essence of this method consists in effecting a change in cons-ciousness, in the common sense attitude to the world. To philoso-phise is not to theorise, but rather to 'see' the objects in an essen-tially different way. The method of reduction involves suspen-sion of belief in the existence that accompanies our everyday life and scientific thinking. Now, this is not merely an intellectual act but involves self-discipline, for, to suspend existential beliefs is to withdraw our commitment to them, to stop identifying ourselves with such beliefs. This ultimately amounts to a total transforma-tion of the personality of the individual comparable to a 'religious conversion'. Yet it is not clear whether phenomenologically re-duced consciousness is morally perfect. In religious conversion it is the moral life which is primarily transformed—a religious person is necessarily morally perfect, but does not appear to neces-

sarily possess philosophical knowledge, whereas phenomenological reduction makes one a philosopher. Husserl, of course,
has claimed that phenomenological reduction goes even beyond
religious conversion and 'has the significance of the greatest existential conversion that is expected of mankind' (Husserliana VI,
140; quoted by Spiegelberg, *The Phenomenological Movement*, Vol. I,
p. 136, note 1). Yet the nature of this reduction has not been revealed.
Hence, phenomenology has sometimes tended to become an esoteric
practice not accessible to the uninitiated.

The existentialist philosophers have emphasised the role of the self
in experience. The self which tends to be overlooked and forgotten
in the scientific attitude comes to the forefront in the realisation
of crisis. It is only when we are deeply engaged, when we are in
the world in the fullest sense, that *Dasein* is revealed. But if the
function of philosophy is merely to make us aware of our authentic existence, then it does not involve any fundamental change
in our personalities comparable to that of conversion. It merely
restricts our tendency to escape into a world of abstractions and
imaginations, to avoid responsibility for our choice and to conform mechanically to social and ethical standards.

This brief survey of some concepts of philosophy shows that
philosophy always involves a change in our consciousness, i.e.,
has a practical aspect according to all these views. The difference
lies in the appraisal of the nature of the change brought about by
philosophy. Yoga and other systems of Indian philosophy
claim a total transformation of personality and cessation of all
suffering as effects of philosophy; Hegel seems to come very close
to such a theory claiming for philosophy the power to produce
moral perfection in man; analytic philosophers claim only a limited therapeutic value for philosophy; Husserl claims a 'total
personal transformation' as a prerequisite, not a consequence,
of philosophy; but the nature of this transformation and its method
remain yet to be explained; the existentialists urge us to eschew
the palliatives of either socially directed responses or intellectualised
acts in favour of responsibility and to live authentically.

The main problem which remains to be solved is: How does
philosophical knowledge produce a practical change in our consciousness or a personal transformation?

We shall not discuss the problem we found in Patañjali's
theory, i.e., How can concentration produce sometimes cognitive

and sometimes non-cognitive results? Patañjali himself states these results without offering any explanation and it is difficult for us either to dispute the truth of these statements, or to justify them.

We shall explain and examine two types of answers to this question, namely, that given by the Nyāya system and that given by the Advaita Vedānta. As both these systems explain their answers only by explaining the nature of self-knowledge, we shall have to understand their theories of the self, the inner sense, the nature of false cognitions and wrong notions and the nature of knowledge.

The Nyāya Theory

Nyāya postulates the existence of two types of selves: one supreme self which is identified with God, and a plurality of finite selves. Both these kinds of selves are conceived as substances possessing consciousness as a quality. Not merely the supreme self but even finite selves are eternal and omnipresent; the supreme self differs from the other kind of selves in being omnipotent and omniscient. By 'omnipotence' is meant not 'the power to create everything', but only 'the power to create whatever can be created'. The supreme self creates the universe, keeps it in existence so long as it exists, and then destroys it—all by one act of will. There is no need to postulate different acts of willing in the supreme self. This one act of will which is postulated is of course eternal. Just as one act of will is directed towards all created objects, so also the omniscience which is postulated in the supreme self is one eternal state of knowledge about everything. Although the supreme self and its consciousness or knowledge are both eternal, yet they are not identical. The self is never identical with consciousness.

Every finite self is eternal and also omnipresent. It is not identical with consciousness, nor is it essentially conscious. Consciousness is only an accidental quality of finite selves. A finite self happens to possess consciousness only when the following conditions are fulfilled: (1) In order to be conscious a finite self has to possess a body; (2) the self has to be related to the inner sense in a characteristic manner; (3) consciousness is always of some object. Let us explain these conditions.

(1) Every finite self is omnipresent. If, in order to have

consciousness or knowledge, a relation between the self and the object be sufficient then every finite self being present everywhere will be related to everything and hence would have knowledge of everything, i.e., every finite self would be omniscient. But it is not omniscient, so at least one more condition is necessary for consciousness. Moreover, consciousness is experienced in the self as associated with the body, no one experiences knowledge belonging to the self beyond the body.

Now, it may be objected that so far as the facts of consciousness are concerned, the finite self is not omnipresent. What do we gain by saying that the self is present everywhere, if we have to admit that consciousness belonging to the self is limited within the body? In order to understand the Nyāya position, it is necessary to know the Nyāya theories of eternal entities and perception of things and their attributes.

According to Nyāya if a thing is eternal, it cannot be composite. For if a thing is composed of parts, then it is always possible for the parts to fall apart destroying the whole which, therefore, cannot be eternal. Nyāya postulates two types of simple entities— atoms of earth, air, water and fire, and infinite substances. Infinite substances are necessarily eternal, and hence cannot be composite. Now, every self is eternal; hence it must be either atomic or infinite. It cannot be an atom, for an atom cannot be perceived whereas a self is perceived in introspection. No attributes of atoms can be perceived, yet we all internally perceive our happiness, sorrow and other internal states of the self. So, the self is not an atom, yet it is eternal. Hence it must be infinite in magnitude, i.e., must be present everywhere.

Consciousness, according to Nyāya, is the same as cognition. The other states of the self, namely, feeling and willing, are not conscious states. But when they occur in the self they are immediately followed by their introspective awareness. So, for all practical purposes, there is no feeling or willing which goes unnoticed. But this introspective awareness of feeling or willing is not identical with either of them.

Consciousness is neither the essence of the self nor is it identical with it. In deep dreamless sleep we are wholly unconscious. This would be impossible if the self were identical with consciousness, or if consciousness were the essence of self. The problem for Nyāya is, then, to explain the nature of our cognition that we slept

well—which we have on getting up from sound sleep. According
to Advaita Vedānta this cognition is memory, i.e., we remember
on getting up from sleep that we slept well. But this memory will be
impossible if we did not have direct consciousness of sleeping well,
i.e., if we did not have experience of sleep during sleep. This implies that we are conscious even during deep sleep. But according
to Nyāya this is impossible; we can never remember that we slept
well. How then can we ever say that we slept well? According to
Nyāya this is an inference, not memory. We infer that we slept
well from the feeling of freshness, etc., which we have when we get
up from sound sleep. If the self is thus unconscious in deep sleep,
then there must be some other condition of consciousness than the
body. For, even when we are asleep, both the self and the body
remain, still we are unconscious. This brings us to the Nyāya
concept of inner sense (manas or antaḥkaraṇa).

(2) The concept of inner sense as distinct from the self is common to many systems of Indian philosophy. The inner sense,
according to Nyāya, as according to all systems which admit its
existence, is material in nature. According to Nyāya it is also an
atom. The function of the inner sense is necessary not merely for
introspection but for cognition, i.e., consciousness as such. In
deep sleep, although the inner sense is there, yet it is not characteristically related to the self, does not perform any function and is
at rest. This is why in such sleep there is no consciousness even
though the self as restricted by the body is there.

The inner sense, according to Nyāya, must be an atom, not a
composite, spread-out substance. For in that case it would have
been related to the self at more than one point, thus giving rise to
more than one cognition at the same time. But according to Nyāya
only one cognition can originate in the self at one time. Sometimes
we seem to have different cognitions at the same time, but according to Nyāya, this is an illusion. What actually happens is that
different cognitions quickly succeed one another producing in us
the illusion of their simultaneity.

(3) Consciousness is always directed towards some object. As
we have already remarked, consciousness according to Nyāya is
the same as cognition. Non-cognitive mental states like willing
are unconscious states; they can be directed towards objects only
through some cognitive state. Thus, desire (aversion) can be
directed towards an object only because desire for an object

involves the belief that the object is good, and that the object is attainable by me. These beliefs being cognitions have their objects and the desire is directed to these objects of belief in a secondary sense. Only cognitions are directed towards objects in the primary sense.

This directedness towards objects takes different forms corresponding to the different forms of cognition. In perceptual knowledge, there is a relation between three entities: (*i*) the self and the inner sense, (*ii*) the inner sense and the sense organs, and (*iii*) the sense organs and the objects perceived. We should note here that Nyāya does not find any difficulty in holding that the self can be directly related with material substances, like the inner sense. This threefold relation between the self and the object of perception is, of course, completely different from the epistemological relation of the knowledge to the object. Nyāya makes a distinction between the relation of the knower and the known and the relation between knowledge and its object. This is possible because according to Nyāya the self is not identical with consciousness, hence the relation of the self to the object is also different from the relation of cognition to its object. Here we shall be concerned primarily with the relation of cognition to its object. Single objects are known according to Nyāya in a way roughly akin to what Russell calls 'knowledge by acquaintance'. Here knowledge is related to its object in one way which is completely different from the way in which knowledge of an objective complex is related to the complex. According to Nyāya all ordinary cognitions are of relations holding between two terms. Thus, when I see a jar, the knowledge is not of the single entity, but of the objective complex, the jar, the universal jarness, and their relation. So the objective complex can be schematically represented by *aRb*. The first term of the relation known (here, *a*) is the *viśeṣya* of the knowledge and the second term, *b,* is the *viśeṣaṇa* or *prakāra* of the knowledge. When we know a complex whole, then although there is one knowledge in the self yet this one knowledge is related to the different elements of the objective whole in different ways. The knowledge is related to the first term of the relation known, i.e., to *a,* in one way (*viśeṣyatā sambandha*), to the second term, *b,* in another way, (*viśeṣaṇatā* or *prakāratā sambandha*), and to the relation itself, i.e., to *R,* in a still different way (*saṁsargatā sambandha*). Conversely, the first term of the objective complex, i e., *a,* is related to the knowledge in one way (*viśeṣyitā sambandha*), the second term, *b*, is related to the knowledge in another way (*prakāritā sambandha*) and the relation is related to the knowledge in a still different way (*saṁsargitā sambandha*). Thus, the converse of *viśeṣyatā* is *viśeṣyitā*, of *prakāratā, prakāritā* and of *saṁsargatā, saṁsargitā*. Apart from these three relations and their converse, there is the fourth type of relation between knowledge and its object when the knowledge is acquaintance. Nyāya admits further types of complex cognitions involving relations of a second order (*viśiṣta-vaiśiṣṭya buddhi*). In this type of knowledge we know that something related by a certain relation to a second term is further related to a third term by another relation. For example, when we know a man wearing a red coat, we know that the coat which is related to the red colour is again related to the man who wears it. But in this type of higher order knowledge, no new type of relation is involved between knowledge and object.

Now we come to the Nyāya theory of bondage and liberation. A man in bondage suffers pain, liberation is the cessation of pain forever. In deep sleep there is no suffering, but deep sleep is not liberation because the painless state ends when we wake up. According to Nyāya, consciousness of objects is a necessary precondition of suffering. We suffer because we do not get the desired object, and desire for an object is caused by cognition of objects together with other conditions. Thus, objective consciousness is a necessary condition of desire, and desire is a necessary condition of suffering. Thus, to be free from suffering it is necessary to destroy objective consciousness. But according to Nyāya consciousness is consciousness of objects, to remove objective consciousness is to become totally unconscious. Thus, in the state of liberation the self becomes totally unconscious. We have already explained the Nyāya theory that a precondition of consciousness is the relation of the self with the inner sense. This relation is due to our ignorance of the true nature of our own selves. If we realise that the self is altogether different from the body, from the sense organs including the inner sense, then the self will cease to be related with the inner sense and thus cease to be conscious, and thus escape suffering. We are ignorant about the true nature of the self, because we have wrong notions of the following objects: (*i*) self, (*ii*) body, (*iii*) sense organs, (*iv*) sensory qualities, (*v*) cognition, (*vi*) inner sense, (*vii*) good and bad deeds, (*viii*) desire and aversion, (*ix*) rebirth, (*x*) suffering, (*xi*) pain and (*xii*) release. About these objects various types of false beliefs are usual. For example, about the self one may believe falsely that there is no self, or that the self is identical with the body, and so on. If all these beliefs are destroyed, the self stays in its pure state, without pain, and also without happiness and consciousness. These false beliefs are destroyed by knowledge about these objects, and primarily of the self.

Now we come to the Nyāya explanation of how false beliefs are destroyed or rendered ineffective by knowledge. Nyāya does this by its theory of preventing (*pratibandhaka-pratibaddha-bhava*). According to Nyāya, cognitions of a particular form are prevented from occurring by cognitions of another form. We have to note here at the outset that this relation of prevention exists only between cognitions, beliefs, knowledge, etc., only so long as they are actual states of the self, but does not exist between mere dispositions. We have already noted that the analytic philosophers of ordinary language hold that it is impossible to be puzzled by knowingly misusing language and the term 'knowledge' is used by them only in a dispositional sense. But it is not a fact that a mere disposition can prevent us from misusing language and being genuinely puzzled. There is, for example, a controversy among philosophers whether any one can think or believe in self-contradictory propositions. Eric Toms says: 'That an object may be said, or *even believed* both to have and not to have a certain property, every one knows to be possible, alas! Thus there is no problem about the actual occurrence of contradictions in language' (*Being, Negation and Logic,* p. 3; italics mine). Arthur Pap, on the other hand, argues: 'Thus explicitly self-contradictory sentences do not express anything that could possibly be believed; that there are round squares, for example, is not something that could possibly be believed, and the impossibility is not just psychological. That somebody should believe both (and at the same time) *p* and *not-p* is itself a contradictory supposition. The frequent claim that people, alas, are capable of holding self-contradictory beliefs notwithstanding, the statement "*X* believes at *t* that *p* and *not-p*" is itself self-contradictory' (*Semantics and Necessary Truth,* p. 173; author's italics). According to Nyāya this controversy can be easily solved. When any one believes that *p* and also believes that *not-p*, at least one of the beliefs has lapsed into

a disposition; that is, one has forgotten that one believes that
p or that *not-p*. Pap uses the term 'belief' not in the sense of a disposition but in the sense of an actual mental state. This is clear
from his emphasis on 'believing at *t*' and 'believing at the same
time'. If 'belief' or 'believing' is used in a dispositional sense,
then one can, and very often does, hold self-contradictory beliefs.
Thus according to Nyāya both Toms and Pap are right, only
Toms uses the term 'believe' in a dispositional sense, whereas
Pap uses it in an episodic sense. Nyāya uses the terms 'cognition'
('cognition' and 'consciousness' are synonyms), 'belief', 'knowledge,' etc., only in their episodic sense. For dispositions they use
other terms like 'trace', etc. Every actual mental state, cognitive
or non-cognitive, has three moments—of origination, of duration
and of cessation. Nyāya bases its theory of prevention on the
moments of origination and duration. We may note here the
following points:

(*a*) When one cognition originates it prevents the origination
of any other cognition. In the case of introspective cognition of a
first order cognition of objects, the objective cognition first originates, then passes into its second phase of duration; it is only
then that the second order introspective cognition originates.
Thus, when the introspective cognition comes into being the first
order cognition endures, and hence is directly known in introspection. But the two cognitions cannot originate at the same
time and cannot endure at the same time.

(*b*) Nyāya then calculates the strength of the conditions of
different types of cognition. In every moment of waking life,
there are conditions which can produce perceptual knowledge;
i.e., the conditions which suffice to produce perceptual knowledge
are always present. Yet we have other types of cognition—inferential, memory, etc.—too. This means that when we have inferential cognition, the conditions which suffice to produce this
cognition prevail over the conditions for perception of some
object or the other. For, as we have already seen, the conditions
of perception are always present, so whenever we infer or have a
different type of cognition, the conditions of inference, etc., have to
prevail over the conditions of perception. For example, when I
infer that there is a man in the next room, instead of performing
this act of inference I could have perceived the table in the room
where I am sitting. As conditions sufficient for perceiving some

object or the other are always present, these conditions have to be subjugated if we are to have any other type of cognition. Here Nyāya gives the following rule: In the case of the same objective complex the conditions of perception normally prevail over conditions of other types of cognition; in the case of different objects, the conditions of inference prevail over the conditions of perception. Let us explain this rule.

According to Nyāya we can cognise the same objective complex in different ways. For example, we can cognise that there is fire on a hill by perception, by inference, or even by hearing reports from others. Suppose we are standing in front of the hill from where we can perceive that there is fire on it, we could also infer fire from perceiving smoke. When conditions for perception and inference are thus simultaneously present, normally we shall have perceptual knowledge. But if we want to infer, then we shall have inferential knowledge, not perception. The desire to infer what can at the same time be perceived will produce inferential knowledge. When this desire to infer is not operative, i.e., is not an actual mental state, then we shall have perceptual knowledge. But when sufficient conditions for perceiving an object are present and also sufficient conditions for inferring a different objective complex are present simultaneously, it is inference which will always take place, not perception. Suppose I am standing in front of a hill, and sufficient conditions for perception of the hill are present as well as sufficient conditions for inferring that there is a fire on the hill at the same time; then, according to Nyāya, I shall not see that this is a hill, but shall have the inferential knowledge that there is fire on the hill.

(c) Now we come to the theory of cognitions of contradictory propositions. The question here is: Supposing that I have a cognition that S is P, can I also cognise that S is not P? When will one cognition prevent occurrence of the cognition of a contradictory proposition? Thus here there are two cognitions, one preventing cognition, the other the prevented cognition, i.e., the cognition which is prevented from occurring or originating. Nyāya enumerates the different characteristics of the preventing and the prevented cognitions of contradictory propositions.

The characteristics of the cognition which is prevented from occurring are:

(*i*)   The cognition can be either true or false.

(*ii*)   It may or may not be attended with belief.

(*iii*)   It must not be a supposition.

(*iv*)   It must not be an ordinary perception, or an illusory perception due to any psychophysical defect.

(*v*)   The cognition must have as its object a complex of the form *aRb*.

Characteristics of the preventing cognition are:

(*i*)   The cognition must be attended with belief.

(*ii*)   It may be either true or false; if false, it must not be known to be false.

(*iii*)   It must not be a supposition.

(*iv*)   It must be about the proposition which is contradictory to the proposition cognised by the prevented cognition.

Let us now explain these characteristics.

We first note that we are dealing here with cognitions of contradictory propositions only. A mere supposition of a proposition can neither prevent nor be prevented by a cognition of the contradictory proposition (characteristic (*iii*) of both). If we suppose that *S* is *P*, then this supposition when it endures as an actual mental state cannot prevent us from cognising or even knowing that *S* is not *P*. So also even if we know that *S* is *P*, this knowledge will not be able to prevent us from supposing that *S* is not *P*. The supposition, in this case, will be a contrary-to-fact supposition. Then an illusory perception cannot be prevented from occurring by any cognition of the contradictory proposition. For example, if we are suffering from jaundice, then even though we know (in the episodic sense of 'know') that the wall is not yellow, yet we shall see that the wall is yellow. Then, also, the preventing cognition can be either true or false, but it must not be known to be false. Suppose that it is false that *S* is *P* . But if we know that our belief is false, then, of course, we shall no longer hold it. i e.. we shall withdraw our conviction from it; then this cognition which has been known to be false will not be able to prevent the occurrence of any cognition of the form '*S* is not *P*'.

These are the three ways in which, according to Nyāya the occurrence of a cognition can be prevented. Now let us see how identical with the body. This is a false cognition which has to be cured by knowledge of the self as it really is. Suppose also that the self is not identical with the body. Destroying the false cognition that the self is identical with the body means nothing but preventing the occurrence of this cognition in the self permanently. The method prescribed by Nyāya to achieve this result is this. First of all, we have to learn from someone, who knows, that the self is not really identical with the body. Then we shall have to strengthen our belief in it by argument, and finally know the truth. Then we shall have to constantly meditate on this truth. Meditating on it is nothing but keeping the knowledge of truth constantly in mind; anyone who desires liberation cannot afford to forget the truth even for a moment. The knowledge of the truth must not lapse into a disposition, for as a disposition it will not be able to prevent the false cognition from occurring and deluding us. When the false cognition has thus been blocked from occurring, meditation on the truth results in illumination or intuition of the truth. Thought collapses yielding place to an immediate apprehension of truth. This immediate apprehension of the real nature of the self may be called self-realisation. Ordinary men do not have self-realisation, because even though they know that the self is not really identical with the body, etc., still most of the time they forget it, and behave as if the contradictory were true. But Nyāya goes a step further and claims that this intuitive knowledge of the self is not the final stage, but is the penultimate stage leading automatically to the cessation of all consciousness and suffering. For, consciousness which is due to the relation of the self to the inner sense ceases as soon as this relation is broken. The relation which is due to false cognition is destroyed by the intuitive knowledge of the nature of the self, etc. If this state of unconsciousness be the state of self-realisation, then it is not a state of knowledge. Self-realisation at the penultimate stage as a state of knowledge has the following characteristics: (i) It comes as the culmination of intellectual and rational arguing, inferring, etc. (ii) It is constantly an actual mental state, which is not allowed to lapse into a disposition. (iii) It is held with the greatest conviction. (iv) It transforms the entire personality of the individual by completely dissociating the self from the body, sense-organs, the inner sense, etc. This it can do only because the self's association with the body is due to false cognitions knowledge about the true nature of the self destroys false cognitions about it, and thus liberates the person who has it.

Suppose, we who are in bondage believe firmly that the self is about the nature of the self, the body, etc. And this ignorance has no beginning, though it ends with the attainment of liberation. Finally, we note the following points about the Nyāya theory of liberation. First, the process of liberation is a personal process—when a person is liberated it is his personality which is totally transformed, but nothing else in the universe is affected. For although the self can be associated with the inner sense, the sense organs and the body, and can have objective cognitions only because it is ignorant, still this transcendental ignorance, which is at the very root of objective consciousness, cannot in any way affect knowledge of the reality of other objects of the world. This transcendental ignorance makes one ignorant only about the twelve objects listed above, and it is this ignorance about these objects which is the cause of bondage. When one attains liberation one is rid of wrong notions, but this does not mean that all objects have been wrongly cognised, or that the entire world is unreal. Objective consciousness is destroyed, but not the objective world.

Second, Nyāya has therefore no difficulty in explaining how if one person is liberated, others remain in bondage. For when a person is liberated, there has been a transformation only within himself, others remain unaffected by his transformation.

The Theory of Advaita Vedānta

According to Advaita Vedānta, the self is identical with pure consciousness which is not essentially related to any object, for it cannot be really related with anything. It is eternal and beyond all change, and is the highest reality. Empirical consciousness, however, is of objects. In order to explain the nature of empirical consciousness it becomes necessary for Advaita Vedānta to introduce some principle which will explain what cannot be a real knowlege of objects, as distinct from the pure, transcendental consciousness, is based on a transcendental illusion. Owing to this transcendental illusion, self-shining consciousness is 'reflected' on the inner sense. This inner sense is, according to Advaita, material, being an evolute of *māyā*, and is spread out, and hence can assume modes which are images of objects. The inner sense with consciousness reflected in it is the empirical self. This reflection of consciousness in the inner sense is due to the transcendental illusion, i.e., a false identification of the transcendental self with the material, unconscious inner sense. According to Advaita Vedānta, in perception of an external object the inner sense goes out to the object through the outlet of the sense organ and assumes the shape of the object with which the sense organ is in contact. This shape or modification of the inner sense is the *vṛtti* of the *antaḥkaraṇa*. This mode is illuminated by consciousness and is known. This means that the relation between consciousness and the external object is mediated on both sides. Consciousness itself is not related with the object, only the inner sense which is illumined by consciousness is thus related. But again it is not the object itself which is related to consciousness as reflected in the inner sense, but only its image in the inner sense which is directly illumined by consciousness. Thus the inner sense acts as the medium where the subject and the object meet.

Now we come to an analysis of the subject-object relation when the object is internal. According to Advaita Vedānta, only external objects need to be copied by the inner sense in order to be presented to consciousness, but the copies themselves are known directly by the witnessing consciousness. The copy theory of knowledge will lead to an infinite regress if the copies themselves have to be copied in order to be known. So the witnessing consciousness is postulated which can and does know the internal states without the mediation of images.

This witnessing consciousness which is sometimes the direct awareness of the internal states is also objectless at times. Thus, in deep dreamless sleep there is consciousness of sleep, but there is no object of consciousness. For, even the internal states do not arise in deep sleep. This direct awareness is independent of the images, and witnesses the passing away of one image and the origination of a new image. The images succeed one another, they are discrete, yet the finite self even in its finitude is a unity. There is a consciousness behind the changing states of the inner sense which remains unaffected by the change and knows everything

that goes on in the mind. No one can deceive this consciousness
which is the witness of all our mental states.

The witnessing consciousness reveals not merely the mental
states but all objects either as known or as unknown. This is why
when one knows a new object for the first time, one has the feeling
that one is knowing an object hitherto unknown to one. This is
possible only because the object was not merely unknown to him, but
was known to be unknown to him. The knowledge that the object was
unknown to him is the function of the witnessing consciousness.

Now, if the witnessing consciousness reveals everything,
subjective and objective, is infallible and unerring, then how is it
that a finite individual still remains ignorant of the true nature
of the self? We have already seen that Nyāya also faced the
problem of explaining why a finite individual should not be
omniscient. This problem arose in Nyāya because it conceived a
finite self as omnipresent, and to solve this problem it had to
postulate a special function of the body in the production of
knowledge. Now, Advaita Vedānta admits that the witnessing
self is omniscient in a sense, for it has direct knowledge of everything. But this direct knowledge is not sufficient to make one
omniscient in the true sense of the term. Omniscience should
cancel all ignorance, but the type of omniscience which the
witnessing consciousness enjoys cannot do this. Ignorance,
according to Advaita Vedānta, is not mere absence of knowledge,
but is false cognition. This false cognition can be cancelled only
by a true cognition which involves modes of the inner sense. We
have seen that the witnessing consciousness is direct consciousness
which does not involve any mode of the inner sense. Hence, it
is incapable of cancelling ignorance. In order to attain liberation
it is necessary to have a mode of the inner sense about the ultimate
reality (brahmākārāvṛttiḥ). This is the last mode which the inner
sense presents to the consciousness of the finite individual.
This awareness of the ultimate reality which is identical with
the transcendental subject cancels māyā, the principle of finitude,
and the individual is liberated.

Let us now compare the Nyāya and the Advaita theories.
We first note the points of similarity. (1) According to both Nyāya
and Advaita, consciousness of objects has to cease if the individual
is to be liberated. According to Nyāya this means that the
liberated self has no consciousness at all; according to Advaita

Vedānta, this means that the liberated self dissolves itself totally with the pure transcendental consciousness. (2) Both prescribe the same method for attaining liberation, i.e., śrvaṇa, manana and nididhyāsana. The self is realised in its true nature by intuition which is the culmination of intense rational activity.

Now let us note the fundamental points of difference between these two theories.

(1) According to Nyāya the finite self is eternal and omnipresent. It cannot be destroyed. According to Advaita Vedānta, the finite self is essentially a mystery; an irrational and unreal relation of the pure consciousness with the material inner sense is at the root of its being. Liberation is not a continuation of the finite self in any form but the release of the pure consciousness from its association with the not-self. The finite self, being a product of māyā, has no beginning but comes to an end when the self is liberated.

(2) According to Nyāya, liberation is just cessation of suffering, while according to Advaita it is not a negative state but a state of pure bliss.

(3) According to Nyāya, the intuitive knowledge of the self, which cancels false cognition, is kept as an actual mental state, whereas according to Advaita Vedānta this final knowledge consists in having a mode of the ultimate reality. According to Nyāya, the inner sense being atomic, there can be no image of anything, whereas according to Vedānta the inner sense is like a plastic substance which can assume shapes of objects, i.e., can have images.

(4) According to Nyāya, the process of liberation is purely a personal affair which leaves the rest of the world unaffected, but according to Advaita Vedānta this is a cosmic process. The ignorance which is the cause of bondage is also the cause of the world. So the process of destroying bondage is also the process of the dissolution of the world. But this gives rise to a problem for Advaita Vedānta. According to this theory the ultimate reality is one transcendental consciousness, the finite selves are many, for māyā, which is involved in the constitution of the individual, though one, is yet the principle of multiplicity thus giving rise to a plurality of finite objects and finite subjects. If liberation is the cancellation of this principle, then liberation is also the dissolution of the world. If māyā is cancelled, then all

finite objects and also all finite subjects would be annihilated. That is, the liberation of one person will be the end of everything, and with the liberation of one person will be the liberation of all. (It is interesting to note that Sri Aurobindo, who differed radically in his interpretation of *māyā* from the Advaita interpretation, accepted this consequence of the Advaita theory. He admitted that the liberation of one person is the liberation of all persons, and it is Sri Aurobindo who will liberate all mankind, indeed, all forms of life, by his own *Sādhanā*.) If *māyā* is not destroyed, then none are liberated. Personal liberation is thus impossible. Advaita Vedānta solves this difficulty by distinguishing between two types of *avidyā—tūlāvidyā* and *mūlāvidyā*. There is a type of *avidyā* which attaches to the individual and is different from the universal cosmic *avidyā*. For the liberation of the individual, it is sufficient to destroy his personal *avidyā*, not the universal *avidyā*. If this explanation of the Advaita school is accepted, then on this point, the difference between Nyāya and Advaita is considerably diminished. For now, liberation is personal according to both, and when a person attains liberation, the rest of the world remains unaffected. On other points their differences remain.

Suggestions for a Theory of the Self and Some Techniques of Self-realisation

We shall now try to explain a theory of the self which will avoid the difficulties of both Nyāya and Advaita Vedānta, and will take into account the various aspects of self-consciousness. The self as a factor of all experience is a conscious principle. There is no point in postulating a self which is essentially unconscious as is done in Nyāya. Advaita Vedānta, on the other hand, has to postulate an irrational unconscious element, *māyā*, in order to explain the appearance of the world. The relation, if any, between *māyā* which cannot be described either as real or as unreal, and the transcendental consciousness which is existence and bliss, is again a mystery. The difficulty is basically the difficulty of dualism. If any unconscious element is admitted, in whatever form with whatever ontological status, in a metaphysical system, it cannot be got rid of afterwards in any way. To avoid this difficulty of dualism we have to say that the so-called unconscious matter is itself really consciousness, i.e., there is nothing but consciousness. The appearance of matter, then, is a false appearance; the difference between Advaita Vedānta and the theory we are explaining here lies in the explanation of this false appearance.

Consciousness, which is indubitable for man, is, as known in introspection, empirical consciousness referring to, or intending objects. The empirical subject knows objects (external or internal, gross or subtle), performs acts (good or bad, moral or immoral), and enjoys pleasure and suffers pain. The empirical subject reveals, on analysis, a composite structure of three elements— (a) the ontological principle of presentation; (b) the ego; and (c) the ontological principle of deliberation.

(a) The very basic feature of empirical consciousness is that it can have presentations, that things and objects can be presented to it. Consciousness at this level is always consciousness of objects which are presented to it. Objects can be presented to consciousness only through mental states. The capacity to have states is thus the fundamental feature of empirical consciousness, and because of this capacity empirical consciousness is intentional, is capable of referring to objects. This capacity is due to an ontological element in the very structure of the empirical subject and is called buddhi.

(b) The second element of the empirical subject is the ego; the empirical consciousness is always known in introspection as personal consciousness, as 'my' consciousness. Because of this element, everything which the empirical subject knows, does or feels, is introspectively known as 'my' knowledge, 'my' action, 'my' pleasure or 'my' pain. But this ego is ontologically derivative, because it is dependent upon buddhi. If there is no mental state, either of cognition, or of conation, or of affection, then there will be nothing which the ego can own; but as the ego is the principle of ownership, of appropriation, it is logically and ontologically dependent upon the buddhi which produces the mental states which are to be owned. This ownership, again, introduces a stable and enduring unity among the different mental states. The mental states are unified as states owned by the same person, as states of the same person. With the ego the person is born. The ego as the principle of ownership is also the principle of unification; and as the principle of unification, it is also the principle of restriction and limitation. The ego delimits empirical consciousness and differentiates one empirical subject from another.

Paradoxically, the ego endows not merely the empirical subject with independence, making it the doer of its own deeds and the enjoyer of its own feelings, but endows the object too with the same degree of independence. This is because when the ego turns the empirical consciousness into the subject of knowledge, it makes the subject owner of its own knowledge. Thus the distinction is made between an act of knowing which the subject performs and owns, the act which is thus subjective, and the object of knowledge which the subject cannot own, or in any way modify by an act of knowing, i.e., an object which is totally independent of the subject. The object of knowledge is generally independent of the will of the empirical subject, not merely of its act of knowing. Thus, the ego delimits the empirical consciousness as the knowing subject by the independent object.

(c) The third element in the empirical subject is that which is responsible for deliberation. Sometimes there is conscious vacillation as in a state of doubt which is resolved only by a deliberate act. This activity is different from mere presentation; there cannot be any doubt unless conflicting descriptions of the same object are simultaneously presented to consciousness. The activity of resolving the doubt by deliberation is due to an ontological element called *manas*. This *manas* is derived from the ego and is dependent, logically and ontologically, upon it. For, conflicting descriptions of the same object can give rise to a state of doubt only if the descriptions are presented simultaneously to the same subject. As the ego is the principle of unification of mental states, without its operation there will be unrelated presentations of mental states; without personal identity there can be no conflict among presentations. Thus if Mr. Z knows something to be *B*, and if Mr. Y knows the same thing as *not-B*, there is no state of doubt even though *B* and *not-B* are contradictory. The law of contradiction, *as a law of thought*, cannot be stated simply as: *A* cannot be thought to be *B* and *not-B* at the same time. It has to be stated as: *A* cannot be thought to be both *B* and *not-B* at the same time by the same person. And because without the ego there cannot be any person, doubt and its resolution are dependent upon its function, and so also is the *manas*.

Thus, *manas*, being ontologically dependent on the ego, is different in different persons. It being the principle of doubt and supposition, of determination and ascertainment, it is the determining factor of logical and philosophical theories. Thus there is always the possibility that philosophical theories will be different for different types of persons, and even for different persons. This is true not merely for philosophical theories, but for all theories, theorising being an activity of the *manas*. In the case of empirical theories, too, there is always the possibility of different theories explaining the same set of facts. Their difference is not, for this reason, merely linguistic; for, the question whether they all explain the same facts equally satisfactorily or not can be raised and it can be answered only if the attitude, purpose and interest of the persons involved are taken into consideration.

The empirical subject is introspectively known to be finite. The finitude of the subject is not so much its exposure to pain and suffering as its essential limitations—its very much limited powers of cognition, affection and conation. The finite individual is a particular person having a body, and is consequently limited by things and persons. The finite person is not all-comprehensive; he is not everything that is there, he is not the universe. He is not omnipotent, omniscient or omnipresent. This limitation is due primarily to the ego which circumscribes the consciousness, ties the mental states into a knot as it were; the body is only the external manifestation of the ego. It is subject to death and decay, but the *manas*, the ego and *buddhi* are not. The birth of a person is simply the assumption of a new body by the empirical ego. The body is ontologically dependent upon the ego, but the ego is not dependent upon the body and can survive bodily death. The finitude of the individual is not due to its bodily existence, but because of the presence of the ego. So long as the ego remains, finitude, in the sense of limitations of personality, remains. Liberation is liberation from the ego and its limitations. The individual is liberated by transcending the ego. Thus, liberation is not primarily a permanent relief from all types of suffering, not even the realisation of an abstract undifferentiated consciousness, but rather the transcendence beyond the ego and its restrictions. By cutting the knot of the ego, consciousness ceases to be personal, it is spread out infinitely, and becomes identical with the universe. The universe is then seen to be identical with the transcendental consciousness, arising from it and again with-drawing into it. So long as consciousness is egocentric, all thoughts, feelings and actions are directed towards furthering the interests of the ego. But when consciousness is universe-centric, thoughts and actions no longer serve the interests of a single individual, they become disinterested. As there can be no sense of want there is no longer any feeling of pleasure or pain; there is only a sense of fullness, unvarying and undying. There is nothing outside this transcendental consciousness, there is nothing to be attained; all actions and thoughts are unmotivated, completely free, not even restricted or governed by the laws of logic. There-fore, there is no reason why thoughts and actions are there; they are there simply because the free transcendental consciousness freely wills them.

The problem which arises here is: If this transcendental con-sciousness be the only reality, how then do objects, the world and individuals, arise? In order to solve this problem we have to explain the nature of transcendental consciousness and the nature of creation.

Transcendental consciousness is self-consciousness; the process of being self-conscious is reflection. This power of reflection is the power of the transcendental consciousness and is identical with it. This reflective power is also the same as its freedom. We should note here the difference of this theory from the Advaita Vedānta theory. According to Advaita Vedānta, the ultimate reality is the self-shining consciousness which is different from the knower and the known. This consciousness is not *of* anything, for *of* involves a relation, and this consciousness transcends all relations. Thus the transcendental consciousness, according to Advaita Vedānta, is pure knowledge without any reference to any knower and to anything known. So although this consciousness is self-shining, it is not self-consciousness, i.e., consciousness *of* itself; it is not reflective consciousness and there is no power of reflection in the transcendental consciousness. The transcendental consciousness of Advaita Vedānta is cons-ciousness pure and simple, it simply is, it is bare existence, but not consciousness in the real sense. For consciousness and reflection are one and the same.

Now let us see how the world can arise from the transcendental consciousness which is reflective consciousness. By reflection consciousness becomes conscious of itself, reflecting is not creating. So the world cannot be said to be created. By reflection what is implicit in consciousness is made explicit; the so-called creation of the world can be nothing but the process of its manifestation, the process of being made explicit. The whole world is in consciousness, the universe is the transcendental consciousness; sometimes it is manifest, sometimes not. Transcendental consciousness is implicit when the power of reflection remains dormant or is dispositional; at this stage there is no world, no creation. Such an inactive, i.e., unreflective, state of transcendental consciousness has to be postulated only if we hold that the universe as a whole can cease to be. If the cessation of the universe is not insisted upon, then there is no need to postulate a state of the transcendental consciousness where it is inactive.

The act of reflecting is the act of making explicit what is already there in consciousness, and this is the so-called act of creating. For, the act of making explicit by reflection is to make what is made explicit stand before consciousness as if it were different from, or other than, the reflecting consciousness. The object is not 'that which stands over against the subject' (Gegenstand) but 'that which stands before the subject' as if it were different from it. Reflection is the act of creating an *appearance of duality* in the subject, the duality of the subject which reflects and the object which is reflected upon. But in self-consciousness, the self which is conscious and the self of which it is conscious are not really opposites; the object self is not really an other of the subject self, nor is it felt to be so. To reflect is to hold before consciousness what is in consciousness. So, self-consciousness is altogether different in nature from ordinary objective consciousness wherein the subject is confronted by an object which is its contradictory, so much so that in ordinary knowledge of objects there seems to be a dialectical unity of opposites. In reflective awareness, there is no such felt opposition between the reflecting subject and the subject reflected upon. The world of objects stands before the transcendental subject just as in reflection the subject stands before itself. This explains why without the act of reflecting the world collapses and vanishes into the inactive transcendental consciousness.

We can now see the fundamental difference of this theory from the Advaita Vedānta theory. Śaṅkara starts with the opposition of the subject and the object, so much so that their apparent unity becomes an insoluble mystery to him. The realisation of this mysterious element in all experience is, for him, the beginning of philosophical thinking. His assumption that the subject and the object are contradictories leads him to postulate *māyā* to explain this contradiction, although his explanation amounts merely to an affirmation that the manifestation of the world is essentially an insoluble mystery. The theory we are trying to explain here does not start with the assumption that the subject and the object are contradictory in nature. This assumption seems plausible only if we take ordinary objective knowledge as the model of all knowledge, but there is no reason to do this. If we take our stand on reflective self-awareness instead of on objective knowledge, then there is no need to assume that the subject and the object are contradictories, and there is no need for us to acquiesce in a dualism even in a mitigated form. There is nothing but reflective awareness; there is no need to postulate even *māyā* in order to explain the appearance of the world.

There is another difficulty of the Advaita theory which this theory avoids. According to the Advaita Vedāntists, consciousness has four stages—waking consciousness, dream consciousness, consciousness in deep sleep, and a fourth and final stage in which consciousness shines in its pure form. Now, self-realisation, according to this school, is consciousness at the fourth stage. But these philosophers also hold that a person who has attained liberation can continue to live in his body; that is, even after rising to the fourth stage of consciousness where the world vanishes, a person can lapse into ordinary waking consciousness, and can again see the world and live in it, talk and communicate with other persons. But then the question arises: How can such a person lapse into the lowest form of consciousness—waking consciousness —after having reached the fourth and final stage ? We have already remarked that self-realisation is such a state that there can be no lapse from it, and it is impossible that a liberated person who has realised his unity with the Brahman can again know the world as the common man does. The change in the personality brought about by self-realisation seems to consist only in a moral transformation, for there does not seem to be any change in his waking consciousness, except that perhaps he has the memory that the world is unreal. But this memory does not prevent the appearance of the world from continuing so long as he is in waking consciousness. That is, self-realisation, on this theory, is incapable of transforming waking consciousness, just as waking consciousness can only contradict and annul dream consciousness, but cannot transform it. The liberated soul can, of course, rise to the fourth stage of consciousness at will, but so long as he is in that state of consciousness, the world and world-consciousness, i.e., waking consciousness, are contradicted and wholly disappear. But the difficulty is, if the state of self-realisation be a state from where there can be no 'fall' then how can a liberated soul at all lapse into waking consciousness ? Advaita Vedānta cannot explain how this is logically possible—for to say that the liberated person continues in his body so long as his *prārabdha* remains is not to resolve the logical difficulty.

The theory which we are recommending here is not involved in this difficulty. In self-realisation the world is not negated, neither is it necessary to remain perpetually in the fourth stage. Self-realisation is not complete unless one reaches a state of consciousness which is permanent and enduring; this realisation will be there even if the person is awake, dreaming or in a deep dreamless state of consciousness. The entire universe is seen to be in consciousness, arising out of it and disappearing in it. The different states of consciousness are likewise seen to be passing phases; the underlying transcendental consciousness shines through all of them. This is a deeper level of consciousness which does not annul the empirical mode of consciousness, but is at the back of everything, every mode of consciousness. This substratum consciousness is reflective self-consciousness; it is the witness of everything as arising out of it and disappearing into it. Once a person attains this stage, he can, or need, not lapse into any other state.

We shall end our discussion by indicating briefly three techniques or methods of attaining liberation in our sense of the term. (1) The method which we first describe is essentially the method recommended by the Buddha as preached in the *Aṅguttaranikāya* (*Rohilasvabagga*). There he says that in the human body which possess *manas* and consciousness, the universe is there—the cycle of its origination, duration and cessation is there; this is not merely the correspondence of the macrocosm with the microcosm. The way out of this cycle is also to be found in consciousness. The method is to attend to the process of breathing (ānāpānasati). This is not the usual practice of breath control. Breathing is the same as living in the body, and the body lives only so long as it is related with consciousness in a characteristic manner. Really everything that is, every action in the universe, proceeds from consciousness; breathing is more obviously so. Yet breathing has become so automatic that it goes on without our attending to it, as in sleep. The process of self-realisation consists in being conscious of every act of inhaling and exhaling; to constantly watch the breath as it comes in and goes out is to attain a deeper level of consciousness, to start on the path of inwardness and be a witness of breathing. The Buddha gives details of this method which we need not explain here. But the philosophy behind it is that to attain a deeper level of consciousness is to be a witness that every action, thought, feeling comes out of consciousness and returns to it. We are not involved in these actions, thoughts and feelings when we become a witness. The highest stage of consciousness is attained only when the ego is transcended and consciousness becomes identical with world-consciousness which again is identical with the world. Consciousness by reflecting on itself witnesses the world. There is no going out, no intending, no referring to, an object outside consciousness, to another which contradicts it. Consciousness is self-contained, it is fullness.

(2) The second method, also an ancient one, is to constantly watch the emergence of the spoken word. Speaking is obviously a conscious act, yet it becomes so automatic that people are constantly speaking, if not loudly then in a subvocal manner, or even in dream. It is a fact that speech arises from consciousness, although we are not aware of it, we do not realise it. Going back to the deeper consciousness is easy if we watch how speech originates in consciousness, in a very subtle form, then passes through various stages before reaching the final stage of audible speech. The practice of watching the subtle form of speech, again, takes the consciousness away from external objects, and thus helps us to attain the state of witnessing consciousness, aloof from the world. The consciousness is not involved in the world, the world is in consciousness.

(3) The third method has been explained in detail by Rājānaka Kshemarāja, a direct disciple of the great yogi, Abhinavagupta,

in his book, *Pratyabhijñāhṛdayam*. We have already stated that in empirical consciousness there is always some presentation or the other. These presentations or mental states are short-lived and they succeed one another, although very quickly. But there is a gap, a split-second interval, between two succeeding states. Through this gap the underlying substratum consciousness, the transcendental consciousness which is beyond all mental states (*nirvikalpa*), shines in its pure form, just as light shows through cracks in a wall. The transcendental consciousness is overlaid with mental states; but because it is eternally there, it cannot be extinguished by empirical consciousness. On the contrary, empirical consciousness is possible only with the permanent support of the substratum consciousness. The method of self-realisation is to identify oneself effortlessly with this fundamental consciousness, to begin with only for brief moments, in the gaps between two mental states. This method is the most direct of all methods, it gives us a direct access to the transcendental consciousness from the level of empirical consciousness, and releases us directly from the limitations, privations, and constraints of the ego. The transcendental consciousness is self-consciousness, not an object-consciousness. We conclude with a rough translation of a famous verse of the *Pratyabhijñā* school:

He, whose mind is tranquil without the support of any object, whose breath is controlled without effort, whose gaze is steady without looking at anything, is in the *mudrā* of the pure *khecari* (i.e., has attained self-realisation).

4

Culture, Language and the Philosophical Enterprise

C. T. K. CHARI

In an earlier paper I contributed to the Proceedings of the Second All-India Seminar on 'Language and Reality' held at the Centre of Advanced Study in Philosophy, Banaras Hindu University, and also in another paper which appeared in *Dialectica* (*Internationale Zeitschrift für Philosophie der Erkenntnis*), Vol. 22, Fasc. 3/4, 1968, I have argued that culturally different philosophies require culturally different languages. In the paper sent for the seminar, I proposed the view as a greatly amended version of the Sapir-Whorf hypothesis. In this paper I should like to suggest some further perspectives for my hypothesis.

Philosophy as a Cultural Self-assessment

I hold that philosophic reflection attempts to sum up its own achievements as well as some other major achievements of the culture which produced it in the related domains of mathematics, science, literature, art, and in social and religious practices. Philosophy, implicitly or explicitly, cannot stop short of cultural self-assessment. The contemporary preoccupation in the West with language, on the one hand, and with the structure of science, on the other, is readily understood when it is realised that language is an essential instrument of culture in all domains and, in the hands of science, has become one of the most potent devices used by knowledge.

Rabelais, who stood on the very threshold of European Renaissance, contributed to the growth of the French language by coining some six hundred neologisms just as Dante Alighieri much earlier had promoted the use of the Italian language as 'The Illustrious Vernacular' (*De vulgari eloquentia*). In the twentieth century the technical vocabulary of science has expanded, according to estimates by authorities, into several millions of items. Some of the newer technical scientific words have flooded even popular speech and obtained wide currency in the East as well as in the West. Vitamin, penicillin, and antibiotic bear too closely on our health for us to forget them. Nylons, televisions, and transistors are popular consumer goods. Stratosphere, supersonic and rocket irresistibly remind us not only of man's travel through the air but of his awe-inspiring conquest of outer space.

Occidental philosophy since the days of Rabelais and Descartes has fallen very much behind science, or even art for that matter, in fashioning new words to express new concepts, objects or attitudes. The vocabulary of modern Western art, e.g., Collage, Frottage, Orphism, Rayonism, Suprematism, Vorticism, if less familiar than the phraseology of science, is no less challenging. It is no wonder that a chastened philosophy in the West tends to assume the complexion of a far-reaching linguistic self-assessment. I must point out that this is only one of the forms that philosophy, regarded as a cultural self-assessment, can take. We should not mistake a parochialism for a universal idiom.

Social and Cultural Systems

Kluckhohn refers to the *embarras de richesse* we confront when we seek to define culture. Ralph Linton's early definition of it as 'the sum total of the behaviour patterns, attitudes and values, shared and transmitted by the members of a given society' is as serviceable as more sophisticated definitions. It has the advantage that it does not commit us to an unwholesome and unnecessary antithesis of 'culture' and 'civilisation'.

Talcott Parsons and Shils have distinguished the social system focus involved in the interaction of human individuals who constitute concrete collectivities from the culture system focus implied by shared patterns of meaning, values, norms, common to members of the society and transmitted through learning processes rather than by way of biological inheritance. The integration and interpenetration of the two systems, the social system and the culture system, is generally through some form of institutionalisation. The terms role norm and value have not received agreed meanings in social psychology. If roles are specific forms of behaviour associated with status or position in a social system, norms are general expectations savouring almost of demands imposed on role-incumbents and values are generalised aspirations.

Human personality can influence social systems in one of three ways. First, it may be a potent determiner of values and social institutions. Second, it may be an integrating link between social institutions. Third, it may not be only a carrier or link, but also a support for institutions by guaranteeing appropriate role behaviour. The importance of personality for any theory of social organisation is emerging from the 'Human Relations Approach' in the Administrative sciences inspired by Elton Mayo and Roethlisberger. The Homans model has a three-layered environment comprising the physical, the cultural and technological factors all producing external systems of interaction and an internal system of motivational patterns corresponding to the informal organisation of Mayo, Roethlisberger, and Chester Barnard. I must stop to point out here that any sociological analysis which takes us far enough is also a philosophical self-assessment of culture. There are *au fond* no uncommitted and detached observers in social research. The researcher is deeply involved in his data; he is a participant observer in his field-work.

Cultural and Philosophical Systems

On almost any theory, philosophical traditions must enter into the culture pattern. Unfortunately, most meta-historians, sociologists and anthropologists, like Danilevsky, Spengler, Toynbee, Sorokin, Kroeber, etc., who insist on a plurality of cultures, have tended to assume that an analogous or homologous trait called 'philosophy' can be located or isolated in major cultures exemplified in India, Greece, China, and modern Europe. Worse still, these authorities tend to construe philosophy as a derivative or a precipitate and not as a fundamental cultural trait.

To single out some meta-historical approaches to philosophy which are clearly insufficient. Spengler, in Chapter 11 of his *The Decline of the West*, regards the earliest phase of a culture or its 'spring' as characterised by a mystical religion. Only in its later phase or 'summer' does culture display forms of pure philosophical thinking. When 'autumn' descends, there is mere rationality. And this degenerates during 'winter' into scepticism, relativism and the chicaneries of understanding. Toynbee, in Volume 7 of his *A Study of History*, seems more concerned with universal churches and religion than with philosophy, even when he deals explicitly with Hindu culture. Sorokin condemns the civilisations of Danilevsky, Spengler, and Toynbee as 'vast cultural dumps'. He maintains that civilisations are never meaningfully unified wholes. He proposes other systems and plays down philosophy. Systems, according to him, differ from congeries. Among the principal pure systems, he admits language, science, fine arts, religion and ethics. Philosophy is dismissed as a *mélange* of science, religion and ethics.

I must register two protests. First, with Toynbee and Kroeber, I dissent from Sorokin's assessment of historical civilisations as 'cultural dumps'. Any historically enduring culture has a certain kind of compactness (*Geschlossenheit*). Erwin Panofsky argued impressively that the logical pattern of the *Summa* of St.Thomas Aquinas with its *partes, membra, quaestiones*, is paralleled by the windows and bays of the triforium in Gothic architecture. It seems not improbable that the cultural milieu of the *disputationes de quodlibet* influenced the Master Builder as much as the thinker. Second, I would claim that philosophy, in some cultures at any rate, is as basic as religion. Louis Renou dwelt on the short-sightedness of treating religion in India as an isolated phenomenon. Paul Mus, at the Third East-West Philosophers' Conference, traced ingenious correspondences between the architectural, magical and religious practices of India. I would extend the parallelism to the religious forms of Indian dance.

Cultural Personality Types and National Character

Are there then as many valid philosophies as there are cultures? Before forming an opinion on this issue, it may be useful to consider certain accepted anthropological methods of contrasting personality types. Ruth Benedict's typologies were largely impressionistic and built up from collective behaviour involved, for exam-

ple in ritual. Kardiner's Basic Personality Structure mediates between postulated primary institutions, such as family organisation
and child-rearing practices, and secondary institutions, such as forms
of art, folklore, mythology and religion. The Modal Personality
pattern of Cora Dubois imports a quasi-statistical notion of a
set of characteristics shared by a large number of individuals in a
group. None of these models is quite satisfactory, especially for
exhibiting philosophies in their cultural setting.

There is a closely related theme: national character. National
character indubitably exists even if, with current techniques, we
can form no precise notions of its nature and function. The
contrasts of Russian geography seem to go with contrasts of mood
and character. Paternal violence, family conflicts, mother-child
alliances, dependence, a sense of guilt, and authoritarianism turning on the written word, have severally moulded Russian character.
Outbursts of emotion alternate with periods of reserve. Is this
a counterpart of the enigmatic Russian foreign policy? Emotional
instability leads to revolt and terror (*ustrashenie*). The French are
passionately ideological. Perhaps their revolution, which is primarily social, has never ended. In the Japanese national character,
there are elements derived from a feudalistic hierarchy, bureau-
cracy, taboos resulting from early techniques of rejection and
ridicule, restraints arising from toilet training. If Lucian Pye is
right, the Chinese impassivity signifies that emotions are not
geared uniformly to action. Action can occur without clues to the
submerged feelings. The varied pictures of the American character
are not altogether discrepant when one remembers the geographical ranges of the USA: we have to do with a 'marketing orientation' (Fromm), a 'a high industrial rationality' (Mead), 'a tendency
to power structure' (Adorno, Brunswick), 'adolescent plasticity'
(Erikson), and 'transport of moral terms' (Riesman).

In the light of recent research we should distinguish syntality
traits characterising the group as a group from the internal traits
of members and both from the population traits which are almost
statistical averages. In delineating national character, we should
be careful to allow for change. The Vikings of yore have become
phlegmatic; the American is no longer a backwood frontiersman;
and the learned and bespectacled Japanese of today is not the 'doll-
like' creature of Commodore Perry's days. If philosophy is bound
up with culture, we must not naively identify it with an unchanging

tradition. In any culture which lasts long enough, traditions change. Every tradition, confronted by new challenges, modernises itself. And every modernity, after the initial bustle and excitement, generates a tradition of its own.

Language, Cognition and Philosophy

I must at this point reiterate the contention of my earlier paper, 'Language, Culture and Reality', that, even if notions of a strict isomorphism between culture, language and thought are exaggerated, the available evidence does suggest that differences in cognitive functions accompany differences in languages. Cultural differences enter into even perceptual tasks. The Europeans are much more prone to the Müller-Lyer illusion than the Africans, the Filipinos, or the Murray Island inhabitants. Brown and Lenneberg, by using the English language and a colour spectrum in their experiments, demonstrated a relation between the accessibility of a linguistic term and recognition. The English vocabulary for colour involves codability of a kind. Zuni speakers confuse orange and yellow, while English speakers never commit this error. The Navaho verbs of handling involve different forms according to the shape of the object handled. e.g., long and flexible or short and rigid. Carroll and Casagrande succeeded in demonstrating significant differences between natives whose only language is Navaho and those who speak both English and Navaho.

Bartlett and others have noticed a comprehensive influence exercised by culture patterns on the matter as well as on the manner of social recall. The influence of culture can be discerned also in legends and myths, e.g., in the type of task the 'Hero' has to perform or in the kind of 'Helper' he has. Content analysis can fix the 'distance' of any item from the cultural motif. The statistical studies of C. Radhakrishna Rao and others in India have disclosed that culture patterns introduce systematic, if unconscious, distortions in answers to questionnaires by importing Hindu notions of the privileged status of the male child, a distinct tendency to regard married daughters and sisters as not members of the 'household' etc.

Authorities like C. L. Dedrick have despaired of securing truly comparable international data through census reports, because of the variable notions of the 'household' when we pass from one culture to another. The Swedish language has a considerable number of words expressing family relationships (*släktskap*). Different words are used according to whether the person designated is a relative on the father's side (*på fädernet*) or on the mother's side (*på mödernet*). An uncle may be *farbror* or *morbror*, a nephew may be *brorson* or *systerson*. Besides the words *faster* and *moster* for 'aunt' in Swedish, there is a word *tant* for a lady used by young people which is an affectionate from of address without implying kinship. I think it would be highly worthwhile comparing these forms of address with the nuances of the vocabulary for kinship in the several Indian languages which vary over the geographical regions.

Can linguistic analysis of kinship terms settle any philosophical questions? I suggest that the ethical systems propounded by philosophers, in spite of all their pretensions, do not soar far away from kinship terms signifying degrees of intimacy and varying pressures of moral obligation. Values are, as I have explained, cultural aspirations in the first place. I would go further and maintain that metaphysical issues about survival of the ego after death and its rebirth presuppose semantic anchorage in a culture so long as the beliefs have implications for conduct. Dr. Ian Stevenson of the Virginia University, USA, has been greatly excited by the fact that quite a few cases of children 'remembering' their 'former lives' have shown up in Ceylon. Buddhist scholars of eminence have vouched for the evidence. We cannot afford to forget here the cultural horizons of metaphysics. Bryce Ryan, in his fertility studies of Ceylon, found that belief in reincarnation was a basic tenet of Sinhalese culture. Theravada Buddhism came to pervade Sinhalese culture so completely that even stories of 'home and childhood' had Buddhism and metempsychosis for their background. Let us consider the culture of Tibet, of course, before the forcible Chinese occupation. A *Kenchung* Lama once told a European traveller that 'all Tibetans concentrate on thoughts of Buddha, *nirvāṇa*, and the next incarnation'. Socio-anthropological and parapsychological research into reincarnation cannot dispense with a philosophical assessment. It is not obvious to me at all that Tibetan wisdom, *Sher-rab Sdon-bu*, is homologous or analogous to Occidental metaphysics, or to the Sanskrit *Brahma vidya* or to the Tamil *madi nalam* as embodied in *Tiruvaymozhi*.

I question whether the Rengma Nagas of the West, some years ago, when they spoke only their language, could have admitted reincarnation in the human form after death. In their vocabulary, the soul travels along the Road of the Dead (*Teronyu Tsong Ksh nü*). It may be born and may die seven times in the other world. A fortunate few after that become crickets on earth. If these crudities are deplored by metaphysicians, I must draw attention to the Rengma Naga belief in an inscrutable 'birth spirit' (*aniza higworawa*) which lives in a man and protects him so long as he lives but dies when he dies. I have not found the exact counterpart of this subtle notion in other languages.

Metaphysics, in its highest flights, cannot do away with its cultural heritage limiting its vocabulary. To suppose either that there is already a consensus about the metaphysics of the human self and its linguistic apparatus or that the metaphysics can be debunked by a discourse conducted with an agreed formal or informal logic is to court an illusion. The ghosts of metaphysics cannot be exorcised in all languages and in all cultures.

Mathematics as a Culture Trait

I have argued in *Dialectica* that mathematics historically behaves like a culture trait spreading by innovation, diffusion, adaptation and borrowal. The Chinese *I-Ching* contains mathematics but embedded in much magic and divination. The earliest forms of the magic square in this quaint book make the mathematics recognisable as such. The Hindus are justly proud of Bhaskara's *Bīja Gaṇita*. But zero, after its transmutation into the Arabic *assifr*, became the *zephiro* of the European Renaissance. George Sarton, in his *A History of Science*, declares that Occidental scientific thinking has been deeply influenced by Hebrew and Greek ideas, hardly any by Chinese and Hindu ones, and what influence came from South and Central Asia reached Europe in a round-about way. Alice Ambrose, in debating Wittgenstein's *Bemerkungen über die Grundlagen der Mathematik,* makes out that the average textbook proof of $a° = 1$ consisting in the twin statements, $a^m \div a^m = 1$ and $a^{m-m} = a°$ is not so much *quod erat demonstrandum* as a decision about language, a linguistic innovation. Log O calls for an excursus into both the negative infinity and the algebra of imaginary quantities which Spengler regarded as the prerogative of 'Faustian' culture. A few modern mathematicians like G. H. Hardy believed that mathematical numbers had a sempiternal existence right outside the human mind. Their arguments cannot be refuted; and they produce no conviction in those who do not subscribe to the Pythagorean mysticism. Even in the philosophy of mathematics, one must preach to the converted only.

The Alleged Universality of Science

It has been said that Latin and Greek became the universal heritage of science after the European Renaissance. From Latin, science lifted bodily terms like *bacillus, corolla, cortex, genus, quantum,* and from Greek it appropriated wholesale *cotyledon, iris, larynx, pyrites, thorax.* Chlorophyll is made up from Greek elements, *chloros* (light green) and *phyllon* (leaf). The term is applied to the colouring substance in the leaf, not to the leaf. Vitamin comes from Latin elements one of which is *vita* (life). In the eighteenth century an enormous expansion of the vocabulary of the biological sciences occurred. In the nineteenth century, the scientific expansion became explosive. In Italian alone, chemistry supplied a host of terms the universal currency of which can be recognised even by those who know no Italian: *boro, cloro, alluminio, calcio, sodio, paraffina, morfina, cloroformio.* The word 'shift' in ordinary Italian is written *spostamento.* But 'Lamb's Shift', associated with W.E. Lamb, the Nobel Prize winner, is not translated at all and is so spelt in Italian.

The point of all this is that the vaunted 'universality' of science did not always exist. It has been attained by a process of cultural diffusion and cultural acceptance. Western mathematics and science have not had any competitors in the older cultures during the last six centuries. The Western Graeco-Latin scientific idiom imposed itself on non-Western cultures. Let me give a concrete instance of the spread of a new idea within the boundaries of science. Modern information theory is a cultural 'style' which appeared first in communication engineering and then infected powerfully other domains of science: thermodynamics, quantum mechanics, astronomy, cosmology, biology and psychology.

Even literature in the West has not been immune to the inter-departmental contagion. Literary style today can be regarded as an informational and statistical construct. Demosthenes, the Bible, Kalidasa, Dante, Shakespeare, can all be analysed along these lines. Sir C.P. Snow once proposed as twin tests of cultural literacy a little knowledge of thermodynamics and some familiarity with Shakespeare's plays. It has been said that, for thermodynamics, we should substitute today the more ubiquitous term 'information'. Nobody will be so rash as to confer 'objectivity' on these tests.

Greek and Modern European Art

Bruno Snell, in his *Die Entdeckung des Geistes*, dwells on the rationality of the Greeks, a trite theme. E.R.Dodds maintains that the Greeks had no instruments for probing the irrational. He thinks that modern man is beginning to acquire such instruments. The rediscovery, during the Renaissance, of the Greek 'Golden Mean' had far-reaching effects. To take another instance: the spiral of Pheidias embodies the ratio $\frac{1 \pm \sqrt{5}}{2}$ which can generate the series $.618$, 1.618, 2.618, etc., approximating to the well-known Fibonacci series each step of which is obtained by adding up the two immediately preceding numbers. Many European master-pieces of painting, e.g., Turner's *Ulysses Deriding Polyphemus*, involve an application of the ratio.

But European art was not simply a rediscovery of Greek forms. Leonardo da Vinci was not content with the revival of the Greek 'Golden Mean'. He anticipated modern Tachisme and Action Painting (as expounded by Harold Rosenberg and Jackson Pollock) by recommending a study of accidental stains on walls for working out new designs. The contrapposto of Tintoretto's *Leda and the Swan* (W.B.Yeats gave the same title to one of his sonnets) is, in its own way, the dialectic of opposites. The *imago pietatis* (image of pity) of the Middle Ages surrounded represen-tations of the Dead Christ with conventional figures of the Virgin, the Angels and Souls. Michelangelo's Rondanini *Pietà* is the very antipode of this. It was so highly charged with trumultuos emotion that Michelangelo's contemporaries regarded it as his *terribilità*. His harsh and mannerist treatment of *The Last Judgment* is also noteworthy.

In my earlier paper sent to Banaras I have referred to Erwin Schrödinger's conjecture that the abstract developments in modern physical theory, e.g., group theory in quantum mechanics, are paralleled by those of modern European art. All art in a sense is abstract in some degree, but twentieth century Occidental art has used form and colour entirely for their own sake. There is a continuous evolution of new styles leading from the work of Monet and Pissarro to Seurat, Cézanne, Gauguin, and Van Gogh. Monet's *Water Lilies* are just shimmering pools of colour devoid of even form and form the starting-point of what is called Abstract Impressionism. With Seurat, we have the beginnings of Neo-Impressionism. Abstract Art can be wholly 'non-figurative' or 'non-representational'.

Chance as a Philosophical Motif

In my earlier papers I have argued that the logic of probability is an exclusively modern European achievement or 'style'. The ancient Greeks, Hindus, Chinese and Babylonians developed no theory of randomness. Galileo, Pascal and Fermat, by contrast, calculated the chances of winning in gambling systems. The preoccupation with chance was not confined to these men. The antithesis of Fortune and Virtue is essential to the whole political teaching of Machiavelli. His Fortune was not Dante's 'Arm of Providence', but a non-rational principle limiting all history, a *principium universalitatis*, as Ferrabino interprets it. I suggest that it is a long yet unmistakable road stretching from Pascal and Machiavelli to thermodynamics and modern quantum mechanics with its well-ordered list of betting odds and its warring schools of Copenhagen, Dublin, Göttingen, Paris and Jerusalem.

The Indian Philosophical Tradition

Is there a distinctive Indian philosophical tradition bound up with the hoary Indian culture ? And must the Indian philosopher of today be concerned with reviving and reinterpreting tradition? My answers to these questions are in the affirmative. I have indicated the lines of my intellectual development as evinced by my published papers and in my essay contributed to *Current Trends in Indian Philosophy*, edited by Professors K. Satchidananda Murty and K. Ramakrishna Rao of Andhra University (1972). In this paper I should like to say something about Indian tradition itself.

The Indian philosophical enterprise is at once metaphysical, ethical, religious and mystical. The differentiation of religion and philosophy, and the delimitation of their respective spheres, is a Western phenomenon, not an Indian trend. *Atma vicāra* is a quest for salvation and withal a metaphysical depth-psychology. The apparently systematic exposition and argumentation of the Indians, resembling the Western style, are confined to *Darśana* literature. And even here one encounters the awkward *drś*, 'to vision', flouting alleged rational bases of metaphysics. The intrusion of animal symbols into the popular Hindu religion is eloquent of the Indian preoccupation with the deeper reaches of the mind. The image of Ganapathi, with the body of a child and the head of an elephant, symbolises the learning (*aparā vidya*) which leads nowhere unless it is crowned with spiritual discernment (*parā vidya*).

Philosophical ideas in India are not always institutionalised in the Western sense. Lord Morley found that universities and public schools in England were agents in moulding secular as well as ecclesiastical politics; as he put it, *c'est toujours le beau monde qui gouverne le monde*. The philosophical situation in India is different. Sri Ramakrishna, Mahatma Gandhi, Sri Aurobindo and Tagore were not professional philosophers at all. Yet, recent Indian philosophy has a lot to do with them. Humayun Kabir hazarded that the nearest equivalent to the Indian *darśana* is the German *weltanschauung*. I am afraid that I must disagree. Lord Morley found that the English have no equivalent for *weltanschauung* and that the French have no single word for it or even a circumlocution. *Weltanschauung* bespeaks the peculiar German zeal for metaphysical circumnavigation. Their encyclopaedic mind of 1700 A.D. was Leibniz; their encyclopaedic minds of 1800 A.D. were probably Hegel and Goethe. Neither Tagore nor Sri Aurobindo was an encyclopaedic mind though each was a learned man by ordinary standards. When we read about the *Ramanāśramam* in South India, we must remind ourselves that is it a community left by a seer who has had no successors but only devotees.

As I view it, the revival of the Indian mystical and metaphysical tradition is not by a simple dogmatic re-affirmation of some *darśana*, e.g., Advaita. Do mystical states occur at all? The question must be squarely faced. Pedestrian scientific research into certain hypnotic, visionary and other states is called for in the first instance. The Indian philosopher must explore the discrepancy between the 'subjective time' of some of these states and 'clock-time'. He must study the altered relation of the ego to perceptual objects in these states. In my opinion, Western writers on mysticism like Zaehner, Stace and Sidney Spencer are little equipped to deal with neuro-physiological and empirical questions involved in studies of mysticism. The Indian philosopher, who is still interested in his tradition, must learn not only from Occidental philosophy (that costs little) but also from the newer and more controversial reaches of Occidental science, hypnoanalysis, depth psychology and parapsychology. Let us consider the 'profane' mysticism induced by drugs. The Indian philosopher is definitely concerned with the blocking effects of LSD–25 on the serotonin action, perhaps concentrated in the autonomic centre of the hypothalamus; the curious fact that lysergic diethylamic acid in which bromine has been substituted in the 2–position, has a potent anti-serotonin effect, but produces no mental disturbance; and the no less curious fact that the optical isomers of LSD–25 are practically ineffective. There are quite a few other states, ostensible 'out-of-the-body' experiences, studied by Celia Green, Crookall, Tart and others in which the subject has the overwhelming conviction, *que je suis autre*. These modern studies, conducted with an eye on the classical Indian tradition, have a profound bearing on issues about the destiny of human selves.

Current Philosophical Trends in the West: Their Cultural Pre-suppositions

I have so far said little about the impact of some influential philosophical trends in the West, notably linguistic philosophical analysis (Whorf and Sapir were linguistic scientists, not philosophers) and existentialism. It is my considered view that the Indian philosopher must view these contemporary movements of the West first of all in their comprehensive cultural setting before deciding what his own reactions to them should be. Bernard Williams rightly points out, in his introduction to *British Analytical Philosophy*, that linguistic philosophy and existentialism, in spite of their self-conscious titles, do not display any straightforward unity of either allegiance or doctrine. Even the unity of method may be disputed.

Wittgenstein was peculiarly a product of the West, notwithstanding his oracular tone 'like the voices of the dead in Japanese films', as D.F. Pears describes it. Logical Positivism, too, was born of the Western *zeitgeist*. Gilbert Ryle has explained that, in Vienna, metaphysics enjoyed a pedagogic domination denied to science until Mach came along. Mach tried to repudiate the superior claims of metaphysics. The questions of mathematics, physics, biology and psychology, he said, could never be settled on metaphysical grounds. Scientific problems are solvable only in scientific ways. In England, if we follow Ryle, the situation was different. The pertinent question here was whether logic and philosophy possessed virtues lacking in science. As Ryle says vividly: 'Philosophy was regarded in Vienna as a blood-sucking parasite; in England as a medicinal leech.'

Among the Western practitioners of philosophical analysis, there are all shades and distinctions. There are those still hankering after a mathematical logic; there are followers of Wittgenstein who think that the investigation of language is a means to intellectual therapeutics. There are ordinary language philosophers who are inclined to a systematic study of the informal uses of language. The Indian philosopher can learn from some or all of these thinkers. I have often used modern mathematical logic as the vehicle of my thinking. Should the Indian philosopher decide that philosophy must be done exclusively in the linguistic or phenomenological 'styles'? No embargo can be laid on him naturally. But any Indian philosopher who decides that his business is to be transacted purely in the Western style must say plainly whether in his eyes anything in the Indian metaphysical and mystical tradition survives. For myself I must disagree profoundly with the verdict pronounced by Feigl in *The Philo-*

sophy of Rudolf Carnap that 'The case of the mystic (theologian or metaphysician) is plausible only so long as naturalistic explanations of religious and mystical experience are not available. "Naturalistic explanation" here refers to the type of account given in the various psychologies of religion—Jamesian, Freudian, etc.' Feigl omits to mention that Freud came to accept telepathy and that James, who delivered a Presidential Address to the Society for Psychical Research, regarded survival after death as not improbable. His Ingersoll Lecture on Immortality has much the same lesson to teach us. Feigl is honest enough to admit that parapsychological phenomena, if admitted, would entail a revision of the 'basic laws of nature' in some 'essential respects'. But he shuts his eyes again to the possibility that this 'openness' of science leaves room for a mystical metaphysic of the Self.

I should like to make a few remarks about the other dominant trend in the West: Existentialism. The cultural framework is again basic. The French version of existentialism, *de l'existence à l'existant*, is said to be a metaphysics, a psychology relying upon phenomenology, a sociology of literature, a therapy and a challenging ethic. Some ambivalent reactions to Husserl's demand for a 'return to things' (*die Sachen selbst Zurückgehen*) must be grasped before coming to terms with Sartre. The Indian philosopher will be sympathetic to the claim that 'the world is not what I think, but what I live'. He certainly was never bewitched by *je pense*. He will consider carefully a metaphysic which is 'a living effort to embrace, from the inside, the human conditions in their totality'. But the Indian philosopher notices in Marcel and others the movement from *je suis* to *je crois*. The German *Schuld* with its double meaning of 'debt' and 'guilt' will bother him. I cannot agree with Sartre that if we admit God it is because we are afraid to be what we are. Heidegger distinguishes his philosophy, or perhaps the several layers of it, from French existentialism. His 'waiting' in the 'forest paths' (*Holzwege*) is exciting; but it does not give the Indian philosopher still interested in his mystical tradition all that he wants. Nor can the superb *Dichtung* of Rilke replace altogether the poetical thoughts of Āṇḍal, Sri Aurobindo or Swāmi Vivekananda. There are parallels to be traced between Indian philosophy and existentialism. I have dwelt on some remarkable convergences between Swāmi Vivekananda and Kierkegaard (*Revue Internationale de Philosophie*, Brussels, 37, 1956, Fasc. 3, pp. 315–31). But all such comparisons are worthwhile only if important differences between the Indian and Western traditions are kept steadily in view.

Indian Philosophy and the Challenge of Modern Ideologies

Has the re-statement and the re-interpretation of the Indian philosophical tradition any practical relevance to living in the face of contemporary challenges? I believe that such relevance can be established apart from all questions about the mystical 'Flight of the Alone to the Alone'. Many issues about contemporary ideologies jostling against one another in India can be disentangled only by a socio-philosophical analysis. The very attempt to define ideology sets a problem for philosophy. Ideologies are total beliefs about the nature of man and of the world having implications for a wide range of human conduct. They are demands rather than descriptions or prescriptions. They say what conduct should be rather than what it is. It is scarcely a matter for surprise that, under philosophical scrutiny, definitions of ideologies put forward by political scientists like Lowenstein, Schleicher, Patrick Corbett, Frankel, Henry Thorne, Padelford and Lincoln, Palmer and Perkins, Snyder and Wilson, Harold and Margaret Sprout, to mention but a few authorities, should be highly discrepant. Why wrangle over metaphysical differences when the divergences are noisier in the theories of international politics? The term ideology is used in a rather special sense by Marx and Engels, Karl Mannheim and Hans Morgenthau. For these writers, ideology has the dual character of concealing as well as of realising objectives.

Ideologies may be religious or political or both. Political ideologies are concerned with political institutions, the relations between citizen and state, the goals of foreign policy, the forms of international action: violence, peaceful coexistence, neutrality or non-alignment. Roy Macridis usefully describes four aspects of any ideology. We have to reckon with the source of the ideology, which may be a national myth or a set of values preferred by the elite; the process of diffusion; the instruments of social control; and the relation of the ideology to the organs of political authority. For the Indian philosopher facing the uncertainties of international politics, it is enlightening to be told by a political scientist like R.A. Dahl that it is fallacious to think of the Americans as a pragmatic and non-ideological people.

India exemplifies the ideological situation in a 'developing country'. If L. Binder is right, the three components of the situation are elite goals, popular aspirations and increasing use of modern media and devices of communication. The ideologies of the developing countries are either highly differentiated ethnocentric symbols like 'Arabism', 'Négritude', 'Pyidawtha', and 'Sarvodaya', or else they are special forms of socialism—African, Destour, Islamic, Syrian, etc. In either case, socio-philosophical analysis of the kind I have recommended is highly pertinent.

On the administrative side, too, there are interpretative issues. Fred W. Riggs locates the 'prismatic structure' of a developing country between the primitive fused societies and the highly diffracted societies of the West. In the public administration of a prismatic society (India seems to be no exception here), the old patterns of status relationships and ethnic groups compete with the new contract-based, work-oriented relationships. Riggs calls the situation 'poly-normative'; the old and the new systems of value are intermingled in a hopeless fashion. Almond and Coleman have provided scales for assessing the efficiency of the governmental apparatus in developing societies. We have to measure degrees of competitiveness (competitive, semi-competitive and authoritarian) and degrees of modernity (traditional, mixed and modern). Philosophy understood as a socio-cultural self-assessment can make a great deal of all this. The concentration of decision-making in a dictator is not always as efficient as it pretends to be. A plurality of skills may be lacking in the elite. Castro's charismatic authority in Cuba could not solve the sugarcane problem. Democracies may withstand longer stresses and strains. Philosophy in India can have practical relevance if the professional distinctions of a highly diffracted Western society are not always remembered. G. S. Brett summed up William James as one who was so far indifferent to formal distinctions that he was scarcely aware 'whether he was treating psychology philosophically or philosophy psychologically'. In my opinion, the Indian philosophical tradition requires something of this freedom. The student of culture cannot afford to be a man of one book. He must be open-eyed, tolerant, and widely read.

5

Prospects of Anthropological Rationalism

DEBIPRASAD CHATTOPADHYAYA

I

World-man relation has been and continues to be a very difficult
problem indeed. It is surprising that this old and very fundamental
problem has not yet received a generally acceptable formulation.
I do not pretend to have myself found a solution to the problem.
I do not even know how to formulate it in a satisfactory form.
But because of this difficulty I do not propose to conclude hastily
that this problem is not a genuine problem at all. The history of
the problem, its formulations and attempted solutions might
prove, I think, helpful in grasping the problem and making it at
least intelligible.

The question, 'how man is related to the world', has been and
may be answered in very many ways. In this paper I shall try to
formulate and answer this question as clearly as I can. It will be
shown in this connection that the critical and growing character
of knowledge owes its rational explanation to a satisfactory
answer to this basic question. And from the proposed answer to the
question, I think, a sound concept of philosophy, which I call
Anthropological Rationalism, emerges.

II

It is always possible to give an account of the world ignoring the
presence of man in it and the difference that human presence
brings about in the world-situation. A 'manless world' is easily

imaginable. One can easily think of (1) a world wherein man has not yet appeared, (2) a world wherefrom man has disappeared, and (3) a world in which, though man exists, his existence is ignored. In fact, the pre-reflective views of the world are marked by some or other, at times all, of these forms of the 'manless world' theory. In this sense, scientific theories—the geological, astronomical and other physical accounts—of the world may be regarded as pre-reflective; and, in spite of their 'manless' character, they are 'complete' and 'satisfactory'. Reflectivity, completeness and satisfactoriness are all relative concepts and matters of growth and degeneration. Scientific concepts, for example, are less reflective than philosophical ones and more reflective than the concepts of ordinary language used in daily life. But in respect of precision and 'operation' the concepts of science are of more satisfactory character than those of philosophy and ordinary life. In so far as scope and 'depth' are concerned, philosophy is of course more 'complete' than science and that is one of the reasons why growth is not so conspicuous in philosophy as it is in science. In richness (i.e., subtlety, suggestivity, etc.) of expressions, ordinary language is superior to both philosophical language and scientific language. It is being admitted by implication that ordinary language serves the purpose of ultimate meta-language, and this meta-linguistic role of ordinary language is due to its immense intuitive resources. Well-defined measures, operations, precision and other characteristics often claimed by 'developed' languages are parasitical in origin and intelligibility. To define a measure or operation we are obliged at some stage or other to fall back upon some indefinable definiens. Neat organisation and precise formulation of experience rest upon some experiences which, though clear and distinct, are themselves neither too neat nor too precise. Intuitive 'foundation' or theoretical primacy of organised experience seems to be absolutely undeniable on reflection. I say 'on reflection', because at various pre-reflective levels man can, and in fact does, withdraw or abstract himself more or less from what he is and does. Pre-reflectivity being, as I have said before, a matter of degree, even at the reflective levels man's ability or freedom to interrogate his own existence, thought and action is only partial. Complete absorption of man in his experience rules out the very possibility of interrogation of experience, and complete abstraction of man's thought and action from his experience keeps the theorised forms of human experience above the board of criticism (untheorised experience, being the practical limit of experience, becomes uncriticisable at some stage or other). Complete absorption and complete abstraction are indeed ideal concepts: in practice we are neither completely absorbed in, nor completely abstracted from, our own experience. While the classical phenomenalist's fallacy consists in believing that he who experiences is (absorbed) in experience, the classical rationalist holds that the experiencer only witnesses or/and unifies experience without being really involved or affected by (not to speak of being absorbed in) it.

The scientist can give and has indeed given an astronomical or a geological account of the world deliberately excluding human phenomena from it. The physicist can well think of a future of the world when all human beings will disappear from it because of unbearable cold or heat or some other calamity. And there is no compelling reason for the scientist to think, as some philosophers do, that the world has been planned by some supreme intelligence only to make the emergence of human phenomenon possible in it. The scientist *qua* scientist is of course free not to reflect on what he is doing in his professional capacity. A scientist can hardly be denied his rightful claim to be regarded as scientist simply because he confines himself to his 'strictly' defined professional tasks and refuses to think over the philosophical presuppositions and/or consequences of his actions and theories.

Two remarks are in order here. First, the authenticity of scientific actions and the acceptability of scientific theories are not to be determined either by deduction from, or reduction to, some more fundamental or 'clear and distinct' ideas or phenomena. Positively speaking, science should be defined by its own aim and method and its autonomy cannot be reasonably questioned. I am speaking of autonomy and not sovereignty of science. And here is my second point. The demarcation between science and philosophy is not very sharp. It is very difficult to identify clearly the 'philosophical' aspects of the scientist's life and differentiate the same from what may be regarded the 'scientific' aspects of the scientist's life. As a result of some practical decision of committing himself to a particular mode or level of activity the scientist tries to disengage himself for the time being from other modes or levels of activities; but his success in this matter is bound to be partial. For, in the obscure unity of human life, different modes of activity tend to overlap and interpenetrate.

III

The concept of a manless world, though seemingly innocent or non-controversial, is open to more than one interpretation. In a sense we can always defend the possibility of a manless world and yet we can deny in a different sense the very possibility of such a world. Roughly speaking, the first sense is scientific and the second philosophical. To me the second seems deeper but less obvious than the first. About the scientific sense of a 'manless world' or 'world without man' something has been said in the preceding section. But a point has not been mentioned at all there. And if that important and reflective point is spelled out, I believe, the not-so-obvious connection between the philosophical sense of 'manless world' and the scientific one of the same will become somewhat clear.

'Manless world' or 'world without man' may be safely construed in two different ways. In one case the difference is due to a similar ambiguity associated with the word without. The world may truly be described as manless (1) when man has not come into existence (in the world) at all and (2) also when he has completely ceased to exist (as man) in the world. One is of course free to take a 'manless' view of the world (3) even when man is very much in existence (in the world) simply by deciding to ignore his existence or, in other words, adopting practically an attitude as if man is not in the world. And in fact it is to this pro-naturalist view of the (manless) world (largely but not exclusively influenced by some need-oriented decisions, well-defined operations, artificial language, and gadgets, etc.) that scientists generally adhere.

If one carefully reflects on these three pro-naturalist interpretations of 'manless' world, it will become gradually clear to one that pro-naturalist world-views, always conceal (but never completely) anti-naturalist ones. True that man is *in* nature but his being is never completely merged or absorbed in it. His ability to know that he is in nature implies that he has also the ability to go and live beyond it. When he thinks of his non-appearance in, or disappearance from, the world he is in fact *in* the world. In other words, his non-appearance or disappearance is after all *his* non-appearance or disappearance. To a pre-reflective man this fact might appear trivial and unimportant, for in his naturalist attitude he might miss the deeper implications of this fact—the fact that man can never think himself out of his own thought. Man can try, as at times he does, to ignore his own existence in the world. But even this trial never proves a complete success. What stands in the way of man's success to dehumanise his relation with the world is a very peculiar nature of his own being. Man is neither completely absorbed in the world nor is he completely free from it. Man's relation with the world is marked by an existential dialectic. In one aspect of this dialectic man's being defines world in nature, and in another world defines his being.

To say as it has been said that world *is* in so far as it *is in* man, is understandable. The *esse est percipi* of the empiricist is an extended version of the above form of what one might call anthropological solipsism. But that is not the thesis I propose to delineate and defend in this paper. I would like to make it absolutely clear that I do not believe that man's existence, however important might it be in the scheme of the world, can define the structure(s) and the process(es) of the world. If this is true, and I think it is, of human existence, it is even more true of human perception. Neither human existence nor human perception is the author of the world wherein man is obliged to live and live within numerous limitations.

However, it would be wrong to derive from what has been said above that a human being does not deserve to be recognised and treated as a non-natural phenomenon. True that the structure(s) and the process(es) of the world are more or less indifferent to our existence in the world and what we do and think. This is only that part of the truth I am trying to explicate. First, the world as we live it includes our existence as its essential (structural and as well as functional) component. Rightly understood, this is not a tautology. Secondly, it is humanly impossible for us to think of a world which is literally 'manless'. Combining these two propositions together one might say, what has already been said before, that man, without ceasing to be what he is, cannot think of a 'manless' world.

A critical philosopher will not fail to see that our world view is realistic. We believe very much in the independent existence of the world of perception and knowledge. Except in a very limited sense we do not create the world we perceive and know. But once we spell out the limited sense in which we believe that our perception and knowledge bring about such a modification—structural and functional modification—in the world we live in, we might characterise our position as pro-idealistic. I for myself will not say this characterisation is totally baseless. But what I will insist upon is a new and different approach—different from both the idealistic and the realistic approaches—to the man-world relations. I call this new approach anthropological approach. This approach is more descriptive and less interpretative than the other two types of traditional approaches.

World is both within and without man. It is both dependent and independent of him. That there is a world without man, i.e., independent of him, is obvious. What is not so obvious is that the world is also within him, i.e., dependent on him. Still less obvious is the sense in which the world is both within and without man. The man in the street, and at times even the pre-critical scientist, does not question the independent existence of the world without man. But once it is pointed out to him that the world he knows is not so independent of him as he thinks it to be, he feels intrigued at first and then on further reflection realises that the being of the world as he knows it owes to him something very definite. This point has been made out in philosophy in very many ways. Kant and his followers argue that 'I think' is the pre-supposition of the world. Cartesians hold that even if everything could be doubted the existence of 'I' cannot be. The sloipsist is certain that 'I' is the sole author of the world. Some teleologists are inclined to believe that the entire process of nature was designed to make the appearance of self-conscious man in it possible. Although we do not accept the above positions, we do believe that man cannot intelligibly or consistently think of a world whereto he has made no contribution and wherein he is not a phenomenon at all. In fact, the pro-naturalist idea of 'manless' world owes its intelligibility to its essential inseparability from the world-in-man. When 'I' as a man try to think of the world wherein I am not, I have to form the idea of that world from the world wherein I am. Manless world is an abstraction from, or an extrapolation of, man-world. This is a true description of the relation between manless world and man-world. This truth might again appear very trivial to a pre-reflective thinker. Before I dispel this misconception of triviality I think we should try to understand the rationale of the proposed 'manless' world itself.

IV

There are different levels of man's existence. One can easily discern different levels in human activity. In some types of activity man is more concerned with objects—objects may be of knowledge, of action, of imagination and appreciation, or of some other mental phenomenon. When I say man's action or knowledge is object-oriented I do not mean to say that he is totally divorced from his subjectivity. There are certain human pursuits, e.g., artistic, philosophical, and moral, in which man is found to be very much involved in his 'own' subjectivity. Careful analyses show that both in subjectivity and objectivity there are different modes or grades. Inlook and outlook of man, subjectivity and objectivity of his body-and-mind are inseparable from one another. In subject-oriented consciousness an objective pull is there, and similarly in object-oriented consciousness the role of subjectivity is not totally absent. Science is said to be the paradigm of object-oriented consciousness, and ethics of the subject-oriented consciousness.

Let us try to understand why science is regarded as the paradigm of object-oriented consciousness. From a common sense point of view we all find that in the matters of art and morals, opinions and even judgements vary not only from society to society but also from man to man. This suggests that whenever human consciousness returns to the extreme end of subjectivity its understanding of objects—factual and evaluational—become blurred and questionable. There is a persistent ambiguity and opacity in pure subjectivity. Some metaphysicians think that subjectivity is a super-human and universal principle running through and somehow unifying all the subjects of experience.

It is not clear how one can escape from the said ambiguity and opacity. The diaphanous character of consciousness is not to be confused with pure subjectivity. Of course, there is a way of postponing or avoiding the problem of subjectivity. In natural science we are mainly concerned with objects 'as they are'. Strictly speaking, as our pursuit of objects is always related to and influenced by subjectivity we can never grasp the objects as such. Within these limitations the scientist tries to understand and explain the objects of nature from a spectator's point of view. May be the ways of apprehending nature are intuitive or emotionally coloured. But, aided by his method, machine, technique, and language, he tries to support, save and abstract the objects of his study from his subjective propensity and inclinations. The scientist wants to discover and disclose the true identity of objects. His methods of testability, well-defined operations, and axiomatic language are all intended to strengthen his abstractionist strategy. The scientist's eagerness to know is always accompanied by his eagerness to let others know it. In other words, scientific knowledge is defined primarily in terms of inter-subjectivity, scientific method and symbolic language. My subjective sense of certitude, however genuine it might be, about the nature of a thing is of no scientific significance unless and until it could be proved or tested in terms of a commonly accepted method and expressible in some well-defined language.

This scientific accent on objective mode of knowledge is undoubtedly very important. Its importance is theoretical as well as practical. From the objective orientation of science one would be wrong to infer that scientific mode of knowledge has no subjective correlate or foundation. Empirical knowledge of objects is founded upon a deep human subjectivity, which on reflection discloses its deeper objective structures. The absolutist is mistaken in his belief that the foundational consciousness of objects is itself absolutely structureless or free (free from objective correlates).

The concept of man-world is very important indeed. One might say man-world is not a single concept at all but a compound of two different concepts—concept of man and that of world. It is to be borne in mind that the concept of world is not to be confused with the concept of earth—a planet on which we live. The concept of man stands very close to the concept of subject, but obviously they are not interchangeable. Similarly, it is to be pointed out that the concept of world and the concept of object, although closely akin, are not synonymous. By way of reduction, i.e., negatively speaking, one might argue that manless subjectivity and worldless objectivity are conceptually incoherent. To say, as I propose to, that there cannot be a subject which is not human is to indicate and emphasise what might appear quite obvious to one. But again what is not so obvious is this. If subjectivity is admitted to be inseparable from man then necessary human characteristics must at least partially define subjectivity. Most of us will agree that (spatio-temporally identifiable) body is a necessary character of man. This suggests, what was not initially obvious, that there cannot be a subject without a body. The body-that-is-subject has a peculiarity of its own which distinguishes it from the objective bodies. Man has a definite place in the world of space-time, yet the spatio-temporal coordinate cannot define the whole of his being. Human body has a depth unknown to the 'physical' bodies in the world. I say 'physical' because the inseparability of man and world, of subject and object, makes it impossible for man to completely withdraw himself from the physical world. What is not physical in man is his ability to exceed the bounds of his body. and senses, to live in a value dimension and survive thereby, of course in a special sense, his bodily death.

Human life and living inject or induct value in physical objects. For example, a building in which my father lived means (or even is) to me something much more than a physical object. One might say it is more than a physical object because I attach value to it. This is partly true but only partly. Even if I like or will to treat it as a mere physical object I cannot, I fail. My inability or failure is a proof of the objective character of what is said to be due to my evaluation, a purely subjective act. This line of argument brings out another point: the actuality of the objective correlate of value consciousness. If even value-objectivity can assert its being in spite of myself, this only strengthens the view that physical objects do not owe their being to my or our merciful perception. In other words, the being of the world, although inseparably relative to our being, is in a very important sense independent of our consciousness. Neither can man incorporate the whole of the world being in himself nor could man be totally merged into the being of the world. Object and subject, man and world, define each other, but never clearly and exclusively and threre is a continuously operative dialectic between the two. And to this is due what we call the growth of knowledge.

Science is generally regarded, and perhaps rightly so, as the best form of knowledge. Certainly one of the reasons why scientific knowledge is esteemed so high is that it is definite, testable, precisifiable and corrigible and modifiable. The man in the street might wonder how what is definite is at the same time modifiable. In science, object is defined in terms of some class properties, i.e., in a general way. However generally an object may be defined in science since the proposed definition is empirical, and not purely formal, it is bound to be modified in course of time and in the light of new relevant findings. In a way, scientific objects, contrary to general belief, are historical and modifiable due to factual considerations. True that historical objects unlike the scientific ones are primarily individual, not general. But it is to be made absolutely clear in this connection that neither historical objects are purely individual, i.e., unique, nor are scientific objects purely general. The generality of scientific objects is effected and corrected by observations of individual cases falling under the concerned general object. From the other end it is to be pointed out that the very possibility of identification of historical objects and passing judgement thereupon indicates the general character (maybe this generality is of a lower order) of historical objects. In brief, naturality or physicality and historicity of objects are not exclusive and cannot be separated from one another in thought. What is historical is natural and whatever is natural may be historical.

The thesis that whatever is historical is natural might appear very strong and difficult to defend. It has been attacked from opposite ends on several grounds. The pro-naturalist holds that the historical has absolutely no autonomy of its own and that it is subjective and imaginary. The anti-naturalist contends that the historical is spiritual; it is not only autonomous but, on reflection, turns out to be sovereign even. Simply because historical object is not a matter of direct perception and does not satisfy the requirements of scientific objectivity it would be rash to conclude that the historical mode of knowledge is invalid. It would be equally incorrect to hold that history is rational re-enactment and gradual disclosure of the timeless spirit in time through human instrumentality.

Whatever we conceive has a perceptual core in it. And, conversely, whatever we perceive has its conceptual orientation. In reconstructing the human past the historian may enjoy relative freedom—relative to the scientist—but he too cannot act as an unfettered agent of a Sovereign Mind. What necessitates review and revision of historical judgement and makes its criticism impossible has no internal relation or pre-established harmony with it. History and its knowledge cannot be more rational than the human being who ultimately accounts for the possibility of either and who himself is subject to the laws of nature or science.

There are different ways of criticising the paradigmatic character of scientific knowledge. One way of doing it is to attack the concept of scientific object as something very abstract. Another way of attacking it is that it is subjective and a construct. Although these two attacks are often launched together, there is no necessary connection between the two. The realist, for example, might agree that scientific object is partly abstract but he is sure to deny the pure subjectivity of scientific object. The concept of subjectivity itself is not free from ambiguity. To the empiricist the subjective is what is psychological and for that reason not testable. Lack of testability disqualifies a 'scientific object'. The empiricist philosopher of science thinks that objectivity is to be defined in terms of some methodological and (formal) linguistic requirements. Underlying this thesis of subjectivity there is a concept of truth, according to which scientific truth can never be self-evident, and it must be other-evident. On analysis it is found that the 'other' on the evidence of which the truth or otherwise of scientific statements is established is itself taken to be relatively unquestionable, i.e., relatively self-evident. But there is another concept of subjectivity inspired and supported by the self-evident theory of truth. According to the proponents of this concept, true subjectivity means freedom from determinate subjectivity. The more a subject succeeds in freeing or withdrawing itself from objective determinates, the more truly subjective it is. The highest subjectivity means absolute freedom. Absolute or God is often taken to be the paradigm of subjectivity and freedom, for it is thought to be beyond all objective determination. It is also the reason why it is said that finite as he is man cannot form an adequate idea of God. It is interesting to note in this connection that this concept of pure subjectivity is acceptable to those who believe in absolute objectivity. There is at least one object, it is said, which is not determined by anything else or by any knowing mind whatsoever and that object alone is to be regarded as absolute. The concept of absolute subjectivity and that of absolute objectivity have one thing in common: they prove inconsistent with the concept of scientific objectivity. Neither subjective idealists nor objective idealists regard scientific knowledge as the best form of knowledge. Both of them define knowledge in a static or substantive way. They think that knowledge *is,* and it does not grow. The concept of growing knowledge is unacceptable to both of them. On close analysis, however, it is found that there is a smooth passage from pure subjectivity to pure objectivity and the converse. Absolute denial of determination brings the pure objectivist and the pure subjectivist close to one another. The smooth passage between pure subjectivity and pure objectivity has at least one very important lesson to offer us.

V

The pure subjectivist and the pure objectivist are engaged in a common pursuit, of course from two different ends. Both of them are trying to develop a theory of Sovereign Mind—a mind in which all other minds and things find their fullest expression, completely or incompletely merge, and in terms of which their inter-relation, own existence, and significance become intelligible. These two views end up in a sort of theocentricism and entail, among others, denial of science as paradigm of knowledge, anthropocentricism and vindication of uncritical metaphysics. Some over-ambitious metaphysicians in their vain quest for certainty try to develop a theory of an infinite and all-comprehensive, or at any rate transfinite, Self, which is very unlike their own selves, finite and mortal, and then offer a speculative explanation of the world as a whole containing all things and beings in it from the point of view of that infinite Self.

Man always exceeds himself and is conscious of his self-exceeding ability. But he cannot exceed himself to the extent and in all the directions he wishes to. He desires to be what he is not and that is both good and necessary for the development of human civilisation and culture. But his achievements, though growing, do not satisfy him. Unfortunately, he does not take the right lesson from his persistent dissatisfaction. Being finite and limited as he is, man cannot own and internalise all that he experiences and encounters. In other words, man cannot comprehend and have in him absolutely the world of objects. Structurally speaking the objective world is not a mere duplication or extension of, or constituted by, the knowing subject. Even in the constitution of aesthetic and ethical objects the subject is not absolutely free. True that in moments and acts of moral will and aesthetic imagination the human mind is more or less free, but even in its self-encounter or solitude it is objectively constrained. The artist is of course less object-oriented than the scientist, but that does not mean that the subject as an artist is free creator or author of his world. And that partly explains the possibility of genuine aesthetic judgement without postulating a sovereign mind and harmony thereof. Similar considerations may be offered also in containing ethical scepticism.

Underlying anthropological rationalism there is a basic concept, human fallibilism. And one must be careful enough to differentiate the concept of fallibilism from that of scepticism. The fallibilist never questions the ontological commitment of scientific and cultural objects, persistent objective constraints, which cannot be completely reduced to experience. Object is largely, but not exclusively, a matter of discovery and description. Partly it is a datum impressing our sense-experience and partly constraining and facilitating our understanding. To what extent an object is datum and to what extent it is not cannot be clearly defined and demarcated. Theoretical orientation of the datum or the given enters into the very constitution of object; and as a result of that human understanding and account of object always leave room for further precisification, modification and improvement. There are some constructionists who think that the forms of understanding or theoretical construction are uniform and immutable and that the matters of experience are completely and conclusively definable by those forms; and, therefore, they conclude that correctly constructed objects are universally and necessarily true. This anti-sceptic argument does not bear logical scrutiny and is not fair to historical facts. Knowledge, whether it is of the knowing and known subjects or of the world of objects, is open-textured and criticisable on reflection or in the light of new findings or both. Whatever factors make knowledge possible—the ontological identity of objects, experience, forms of organisation and even the self that brings about some sort of uniformity in the use of those forms—are open to re-identification and revision.

Self is a sort of bottomless depth and boundless (but not structureless) unity. But we can never encounter self *qua* self. We know it either as subject of knowledge or agent of action or in some other objectified mode. In its pure or absolute subjectivity self is unknown to man. To postulate the unknown existence or idea of absolute self opens the flood-gate of speculative and uncritical metaphysics. Man cannot claim to have achieved intellectually what is existentially impossible for him. True that he is a self-exceeding animal and that there is no permanent limit to what he can possibly achieve. But one must not think, as the classical rationalist did, that he can usurp the position of God and have a view of the world as a *totum simul* and under the aspect of eternity. In order to lend theoretical plausibility to a purely speculative view which is otherwise practically untranslatable it is argued (1) that space-time framework is ultimately unintelligible or self-contradictory, (2) that the sensible is confused, irrational and ultimately unintelligible, (3) that the true identity of self is disembodied and (4) divine. The no-ownership view of self, i.e., nothing is really owned by human self, has been defended from two extreme ends of empiricism and rationalism. Anthropological rationalism is inconsistent with either.

Man learns from experience, but from experience-as-such, if any, he has nothing to learn. It is experience of object or objectward experience which alone contributes to human knowledge. Conscious of problems, mind interrogates the world of objects, and then experience assumes a definite role in the knowledge situation. So far as man is concerned experience as such is a limiting concept. To man, absolutely structureless experience is unknown. Even his self-knowledge assumes of necessity an objective structure. Otherwise, experience could not have any critical say in the growth of knowledge. Had sense manifold been really 'blind' it could be at best a passive partner and not a critical collaborator of reason in the mind's quest for knowledge. Man does not know by experience alone. Nor can he know without experience either. He can anticipate the objective structure (not all details) of his possible experience but the actual details of experience may prove inconsistent with and, therefore, critical of *a priori* anticipation. Human knowledge (unlike God's) is not necessarily valid or deductively systematised. For, the details or sub-structures of experience do not uniformly duplicate and corroborate the structure of objects anticipated by reason. There is always a possibility of surprise in what we come across in our experience, indicating thereby the limitations of the purely *a priori* functioning attributed to reason. The limit of reason cannot be lightly dismissed as the cunning of reason or *avidyā* or something purely subjective. There is an objective, though historical, i.e., changing, ground of human knowledge being limited, corrigible and growing.

The history of all intellectual disciplines in general and philosophy in particular is a standing refutation of the view that knowledge is timeless, knows no growth and is ultimately indifferent to what is empirical. Indifference to the empirical entails indifference to the human model of knowledge and tacit acceptance of the divine model. This criticism is sought to be met by dogmatically denying the validity of historical mode of knowledge and uncritically isolating the historical and/or transcendental from the empirical.

I admit it is not easy to define the empirical. Metamorphoses of the criteria of the empirical make the point abundantly clear. If verifiability is too wide, falsifiability is too narrow, and confirmability is vitiated by paradoxes. But falsifiability, unlike the other two inductive concepts, could be further liberalised and usefully applied to the mixed domain of the empirical and the transcendental, science and metaphysics. The metaphysical rightly understood is not indifferent to the empirical. Metaphysical statements containing less saturated concepts are corrigible and criticisable by scientific statements containing more saturated concepts. Properly analysed, no statement, neither metaphysical nor scientific, is found to contain an absolutely saturated concept. The notion of basic statements, advocated by the rationalist and the empiricist, is ultimately untenable. The so-called basic statements are all criticisable and only relatively basic.

Some philosophers have been overimpressed by the model of physical science, its precision and testability, and some others by the analogy of God, his comprehensiveness and power. Underlying all philosophical positions there is a more or less inarticulate anthropological presupposition. Philosophy being essentially a reflective enquiry, every philosopher in the course of rounding up his position consciously or otherwise touches upon its anthropological root or principle of unity. Man is obliged to be present

in all his thought and action, and this obligation is existential.
The more he deepens and wilfully explores the consciousness of
this obligation the more he realises the human foundation or pre-
reflective presence and function of his being in all his works, theoretical and practical. In philosophical reflection we get what we
have already got in a pre-reflective form. It is a sort of getting the
got, *prāptasya prāpti*. The more he can bring the general results
of his reflection to bear upon the acceptable empirical findings the
more rationally satisfied and fulfilled he feels. Criticised, corrected,
and corroborated by the objective details of experience the philosopher broadens and deepens his theoretical visions. Knowledge
cannot grow in vacuo; growth demands an objective correlate.
Unless their fuller identities are disclosed in course of time it cannot
be ascertained *a priori* whether the relevant objective correlates of
a theory would turn out to be corroborative or corrective. Yet
pressed by practical necessity the philosopher confronted with a
set of competing alternative theories has to make his choice clear
(without knowing the consequences thereof). He is thus initially
obliged to fall back upon his intuitive resources. But intuition is
no truth-guarantee of what is 'entailed' by it. What is proposed
a priori by intuition may be disposed by experience. The dialectic
of difference and unity between experience and intuition in human
self accounts for the self-critical character and growth of knowledge.
Philosophical knowledge is very much like the philosopher himself, self-critical and fallible. In his work he is partly concealed
and partly disclosed.

6

Towards an Anthropological View of Philosophy

MARGARET CHATTERJEE

I shall begin with some methodological considerations. I am sure that the philosopher needs to use different methods depending on his field of investigation. What befits the formal logician can scarcely befit someone working in the field of philosophy of history, for example. Perhaps this will be readily conceded. What people mean when they talk about philosophical method perhaps concerns rather metaphysics, whether metaphysics is possible, if so how, and so forth. I believe that the attempt to make philosophy scientific was understandable—such being the prestige of scientific method and so numerous its practical results since the seventeenth century—but on the whole mistaken. What I call 'inductive philosophising',[1] is not on all fours with inductive procedures in science. The philosophical example is not like an instance, and an accumulation of examples does not establish anything in the way in which the accumulation of instances probabilifies a scientific hypothesis. The high-level generality character of both philosophical and scientific theories lends a spuriously scientific air to the former. One can scarcely do better than follow Kant in pointing out the regulative character of the former and the weakly verifiable nature of the latter. The 'going beyond' in each case is different. But if philosophy cannot be scientific this should not be a matter for regret. The *Geisteswissenschaften* have methods of their own and criteria of their own validity. Let us first see what classifying philosophy among the 'sciences of the human spirit' amounts to. It amounts to classifying philosophy with disciplines like history and the social sciences. These are disciplines where the data are not sensible simpliciter. This is obvious in the case of history. The historian has to discover his facts by going over written records with a view to reconstructing the events and characters of the past. In this task the role of imagination is indispensable. This is not the imagination which deals with replicas of sense experiences, nor, needless to say, with fantasy, but a capacity for 'entering into' a period or, to use a medical analogy, uncovering the nerve that lies beneath the flesh of mere diary and record.

That the data of the social sciences are not sensible simpliciter is less palpable. Men, their speech and behaviour, are perceptible. But social norms, attitudes and institutions are not. Here again a kind of 'understanding' is called for which has more of an imaginative component about it than had the *Verstehen* of which Kant spoke. We are not, however, too far from Kant in what has been said above. Of the historical understanding it can very truly be said that it constrains the world of men and events to give answers to questions which are of its own framing. Kantian also is the ambiguity between understanding and imagination which shows through in some of the most suggestive passages of the first *Critique*. So much by way of situating philosophy among the *Geisteswissenschaften*.

A little more perhaps needs to be said about past attempts to make philosophy scientific. Although mistaken, these attempts were useful. A geometrical model was an advance on a theological one in that reason tried to stand on its own. Seventeenth and eighteenth century philosophers were of course unable to be sufficiently tough-minded about this. The scientism of the empiricists on the other hand came to grief over mathematics, the nature of which they misunderstood. The more recent verificationist challenge, however, has to be met. To say that the philosopher is in any way 'describing' is to fall at some stage into the verificationist's trap. The idiosyncrasy platitude makes room, presumably, for a non-descriptive, meaningful metaphysical use of language. The philosopher can, with a sigh of relief, realise he is not a duck but a swan.

But this jubilation is short-lived. If the theologian goes in for God-talk, what sort of talk does the metaphysician go in for? Talk has to be about something. Let us bring in the point about the 'sciences of the human spirit' again. Let us say (by way of experiment) that talking about metaphysical matters is like talking about the revolution of 1917, or the institution of marriage, or like talking about public opinion. Does this help? Let us see. No one maintains that because none of these are perceptibles none of them 'exist', or denies that there is such a thing as a revolution, an institution, etc. We 'know what we are talking about'. Does the word 'real' or 'reality' or 'really' apply to any of our three examples? The revolution of 1917 'really' took place. The institution of marriage is a 'reality'. Public opinion is a 'real' thing. It has 'force'. We can employ all these words without artificiality. This is because although revolutions, marriages and public opinion are imperceptibles they are 'to do with' matters which are very perceptible indeed. But these perceptibles may be of different orders. Consider, say, the difference between pictures of revolutionaries in old St. Petersburg, the visible cohabitation of X and Y, and the refusal of a group of people to abide by Section 144 of the Criminal Procedure Code. They all constitute evidence, but in different ways. The validation of talk about our three cases will be round about and herein we find the family resemblance with talk about metaphysical matters. Talk about all three would come under the heading of 'describing' (as long as 'describing' is allowed to involve interpretation) but the 'what' which is to be described is in each case 'queer' in terms of orthodox empiricist requirements for describability. The data cannot be simply appealed to, they are not terminals or stoppers, but themselves points of departure for further enquiry. I hope it is clear that I am not saying that thinking metaphysically is absolutely on all fours with thinking about history, sociology and the like. I wished to point out rather why I think it more like this than it is like describing the heavenly bodies, looking down a microscope or even doing theoretical physics.

I move next to two cases which, from my point of view, throw a lot of light on what the metaphysician tries to do, for they deal with fields where we quite patently leave the field of describing altogether. First let us look at translation. The translator aims at getting as close as he can to the original. When he gets close we have 'a good translation'. Sometimes he gets stuck over idioms or proper names (imagine, say, the difficulty over trees in Bibhutibhusan's novels). What does he do then? Either he leaves the word as it is and puts it in inverted commas, or he puts the nearest word he can find. Translations are never perfect copies. They approach the limits, good or bad. The translator does not give a description of what he experiences as he works on the original, but he aims at an over-all fit which is strictly neither a matter of correspondence or coherence but which contains elements of both. Let us apply this parallel to a metaphysical theory. A metaphysical theory does not describe anything but it expresses an attempt to put into words a vision of things which the philosopher himself has experienced. It is an essay in communication, a communication of something which is itself progressively articulated through the verbal expressions used, be these arguments, examples, imagery or all three. To try to 'verify' a metaphysical theory is therefore as misguided as trying to 'verify' whether a translation is satisfactory or not. There is another pertinent parallel. Just as a translator often has to incorporate the 'untranslatable' (the proper name, the idiom, the word which is highly culture-determined), a metaphysician may find himself having to accommodate the 'undigested' elements. For example, a behaviouristically inclined philosopher may admit (somewhat uncomfortably of course) after-images, or an optimist who believes that this is the best of all possible worlds may have to admit incomprehensible surd elements in nature. Furthermore, just as there are alternative translations, so there are alternative metaphysical theories. The touchstone in the one case is the 'original' and in the other experience. Now, our experience does have a common structure to be sure. But differences of temperament go a long way in conditioning our reactions to this common structure. It has often been pointed out that the difference between the idealist and the realist, the monist and the pluralist, has much to do with differences in overall orientation to life. If in the physical world the possibilities are so vast as often to make prediction and control hazardous, the possibilities in the case of man (whose endowment includes and goes beyond the physical) are infinitely more. To read conflicting metaphysical statements is to read diverse records of human experience. Some men are overwhelmed by the suffering that pertains to human existence and react with dismay. Liberation-philosophies are born of this dismay. The outward-looking cosmologies of the early Greeks were born of a different reaction, that of wonder, which in turn was closely linked to curiosity, an attitude which fathered the scientific outlook. The case of translation shows the difficulty of approximating to an original. The original is to the translation what experience is to metaphysical theory. My second case comes from the performatory arts. Those who perform a drama or musical work scarcely have an original before them at all. They have the text, the score, an organisation of symbols on paper. The rest has to be constructed, interpreted, performed. The situation is even more complicated than it is in simple perception which, as the phenomenologists have shown, is hardly simple at all but is closely determined by our noetic stances, affective, volitional and the rest. Each performance yields new disclosures (each good performance that is); each metaphysical theory expresses new insights. Just as we saw that the translator is not-describing, so also the actors or the orchestral performers are not-describing.[2]

Next we need to ask if there is anything in common between the two sets of examples, those from the social sciences on the one hand, and translation and interpretation in the performatory arts on the other. The common element seems to be this, that in all the cases mentioned we approximate towards something the full nature of which is not fully disclosed to us. In each case the 'given' is of a different kind and in each specific endeavour the given cannot be ignored, e.g., the data, the text to be translated, the score from which the musicians play. The metaphysician reads the 'signs', situated historically as he is, and within the limits of his own archaeology of thought.[3] This is why I find unintelligible any claim a philosopher might make to speak of 'ultimate reality', a phrase to which I find it hard to attach meaning. That my inability does not rest on verificationist grounds should by now, I hope, be clear. The philosopher should be in the best position to realise how fragmentary his view is, how time and space-bound. His terminology is usually borrowed from disciplines outside philosophy and his starting-point is usually the criticism of theories other than his own. His *terminus ad quem* is a view of men and things dependent on his own limited experience and the strength of his own creative impulse. What results is no doubt an extrapolation. This extrapolation resembles the artist's work of art far more than it resembles the scientist's extrapolation on the basis of instances. Like the artist, the philosopher has to walk the triple tight-rope of the critical, the creative and the authentic. The philosopher is a craftsman in words. But the medium is not the message either for the artist or for the philosopher.

Whatever I have to say about ethical and religious matters, and I am sure I have not progressed far in either field, I classify as 'anthropological', although in a wider sense the adjective also applies to the methodological enquiries essayed above. I am sufficiently influenced by analytical approaches to feel rather embarrassed if pressed to express an opinion on 'human values' just like that. I believe (1) that certain values exist; (2) that they need defending, not theoretically, but through appropriate forms of action. What 'defence' and 'appropriate' mean here would take us into social philosophy. Without man there would be neither values nor disvalues. Values in some sense 'depend' on man. I believe it very salutary to encounter cultures with different value-systems from our own, for all values seem to me to be culture-bound. I find it difficult to arrange values in a hierachical way because one can always produce an awkward example which can set the whole pyramid toppling.

My thinking on ethical matters, therefore, begins at a suspiciously naturalistic level and continues on the lines of some of the tentative directions indicated earlier. These are:

(1) That there is no one method for arriving at ethical decisions. The kind of thinking involved in ethical perplexity and its resolution perhaps should not be classified as a type of 'reasoning' for such a term seems to overestimate the logical component. We invoke all sorts of queer reasons (often poor ones) for decisions which are made neither on the basis of grounds or instincts but something infinitely more complex—a mixture of reflecting, feeling and cultural conditioning. Sometimes we may 'read off', as it were, from rules, sometimes weigh different people's goods, including our own, and sometimes just take a leap in the dark. Ethical insight, like metaphysical thinking, is in great part a function of imagination. The reflective component in it veers between poles—right and wrong, good and bad, etc. Often this fails us and we have to resort to criteria like 'what is best in the circumstances', 'what is the lesser evil' and so on. If it is pointed out that to appeal to criteria of any kind is to use reason and 'to reason', then I would say that two alternatives are possible. Either to extend the concept of reason so that it includes all the traditional

non-rational components like feeling, etc., where the snag is that in hitting a rock-bottom base out of which sense, understanding and reason (intellect) all spring we are probably hitting something pre-reflective. Or to admit that what falls outside reason (feeling, etc.) may eventually win the day. If we take the first alternative would such an extended 'faculty' be capable of reasoning in any usual sense? If we take the second alternative we need to admit that reasoning is only too often abandoned en route and that choices are often made according to impulse, habit and the like, all of which, I should imagine, do not qualify as grounds.

(2) That it is the ambiguity of facts and situations which gives rise to the possibility of multiple metaphysical stances and varieties of ethical positions. This ambiguity exists both in the external and internal spheres, i.e., the world which is common to all men and the private worlds which vary from man to man.

(3) That the approximative character of all human enquiries is carried over to the field of ethical insight. Our awareness on all fronts is fragmentary. There can therefore be no occasion for dogmatism. There is always the possibility of being mistaken. What being ethically mistaken amounts to, I admit, is philosophically very hard to give content to. The hard-liner here has an advantage. Appeal to consensus will not do because there have often been situations in history where the group, the collective (the lynching crowd, for example) were, we would usually agree, wrong. Again we fall back on cultural conditioning. The competent judges in a head-hunting community no doubt judge in a different way from us. The liberal, still more the believer in non-violence, is in a quandary here. Heart-searching may in fact result in the question whether head-hunting is any more reprehensible than the slaughter involved in sophisticated warfare. The numbers killed are certainly less. This of course does not provide a justification for head-hunting. We take a stand according to our light and not because of any superiority. I see no rationale for admiring the man who, usually thanks to his favourable economic circumstances, constantly makes free decisions, more than the tribal who, with perfect discipline, takes his herd up to the mountains to pasture in the hot weather and for whom no question of doing otherwise arises.

What else belongs more specifically to the ethical situation ? I believe ethical responsibility to be a function of our relations with others and our knowledge of them. To say this seems to presuppose some kind of theory of the self. Our selfhood is won through our commerce with things and with other persons. Relations with others are not to be seen as forays from the fastness of an essentially individual identity. Self-discovery springs from our awareness of and our dealings with others. The linguistic circularity here is intrinsic to the situation. It is others who provide us not only with the context of possibility but with its very *raison d'être*. It is because this is so that bereavement, friction or divorce (to take only a few examples) shake a person to the very foundations. (Cf., the common expressions 'I am not the same since he died', 'He was much affected by the breach between them', 'She was shaken to the core by his disloyalty'.)

At this point an aside is necessary on the concept of 'awareness'. Man's awareness I see as the outcome of a long process which begins in the simple movements of unicellular animals and the tropisms of plants. Plant life I find especially illuminating, with its basic movements of 'towards' and 'away from' (the shoot moving toward the sun and the root away from it), its cyclicality, its proneness to disease. Man's awareness is intentional in a heightened sense, needless to say, and this we usually refer to by speaking of him as being self-aware. His ethical awareness is born of his imaginative understanding that others suffer as he does. The mark of the ethical seems to me to be the willingness to suffer in the cause of others' good. The desire to get rid of one's own suffering, natural though it be, does not seem to me any more ethical than the animal's efforts to remove burrs from its fur or a thorn from its foot. Not, however, that I see any intrinsic virtue in suffering for its own sake. Physical pain, for example, beyond a certain point does not ennoble, but degrades. Only he who has not experienced it, whether himself or through the sight of others' sufferings, can think otherwise. The implication of all this, as may be clear, is that I am in favour of an activist ethic which recognises our involvement with others and regards the main directive of morality as the obligation to lessen the load of human suffering. It is here that the 'defence' of values, to which I referred, comes in. A philosopher may be able to articulate *why* this is the case, but he has no special gifts which qualify him to remedy situations. Professionally we are addicted to talking rather than acting.

Religious life, too, I cannot classify under any heading other than the anthropological. I shall try to explain why. I do so by beginning, as I did in discussing ethical matters, by referring to three preliminary headings. It seems to me that (1) There is no one type of religious experience but many, no *one* being superior to the others, one 'true' while others are false and so on. Religious experience, like ethical experience, is a complex of many elements which are 'vital' rather than logical. (2) It is the ambiguity of man's situation, especially with regard to his experience of wonder at one pole and dismay at the other, which gives rise to his religious outlook. The varying weightage of these two is a leading clue to the varying emphases of the different religions. (3) The fragmentariness which we found to be typical of man's perceptual experience and his ethical insight is continued into his religious life. Here the question is not that of being 'mistaken' but that there is always a 'more' which lies beyond us, an aspect of 'man's position in the cosmos' which we have not taken account of. For example, a religious 'Blik' centred on the fact of human suffering may be less sensitive to other equally undeniable elements such as delight, joy, confidence that all things work together for good, hope, etc.

What then do I mean by an anthropological understanding of religious experience? I believe religious experience to be an extension of experiences of transcendence which we are familiar with in a variety of dimensions. Such experiences are at the same time experiences of incompleteness and yet experiences which contain the promise of more. Let me hazard some examples of different kinds—the expectation of continued landscape, on the other side of the mountain, the resonance of musical sounds which taper beyond the reach of the human ear, the assurance of love which endures death, the sense of history which links us to those who went before and those who will come after. These are 'intimations' something in the sense in which Wordsworth and Jacobi variously use this word. I call all these experiences of revelation, of disclosure. What I am suggesting could perhaps be described as a 'cosmo-phenomenological' approach. Revealed scriptures are to me records of human experience of further revelations or disclosures which, however, I would not regard as discontinuous with the rest of human experience. There are, as C.D. Broad once said, religious 'specialists' whose disclosures are remarkable in one particular sphere. Similarly, a person who is musical is sensitive to a dimension which is closed territory to the unmusical. In the last resort, though, the philosopher can only philosophise authentically on the basis of experiences which are his own. This philosophising is not a matter of merely 'describing experience'. The patient 'describes' his experience to the doctor, although what he does is to bear witness perhaps rather than to describe. If a philosopher merely described his experience (even this would be extraordinarily difficult to do) I wonder if his description would have any interest other than a clinical one. Philosophising is a queer kind of extrapolation on the *basis* of experience, as I have tried to explain earlier.

It is natural, at the terminus of the long evolution of intentionality from tropism to aspiration, that man should seek for, indeed sometimes posit, a spring behind the spectacle.[4] But the philosopher has no special tool nor special talent for probing this spring. He is neither saint nor sage. The simple man of faith or the poet may go further than he. Where religious, poetic and philosophic impulses converged, as in the Upanishads, the result had a certain grandeur that we have not been able since to come anywhere near. For, the deliberately chosen myth is never as felicitous as the one which is the spontaneous efflorescence of an entire culture. Of the three worlds, man has, perhaps irretrievably, lost two. What remains is inescapably spatio-temporal. But this very world, or rather our experience of it, is shot through with possibility. These possibilities point not to another world but to fuller experience of this same world of which life and death, happiness and distress, are all parts. The broken arcs (in Browning's phrase) which we experience, are sufficient to enlist all our powers, feeble as they may be. These powers can include a stoical endurance of misfortune, an enjoyment of the intricate tapestry of nature, and a modest endeavour to change the social situation in desirable directions—here are but a few of the possibilities. The larger possibility cannot be excluded, that such fragments of light as we possess (especially the light of friendship and of aestic the experience) are fragments of a larger light of which we have an inkling, and which, instead of receding horizon-wise as we move, meets us half-way, and from which we are not, in any case, permanently exiled.

Notes

1. Vide my paper 'Two Views of Inductive Philosophising', *Kant-Studien*, 58 Jahrgang, Heft. 3, 1967.

2. This theme is more fully worked out in my paper presented at the seminar on 'The Meaning of Metaphysics' held in the autumn of 1967 in Madras.

3. Vide my paper on 'The Archaeology of Philosophical Thinking' in the seminar on 'The Role of Presuppositions and Assumptions in Philosophy' in the Centre of Advanced Study in Philosophy, Banaras Hindu University, March 1971.

4. This is the name of the title poem in my first book of poems. The idea of 'going further', taken from a well-known Bengali folk tale (told by Sri Ramakrishna), is utilised in the title poem of my third collection called *The Sandalwood Tree*.

7

Notes Towards a Definition of Philosophy

N. K. DEVARAJA

It is symptomatic of the deep cultural crisis of our time that the modern mind should feel altogether uncertain and greatly confused in regard to the essential meaning and significance of the activity called philosophy, a discipline that has, until recently, constituted the core of man's cultural consciousness. The uncertainty and confusion is attested by the utterances of some of the accredited representatives of that discipline in modern and recent thought. Thus when David Hume advised in his *Treatise* that any volume of divinity or school metaphysics which does not contain 'any abstract reasoning concerning quantity or number' or 'experimental reasoning concerning matters of fact and existence' should be committed to the flames, he did not suspect that the work being written by him did not belong to either of the two worthwhile categories. While it may be admitted that recent and contemporary thinkers have greater awareness than Hume of what they are doing as philosophers, it may be doubted if they have succeeded any better in clarifying the concept of philosophy and in explaining its aim and method. This is evidenced as much by the failure of logical positivists to ascertain the status of the verification principle as by the startling declaration of Ludwig Wittgenstein that the statements making up the *Tractatus* were 'nonsense'. All these philosophers tend to give descriptions of knowledge and meaningful discourse that make them as philosophers liable to the charge of self-disqualification.

The recent conception of philosophy as analysis or clarification of language was wrecked by the failure of its advocates to give an intelligible account of the nature and aim of analysis. On the other hand, the later view of Wittgenstein which bids philosophy fight bewitchment or puzzles produced by the abuse of language by previous philosophers, sounds cynically negative. By reading these accounts of philosophy one wonders if that discipline has any organic relationship with or relevance to the business of man's living, or the onward march of his intellectual and spiritual life. Resenting this last type of criticism some recent writers have pleaded that, like so many academic subjects in which the general public 'neither finds nor could well be expected to find any sort of interest',[1] philosophy should be looked upon as having a professional status, which means that philosophers should be permitted to think and write for one another. However, even a professional discipline should be able to make intelligible its aims and methods. The suspicion may arise that the desire to keep philosophy away from public gaze is due to the philosopher's lack of confidence in the meaningfulness of his enterprise. If the only function of philosophy is first to create puzzles and then to try and resolve them, one wonders why the disposition to philosophise be rather not checked than encouraged.

It is not so much the general public who are most of their time preoccupied with the mundane or practical concerns, who need philosophy. They are credulous enough to acquire the needed sense of direction in their life either from an unscientific theology or from prevalent fashions and tastes. It is the restless intellectuals who want to think for themselves on all important issues affecting the course of their life that stand in need of philosophy. Such intellectuals may be found as much among the students of the social sciences as among the votaries of the physical and biological sciences or the lovers of art and literature. Surely, it will be a poorer world if our intellectuals ceased to take interest in the meaning and direction of different intellectual disciplines and artistic endeavours.

Nor can it be shown that the philosophers, e.g., Plato and Aristotle, Thomas Aquinas, Kant and Hegel, the Buddhists and the Advaitins, who raised, discussed and meditated upon issues relating to central concerns of life, were worse off as philosophers than many a professor of philosophy teaching as professionals in modern universities. Likewise, it seems difficult to maintain that literary writers would be able to achieve better results if, aiming at formal perfection, they eschewed involvement in social and moral values and decided to write just for one another.

Nor is there any sign that, even within the camp of purely analytical philosophers, scholars and thinkers in philosophy would cease to occupy themselves with moral and aesthetic matters. While not denying the relevance of questions relating to the language of morals, religion and art criticism, it may be doubted if exclusive emphasis on these has not contributed to the impoverishment of the disciplines concerned.

Nor can we ignore the powerful movements of phenomenology and existentialism while seeking to frame a proper conception of the philosophic activity. In their own way the existentialists in particular have been very much concerned with the aspects of life and consciousness that interest us all as bearers of values. Therefore, it does not seem possible, except by an arbitrary fiat, to deny the name of philosophy to reflections concerning values, or forms of life and consciousness involving awareness or judgements of value. A most important reason that philosophy should not dissociate itself from the values cherished by mankind is that these values do not fall within the purview of any other systematic inquiry. We are constantly using the terms culture and civilisation in judging the worth of individuals and societies; these terms comprehend a variety of values. The question is: Should or should not there be a discipline that could rationally regulate the pursuit of the values in question? Traditionally, philosophy has acted as such a regulative discipline. If philosophy in the future decides to abdicate the functions of reflection over and systematisation of values, by refusing rational guidance to individuals and societies, then man will be left to the mercy of either clever demagogues and unscrupulous rulers or pseudo-visionaries and egoistical prophets claiming divine wisdom. Philosophy alone, it may be submitted, can impart a proper and disciplined sense of discrimination to men and women exposed to bewildering diversities of propagandist suggestions.

This is not to deny that the activity called philosophy or philosophising has a charm and fascination of its own and may justifiably be pursued for its own sake. But this is not a distinguishing mark of philosophy, for, art and literature and each and every science, theoretical physics and economics no less than mathematics and logic, are in the first place pursued for their own sake. And yet all these disciplines have a bearing on the quality of the lives devoted to their pursuit.

II

The insensitivity of Hume to the problem of characterising philosophical knowledge and discourse and the incapacity and puzzlement in regard to the question professed respectively by logical empiricism and Wittgenstein testify to the complexity and magnitude of the problem of framing a conception of philosophy acceptable to the modern mind. The situation is made more complex by the practice of existential philosophers on the one hand and by the attempts at the revival of such idealistic and religion-oriented systems as Hegelianism and Thomism on the other. Added to this is the fact of increasing fascination for philosophies such as Zen Buddhism and Taoism being felt by the intelligentsia the world over. While it may be granted that the greatest cultural influence in modern man's life is science, it cannot be denied that science has failed not only to yield a substitute for the wisdom and the sense of direction that religio-philosophical world views have always professed to offer, but has also failed to suppress the need and conscious quest for such wisdom and sense of direction. Granted that it is one of the functions of philosophy to reflect over a situation like this, it may be pointed out that the philosopher, while redefining the nature and aim of his vocation and its role in human society and culture, can ill afford to ignore the claims of science and scientific method on the one hand and those of man's irresistible need for a connected sense of values on the other.

III

The history of philosophy (like the history of art criticism and the theory of art) has presented us with a number of conceptions of that discipline, some of which stand out prominently. For a long time, when the sciences had not yet come into prominence as respectable intellectual disciplines, philosophy was described as an inquiry into the nature of reality or ultimate reality. This quest for the knowledge of what was ultimately real merged into the quest for the comprehension of the ultimate meaning or significance of life. Quite a few idealistic philosophies—for instance, the Advaita Vedānta, the Mādhyamika and Vijñānavāda systems and the philosophy of Hegel—identify ultimate value with the contemplation or realisation of ultimate reality, variously called *Brahman*, or *Śūnyatā*, or *Vijñaptimātratā* or Absolute Idea or Reason.[2] At a later date the business of philosophy was conceived to be the unification or synthesis of all knowledge, particularly scientific knowledge. While Plato had declared wonder to be the origin or source of philosophy, Wittgenstein thought that philosophic reflection arose as a result of puzzling bewilderment produced by language. It seems that the sense of wonder, referred to by Plato, is evoked primarily by the spectacle of existence, while that of perplexity and puzzlement, as envisaged by Wittgenstein, is aroused by the bewildering entanglements or snares of language. However, neither the attitude of wonder nor the sense of puzzlement is characterisable each with reference to a single type of situation, nor can they be claimed to be the exclusive attributes of the philosophic mind. Thus, the sense of wonder may equally characterise the scientist and the poet and one may feel puzzled by the results of an election (e.g., Indira Gandhi's landslide victory in the parliamentary election held in 1971) or by a moral situation, involving pulls of conflicting loyalties (e.g., in the case of Sartre's young man called upon to decide between going to the front to serve the country in crisis and continuing to take care of his aged mother). Both the attitude of wonder and the sense of puzzlement or bewilderment, as visualised by Plato and Wittgenstein respectively, however, have one thing in common: they arise in a mood of contemplative leisure, when our mind is relatively free from the cares of day-to-day life and existence. Now, the values to which we attend in a mood of leisure make up what has been called the life of culture; philosophy, therefore, is a pursuit that has a peculiar relationship with our cultural life.

To start with, the attitude of wonder seems to be a non-serious type of response; however, it may gradually pass into serious preoccupation with the object of wonder, when an attempt is made to comprehend and spell out the character of the latter. Similarly the initial sense of bewilderment evoked by conceptual confusion may gradually give rise to the consciousness of a felt challenge. Thus it is that sensitive thinkers, having been powerfully assailed by the feelings of wonder and perplexity, find themselves turning into serious philosophers. The so-called philosophers, indeed, are persons who take their sentiments of non-utilitarian wonder and bewilderment too seriously, so much so indeed that the sentiments in question render them unfit to attend to what are supposed to be the really important concerns and affairs of life.

Philosophy may be viewed as the self-awareness of culture; it consists of reflective acts whereby the activities that make up culture achieve critical awareness of themselves.

Cultural activities are the activities that contribute to the enrichment and/or refinement of personality. The term culture, as used here, signifies certain types of values, and is a different concept from the one used by anthropologists and sociologists. However, both these concepts have reference to a common element in the life-activities of man, viz., creativity.

The activities called culture are, in the first place, intrinsically interesting; secondly, these activities are important without being useful. The useful is that which is helpful for the business of living or for the survival of man. Cultural activities, on the other hand, contribute primarily to the qualitative improvement of man. In the third place, the activities constituting culture, or the products of those activities, are in principle shareable by the whole of mankind. Culture is inter-subjective.

The inter-subjective or shareable character of cultural activities and their products imparts to philosophy the status and strength of an objective discipline. The cultural activities on which philosophy reflects are generally carried out with the aid of symbols; this enables philosophy to have a steady view of its subject-matter, it also makes possible the existence of philosophy as a cooperative enterprise.

Men cannot share each other's sensations or sensory experiences. Communication about external objects, forces and energies is possible because they connote identical *meanings* in terms of common human interests and purposes. Propositions do not picture facts; they convey or communicate the meanings that objects and facts have for human beings. In other words, all discourse is purposive; the purpose determines the character or type of the content of a discourse.

A purpose is not necessarily utilitarian. I can comprehend the meaning of the statement mentioning the speed of light by effecting an extension of my awareness or knowledge of speeds of the vehicles used by me in actual travelling. My knowledge of the speed of light serves no purpose in my day-to-day life, unlike my knowledge of the speeds of cars, fast trains and aeroplanes; that knowledge, as also the knowledge of the distances separating the planets and stars, contributes mainly to my contemplative delight.

Here we may distinguish between three types of meanings: empirical meanings, pragmatic meanings and spiritual meanings. Empirical meanings consist of references to collocations of objects, actual or possible, that may be encountered in the realm of experience. The collocations in question are facts comprising objects and their powers and properties in diverse relations. Pragmatic meanings are superimposed on the factual meanings of statements when the facts are interpreted and apprehended as relative to man's practical concerns. Thus, if I want to reach a place fifteen miles away from where I am in not more than fifteen minutes, then I hire a conveyance whose speed is near about sixty miles an hour. Thus, factual, empirical statements convey pragmatic meanings to men and women seeking different goals. In order to appreciate the pragmatic import of an empirical statement, it is not necessary that I should have a practical concern at the moment when I hear the statement. Even without having a purpose of my own, I may apprehend the sense of a statement with reference to a possible context of pragmatic meanings. The pragmatic bearing of an empirical statement may be separately explained by another set of statements, it may also be simply suggested by one or more factual (empirical) statements. The point to be noted here is that a large proportion of factual and pragmatic discourse is carried on simply with the aid of words and other symbols, without our being required to actually look at or point towards objects present in our environment. However, as already indicated, the so-called empirical discourse has potential, if not actual, reference to possibilities of behaviour of objects and forces conceived as existing or being capable of existence. Empirical discourse, therefore, is in principle capable of being confirmed or disconfirmed in a pragmatic sense.

Pragmatic meanings we have stated, can both be suggested by

empirical statements and also expressed by an independent set of statements. The reason is that the pragmatic meanings relate to needs or desires on the one hand and to the manipulation of means for the satisfaction or fulfilment of those needs and desires on the other. All these phenomena refer to experienced, tangible facts. However, the spiritual meanings, which category includes all types of non-empirical and non-pragmatic meanings, cannot be stated or expressed directly; they can only be suggested or shown. Thus, the moral quality of an act does not inhere in that act as greenness does in leaves—that quality is either suggested to observers endowed with moral sensitiveness by the movements or activities constituting the act, or it is shown to the observers by interested speakers through the indication of facts (e.g., enmity of long standing between two persons or families) and actions (e.g., the acts of insulting, aggression or revenge) that are relevant for the moral assessment of the situation. These moral meanings constitute a realm of their own, which is quite distinct from the realm of empirical phenomena that consist largely of movements and interrelations of objects. For the moralist these latter phenomena have interest only as vehicles of moral meanings. A moral judgement may refer to the fact of (unmerited or avoidable) suffering caused by an action. But that reference, too, only suggests the moral quality of the action concerned, and the declaration that a certain action is bad is hardly an improvement on the suggestion of the moral quality accomplished by the narration of relevant facts and activities. In a like manner, the words and symbols used by a literary artist convey emotions and feelings by depicting the situations in which those feelings or emotions are embedded. It is noteworthy in this connection that neither the moralist nor the poet can communicate the moral and emotional (or aesthetic) meanings to persons devoid of moral or aesthetic sensitiveness. There is a sense in which it is correct to say that the perception of the moral qualities of a complicated chain of actions depends on experience and training, and also on the knowledge of relevant details relating to the history of the actions under consideration, even as the perception of the aesthetic qualities of a work of art depends on the critical training of the connoisseur, as also on the range of his acquaintance with other works of art and/or the history of the art concerned.

IV

Philosophy, then, is concerned with interesting and exciting forms of life that are shareable, which implies that they refer not to any actual life but to the possibilities of life. We shall also see that the forms of life that are of interest to philosophy are those created by men through free choice; consequently, those forms are being constantly submitted to assessment and evaluation.

Philosophy and the Human Sciences

How is philosophy related to other human studies? We have said that philosophy is concerned with meanings—spiritual meanings or values and not with facts as revealed to the senses. In a way, all human sciences are concerned with meanings though not necessarily with spiritual meanings. Prof. Hayek hints at this fact, though in a rather paradoxical manner, when he observes that the facts of the social sciences 'are mere opinions',[3] views held by the people whose actions we study. So far as human actions are concerned, 'things are what the acting people think they are'. In other words, what the human sciences occupy themselves with are not so much the visible objects or empirical facts as the meanings or values that those facts symbolise for, or convey to, human beings. This being so, the difference between philosophy and other human sciences is explainable with reference to the types of meanings studied and the types of understanding sought by them. The meanings studied by the human sciences are what we have designated as the pragmatic meanings. These meanings are directly involved in man's pursuit of various goods that are apprehended as relevant for his survival and effective existence as a biological and social being. The social sciences such as economics and political science deal mainly with the goods and values that are competitive and unshareable; on the contrary, philosophy concerns itself with the values that are non-competitive and so shareable. Thus, while everybody cannot own the same car, it is open to all to enjoy a poem (or even a joke, when it does not concern the parties) and to feel puzzled about a moral situation. (It seems that a person is a moral agent in one capacity and a moral philosopher in another. As a moral agent I find myself involved in a particular situation which is unique and unshareable. On the other hand, a philosopher is an uninvolved spectator reflecting on shareably puzzling situations.)

In as much as the pragmatic meanings are superimposed upon empirical meanings, the human sciences have a more direct reference to the world of empirical objects. This makes them conspicuously different from philosophy. Thus, while currency notes or metallic coins may be mere tokens for money or wealth, the commodities purchasable by money are certainly bearers of actual values. Similarly, institutions studied by sociology or political science have a physical dimension, in addition to the dimension of meanings or meaningful relationships. In contradistinction to these, the meanings studied by philosophy are merely suggested by observable physical symbols, e.g., written or spoken words.

Another point of distinction between philosophy and other human sciences is that the standpoint of the former is evaluative without being utilitarian; the approach of the latter, on the contrary, is factual, since the pragmatic meanings or values that interest them are closely bound up with the actual nature of physical objects or facts.

Philosophy Excludes Ontology

On our view philosophy is concerned solely with meanings, as such it excludes ontology as traditionally understood. Philosophy is *not* an inquiry into the nature of empirical objects or facts, which are studied by the different sciences. Nor has anybody succeeded in showing how philosophy can lead us to investigate the nature of the so-called transcendental objects. It is noteworthy that in Advaita Vedānta *Brahman* or *Ātman* is considered to be beyond the reach of the *pramāṇas* or means of knowledge. The *Ātman* or *Brahman* is not regarded as being an object of cognition or knowledge at all. As a matter of fact, the existence of the *Ātman,* as described by the Advaitin, is a postulate taken from the Upanishads. In another sense, as we have shown elsewhere, the *Ātman,* conceived as pure awareness or consciousness, is nothing but a reification of the attitude of total detachment characteristic of the saint who remains undisturbed by the vicissitudes of his mundane life. Philosophy can certainly undertake analysis of the attitude characterising the detached saint, but it cannot, without becoming highly speculative, trace that attitude to the spiritual principle as its source. Such a procedure, which takes its clue from the intuitable characteristics of man in order to frame a conception of ultimate reality, is likely to lead to conflicting views of that reality. According to us, while philosophy should occupy itself with all manifestations of values, and disvalues, it is incapable of telling us anything either about the existence or about the nature of an ultimate first cause.

An important implication of our view of philosophy is that it concerns itself only with the values involved in man's actual, historical life. While not denying that there is beauty in nature, we maintain that aesthetics, or the so-called philosophy of beauty, can reflect only on the beauty as embodied in works of art. Likewise, moral philosophy can deal with the moral or ethical values only insofar as they manifest themselves in the moral actions and judgements of men.

Our statement that philosophy excludes ontology does not imply that the philosopher may not reflect on the categories used by man to describe and make sense of his empirical experience. For the attempt or activity involved in such description or explanation of experience, when undertaken in a spirit of disinterested inquiry either by common sense or by science, is intrinsically interesting. It is immaterial whether this enterprise is called metaphysics or not. P. F. Strawson, in the introduction to his *Individuals,* designates reflection on the categories embodied in everyday language 'descriptive metaphysics'. He says:

... there is a massive central core of human thinking which has no history.... there are categories and concepts which in their most fundamental character change not at all. Obviously these are not the specialities of the most refined thinking. They are the commonplaces of the least refined thinking and are yet the indispensable core of the conceptual equipment of the most sophisticated human beings. (p. 10)

Strawson thinks that descriptive metaphysics is concerned primarily with concepts and categories and their interconnections. This description of the business of metaphysics may be accepted, provided that philosophy as a whole is not identified with such metaphysics.

According to Strawson, the central subject matter of descriptive metaphysics does not change, though 'the critical and analytical idiom of philosophy' changes constantly. Here it may be noted that, since even descriptive metaphysics attempts to draw a consistent picture of our everyday notions and their interconnections, it is compelled to make assumptions and propound theories that are not quite as commonsensical. In this connection another complicating factor may be noted. Even the so-called commonsensical notions may differ in different language systems. Thus we are informed that there are languages (e.g., Russian, German and Italian) 'which render colour by means of verbs'. Thus, while in English we say 'the sky is blue', in the above languages it will be said, 'the sky blues', or something like that. Obviously the situation would affect philosophising based on everyday language.[4] Quite a few philosophical systems take the distinction of substance and quality seriously; the above example shows that, after all, there is nothing sacrosanct about the distinction. Indeed, it would be a boring business to go on reflecting on the concepts used by Everyman. But for the fact that thinkers like Kant and those who invented non-Euclidean geometries and quantum mechanics necessitated rethinking about such concepts as causation, being determined, etc., I suggest that the philosopher, with his fastidious taste, cannot be induced to think over a concept or a conceptual situation unless it is seen by him to be exciting or interesting. For this reason the philosopher cannot be prevented from reflecting over an exciting situation in, say, scientific theory and art criticism.

There are other factors affecting the common sense of mankind. Under the influence of religion, questions relating to the origin or creation of the world, God, and the other world have often formed part of man's commonsensical beliefs and prejudices. In India, for instance, where the law of *karma* formed part of peoples' stock of commonsensical beliefs as much as the law of causation, differences of fortune among men were automatically attributed to actions supposed to have been performed by them in their past lives. The best philosophers of India found it difficult to ignore this so-called law of moral retribution.

Are Philosophical Statements Analytic?

The analytical philosophers, headed by Russell and Wittgenstein, gave currency to the view that the main function of philosophy was elucidation, clarification, or analysis which was effected by a series of analytical statements. Are we to believe that philosophical statements in general, and philosophical theories in particular, are analytic in character?

When Wittgenstein said in the *Tractatus* (4.112) that 'the object of philosophy is the logical clarification of thought. ... A philosophical work consists entirely of elucidations', he was proposing a new definition of philosophy or making an assumption about the nature of philosophy. Since the definition of philosophy is a controversial matter no such definition can be taken to be a self-evident (analytical?) truth.

One definition of an analytic statement is that it is a statement whose negation is self-contradictory; according to another definition it is a statement whose truth can be determined solely by an analysis of the meanings of the words constituting the sentence expressing the statement (or proposition) in question. None of these definitions would seem to apply to the aforesaid statements of Wittgenstein. Unless a definition is merely stipulatory, it has to prove itself to be adequate by successfully indicating the defining characteristics of the concept sought to be defined. In as much as the adequacy of a definition is liable to be judged in the light of the examples or area covered by the concept that is being defined, no definition may be taken to be an analytic statement. These remarks would seem to be applicable as much to a particular definition of philosophy as to a definition of right action, or poetry, or criticism, or religion.

Nor can the examples of analysis presented by this or that analytical philosopher claim to consist of purely analytic statements. For no piece of analysis that claims to be at all (philosophically) important, can be seen to be analytically true and so non-controversial. As an example, reference may be made to P. F. Strawson's criticism of the famous theory of descriptions proposed by Bertrand Russell (vide Strawson's paper entitled 'On Referring'). We are not concerned here with the merits of the controversy between Russell and Strawson. The point that want to make is that a piece of analysis presented by a philosopher may be questioned as to its correctness, from which it follows that no such analysis except in trivial cases cited in logic books is an example of making analytic statements.

In a paper entitled 'A Study of the Irrefutability of Two Aesthetic Theories' constituting Chapter Six of *Aesthetic and Language* (ed. William Elton, Basil Blackwell, Oxford, 1959), Miss Beryl Lake has put forward the astonishing view that aesthetic theories, such as those of Croce and Clive Bell, are linguistic or *a priori* in character. In support of her thesis she tries to argue that the theories advanced, e.g., by the two thinkers mentioned above, are both 'irrefutable and unconfirmable' by reference to any facts about works of art. According to Croce, the real work of art is (1) an imaginative or spiritual or mental, and not a physical thing; also (2) the real work of art is an intuition which is also an expression and an occasion of intuitive knowledge. According to Clive Bell, all works of art, properly so-called, have significant form. Concluding her exposition of the two theories Miss Lake remarks: 'It seems to me that Croce will allow nothing to count as an example of a work of art which is not what he calls an intuition, and Clive Bell will allow nothing to count as an example of a work of art which has not what he calls significant form' (p.3).

Miss Lake seems to concede that the authors of particular theories are also the ultimate judges of the correctness of their theories as also the arbiters between the claims of their own theories and of those advanced by their rivals. If that were so, no theories, e.g., those of logical atomists and logical positivists, would ever be discredited. The truth is that there are limits to which a theory can accommodate the perceptions of factual data admitted by competent observers, that are seen by those observers to be recalcitrant to the theory in question. For instance, Croce's view of art can scarcely do justice to such powerful poetic lines as: 'To be or not to be that is the question' (Shakespeare); or 'Of all these young women not one has enquired the cause of the world' (Ezra Pound). Likewise, the view of Clive Bell will remain unsatisfactory as long as the phrase 'significant form' retains any degree of ambiguity. Our view is that philosophical statements and theses are neither analytic nor empirical which distinction of statements is not exhaustive. A sort of being or subsistence is enjoyed by man's modes of behaviour or life that are made possible by the use of symbolism. It is against these modes of symbolic life and behaviour that the statements made by philosophers are checked as to their validity or adequacy. This fact is rather imperfectly expressed by saying that philosophical statements are about concepts. It would be odd, for instance, to refer to a work of art or a system of morals as a concept, or even as a congeries of concepts; it seems better to describe these as forms of life, or as modes of meaningful or value-directed response or behaviour. This latter description would aptly describe the behaviour of a person passing moral judgements or a scientist engaged in theorising.

Philosophical Questions, Statements and Facts

Philosophy, in our view, is concerned with meanings or complexes of meanings that are considered interesting in themselves. It seems that there is no limit to new and exciting questions that can be asked about aforesaid meanings. In philosophy every important thinker manages to ask new questions, and so make new statements, about the units and complexes of meanings and their mutual bearings. However, we may roughly distinguish two types of philosophical questions and problems, which may be designated as first order and second order philosophical problems. Problems of the first type have direct reference to what may be called the universally visible or observable subject-matter of philosophy. This subject-matter comprises: aesthetic experiences as embodied in works of art; moral and religious experiences as expressed in moral and religious perceptions and judgements; logical experiences as manifested in the perception and use of different forms of valid reasoning, and the perception of fallacies in reasoning; and the perception and pursuit of values involved in our socio-political organisations.

The science of logic may be looked upon as forming a part of epistemology or theory of knowledge, so-called, which attempts to investigate the nature of different kinds of cognition, regarded as being bearers of values positive or negative.

It should not be supposed that the number and character of the first order problems are fixed and invariant. The reason is that the experience, with reference to which these problems arise, is itself not a fixed stock but a changing and growing entity. The advent of new geniuses in, and the addition of new masterpieces to, the realm of art, for example, inevitably modifies the character of the art experience enjoyed and contemplated by the connoisseurs and philosophers of art. The appearance and the career of a new genius in religion similarly modifies our perceptions or experience relating to religious values. The Buddha and Jesus Christ were religious geniuses of the highest calibre who combined action, contemplation and detachment in different degrees, and were inspired by different kinds of faith.

The second order problems of philosophy do not relate directly to the subject-matter noticed or contemplated by different branches of philosophy. They arise rather out of reflection on conflicting sets of explanatory concepts, principles or postulates, formulated by constructive philosophers. These problems are mainly critical or methodological. Our age is peculiarly conscious of problems of this type.

Philosophical Facts

All sorts of philosophers, while criticising their rivals in the field, appeal to considerations that are taken, often without sufficient awareness, to be some sorts of facts. The question may be posed: Does the subject-matter of philosophy comprise any facts? We have already stated our view that all sorts of statements in philosophy are about units or complexes of meanings. We earlier quoted the view of Professor Hayek that in the human sciences, facts are mere views or opinions held by men. In that case a fact would be an opinion or view of a matter that all human beings are under the compulsion of their nature to hold. Philosophers often introduce such facts with some expressions like: 'it is plain' or 'clearly', etc.

Let us notice some types of facts appealed to by philosophers:

(1) That it is a bad thing to be tortured or starved, humiliated or hurt, is not an opinion: it is a fact. That it is better for people to be loved and attended to, rather than hated or neglected, is again a plain fact, not a matter of opinion. (G. J. Warnock, *Contemporary Moral Philosophy*, Macmillan, 1959, p. 60)

(2)... Surely no one would seek to deny that a man may, in the day-to-day conduct of his life, be so changeable, volatile, whimsical, and inconsistent that he could not be said to hold, and

perhaps, for what it is worth, he does not even profess any principles at all. (Ibid., p. 48)

(3) The fact is that expressing and appealing to the feelings is
incidental to, and actually quite rare in moral discourse, much as
exerting influence is incidental to, and often quite absent from,
making moral judgements. 'It would be monstrous to do that'
expresses my feelings, and may stimulate yours; but 'It would be
wrong to do that' is most unlikely to do either. It expresses an
opinion, not a state of emotional excitement; it gives you, perhaps,
my advice against doing something, not a stimulus towards
emotional revulsion from doing it. There is nothing, in short,
necessarily emotive about moral criticism or approval; moral
advice may be given in entirely dispassionate terms. (Ibid., p. 27)

(4) A man might regard considerations of some kind as more
important than considerations of morality, and hence might
take himself, on occasions, to be fully justified in not doing
what he sincerely recognises to be right from the moral point of
view. (Ibid., p.52)

We have quoted the above passages from a single book for con-
venience of reference and also because they are thoroughly representative of philosophical comment and criticism.

We may pause here to take reflective notice of the above passages.
Of these the assertions made in (1) seem to be most emphatic.
Mr. Warnock takes it to be axiomatic that certain things are bad.
However, it is not clear from the context whether the badness
attributed to certain actions or states of affairs is equivalent to
psychological undesirability merely, or whether it includes moral undesirability also. Indeed, in some cases, it may be morally desirable
to humiliate and even to torture a person, e.g., in the case of a
person who betrays the country's vital interests for personal gain
during a war. It seems that there is no end to possibilities while
considering or judging human conduct!

The assertion made in (2) seems to be a reasonable claim about
the possibilities of human conduct or behaviour. Similarly, in
passage (4) a possibility of conflict between moral and other considerations has been visualised. The passage constitutes another
illustration of how possibilities count as facts in human studies.
The passage (3) seeks to refute the emotive theory of ethics by

questioning its assumption as to the intentions of moral discourse.

In his 'A Reply to My Critics' G.E. Moore avers: '...from the fact that it seems to be the case, it does not follow that it really is the case' ed. (Philippa Foot, *Theories of Ethics,* Oxford University Press, 1968, p. 52). As against this, I am of the opinion that, in the human sciences, it is difficult to separate actualities from possibilities. Even the historian has to depend on his sense of possibilities or probabilities while taking something to be a fact. In particular, as we have seen in commenting on (3) and (4) above, assertions of possibilities count as arguments from facts in the domain of the human studies.

Moore makes a significant remark while commenting on some views of Mr. C. L. Stevenson. He says that when he wrote his *Ethics,* it simply had not occurred to him that, in the case of persons making incompatible moral judgements, the disagreement might be merely that in attitude (see, *Theories of Ethics,* p. 42). When actions and attitudes of human beings are under consideration, it is extremely difficult, if not altogether impossible, to visualise *all* the possibilities of the combinations of motives and intentions, attitudes of valuation, selection of means, etc. For this reason, our observations and statements about the possibilities in question have varying degrees of plausibility. However, we are able to see whether the anticipated possibility is genuine or not. We somehow see this, and when a thinker or critic makes reference to a possibility, he tries to make us see the genuineness of the possibility visualised by him. In this sense, proving and disproving in philosophy (particularly when it is done with reference to possible facts) is a matter of 'showing' rather than of strict deduction from well-known premises.

Mr. Warnock's criticism of the emotive theory of ethics consists in showing its incompatibility with some facts, or possibilities, about human behaviour. On the other hand, the emotive theory itself is based not so much on the observation of that behaviour (which mainly consists in visualising the possibilities) as on deductions made from the verification theory of meaning. The history both of logical atomism and of logical positivism is an illustration of the fact that in philosophy the method of 'deductive development of hypotheses' is not only not useful or dependable, but is also misleading. Philosophical insights and truths, it appears, are not susceptible to strict, implicational connections.

A creative writer invents new ways of achieving emphasis and effect, and of promoting awareness in his readers; the author himself cannot anticipate these ways. Probably no two important authors employ exactly the same means to achieve greatness in their writings: the same author may vary his technique in his different works. Analogously the pursuit of virtue expresses itself in a thousand ways of life. This is the reason why creative achievement both in the arts and in morals eludes the grasp of strict rules and canons.

And here we are led to see another kind of facts, or visualised possibilities, that affect the course of the development of man's value pursuits. When Jesus Christ exhorted his followers to offer their other cheek to the person who struck them on one cheek, he ushered in a revolution in man's moral outlook by visualising a new code of conduct that could be seen to be better than traditional modes of response. Likewise, a novelist like James Joyce revolutionised the practice of an art by making daring innovations in ways of looking at life and representing it. In fact, every great literary writer looks at life in his own way, with a new emphasis on this or that aspect of life or its values, thus achieving a new style in the organisation and depiction of the experiential material at his command.

By merely visualising a new form of behaviour involving greater magnanimity, forgiveness or self-abnegation an ethical writer like Aristotle, or a moral genius like Christ or Gandhi, effects a refutation, as it were, of the previous moral theories and practices. In a similar fashion a creative logician or theorist of logic refutes previous views about possibilities of valid reasoning by visualising or creating new, sometimes better, modes of reasoning than those that had been known to his predecessors. Thus modern science invented and successfully applied the hypothetical-deductive method of reasoning that had not been clearly visualised by ancient and medieval thinkers. In India, e.g., philosophers and thinkers in other fields aware only of the method of inference as an instrument for proving the existence of entities not given in direct experience.

Rules and norms indicated by thinkers in different spheres of values consist generally of visualised possibilities that are seen to be better or preferable in relation to other possibilities in conduct or practice.

Generally speaking, it may be maintained that all statements that are claimed to be true are intended to be factual, i.e., statements of facts. Russell and others debated whether there could be negative and general facts. So far as general statements are concerned they are either about dispositions of things or about behaviour, calculated, with varying degrees of certainty, to result from the more or less fixed dispositions. Such statements presuppose the prevalence of uniformity in nature. Statements about values, norms etc., similarly presuppose uniform tendencies of preference in men and women. Without such presuppositions it would be absolutely impossible for us to make any statement about moral or even logical matters with any degree of confidence. Thus, when I assert that the person who pays the debt owed by a poor neighbour is morally superior to the person who pays back his own debt in not very unfavourable circumstances, my confidence in the truth of the assertion or judgement presupposes my faith in certain possibilities of perference in the moral responses of men and women. Our confidence in certain forms of reasoning likewise depends on our faith in the fixed possibilities of logical response in all right thinking persons. Here it may be added that my confidence in the shareability of my moral opinions is partly derived from my intimate knowledge of the cultural milieu to which I am related. It happens that the logical responses of human beings do not exhibit variations comparable to their moral responses. Hence the illusion that logical truths enjoy a necessity unattainable in the sphere of moral opinion. But it should not be supposed that there can be no alteration in the domain of logical truths. Some of the principles of inference formulated by Aristotle have been found defective by later logicians. Thus Bernard Bosanquet, criticising the Aristotlean view that 'from two negative premises no conclusion can be drawn' offers the following argument that seems to go against the rule in question:

Good workmen do not complain of their tools; my pupils do not complain of their tools; therefore, my pupils are probably good workmen.[5]

To the question, can an eternal entity act as a cause?, the Buddhists replied in the negative while the theists all over the world seem to reply in the affirmative. Shall we say this is a case of ambiguity or uncertainty in the perception of logical possibilities?

We may summarise the results of our discussion in the present chapter as follows. Philosophy may be looked upon as the critical awareness (or self-awareness) of the activities (involving use of symbols) that are seen to be intrinsically interesting. The physical movements involved in actions embodying moral values are symbolic of those values and so fall beyond the purview of the physical sciences. (Human actions in general are beyond the scope of these sciences.)

All philosophical statements are general and related to the possibilities of some area of man's shareable symbolic life. The possibilities of this life go on expanding under the creative activity of man. Hence the necessity of continuing an analysis of these activities by philosophy. Philosophical analysis, however, like every other species of analysis, is controlled by a viewpoint, which is the viewpoint of assessment and evaluation. The analysis carried on by philosophy is never final, for the simple reason that the activities or processes analysed by it are ever in a state of expansion and growth. The growth of a spiritual form of activity is directed towards greater depth and elevation, and subtler forms of critical awareness. This is true of both man's logical, and aesthetic and moral awareness.

Philosophical discourse produces the illusion of being purely analytical and *a priori* because it is about symbolic and not observed phenomena, about manipulation of symbols rather than that of physical objects and energies. This, indeed, is the distinguishing feature of the so-called human studies in general, philosophy being marked off from humanistic sciences by its emphasis on value. Philosophical statement are synthetic in the sense that its subject-matter, unlike that of mathematics, is not limited by its defining properties and their possibilities. For this reason philosophy cannot attain final and necessary truths about its subject-matter. Even if it be granted that all mathematical statements are necessary truths, this particular statement about mathematics cannot itself claim to be a necessary and analytic truth. In other words, no philosophical theory about mathematics can claim to be the necessary and final truth. The same is true of philosophical truth about art, morality and religion.

Philosophy makes assertions about those realms of meanings whose truth is revealed by a sort of inspection. This inspectional truth has to be modified in view of new, unforeseen instances of possibilities visualised and presented by rival analysts and thinkers. In this manner while philosophical truth grows richer and more comprehensive, its formulation is never definitive and final. In a sense this is true of the formulations of scientific truth as well. This means that there are no ultimate or complete truths, either in science or in philosophy. And yet there is an important difference between the ways in which science and philosophy can claim to be true as well as interesting. Science deals with phemomena that are intrinsically value neutral. On the contrary, philosophy deals with modes of life and response that are intrinsically interesting. An important consequence follows from this difference between science and philosophy. Once a scientific theory has been repudiated, the formulations or records of the data that supported it become uninteresting to later scientists. Not so the data of philosophy. After we have thoroughly discarded the theory of a Plato, Hegel or Wittgenstein, we still contemplate with pleasure the questions raised and the aspects of spiritual experiences or phenomena noticed and recorded by them. This accounts for the perennial charm of philosophical writings, old and new. In the last analysis a philosophical theory or thesis is nothing more than a device for connected contemplation of a large number of intrinsically interesting phenomena, logical, aesthetic, moral and religious. The final repudiation of a philosophical theory has no tendency to detract the charm of the life-phenomena that seemed to have necessitated the formulation of the theory in question. This is the secret of the fascination exercised on our minds by such writers and works as Hegel and the *Tractatus* of Wittgenstein. Here it may also be noted that some fascinating phenomena, sought to be systematised by a philosophical theory, consist of the questions and problems raised, or created, by the thinker concerned himself. Probably every great thinker asks some questions for the first time, thereby extending the bounds of critical reflective life and setting new tasks for subsequent philosophers. Apart from the questions consciously asked by a philosopher, questions and problems are also generated by the peculiar method that he employs in handling new or traditional problems.

Here I would like to differentiate between the view of philosophy presented here and that upheld by leading existentialist thinkers. The existentialists, while differing from one another in details, agree in characterising philosophy as the study of man's subjectivity. The existentialists are inclined to lay emphasis on the uniqueness of the individual and his subjective life, though that life is supposed to be constituted by the individual's relation to the world and to his fellow beings. This view of philosophy has obvious affinity with the conception of philosophy presented here. Our view, however, differs from the existentialist conception in at least two important respects. We have emphasised that the forms of life studied by philosophy are symbol-bound, and so shareable in principle. The symbolic or symbol-bound life of man is constantly expanding into new possibilities, but any such expansion, though initially achieved by a creative individual, becomes the common property of all properly trained persons who attend to it. We have also said that such possibilities of life are contemplated by philosophy in a spirit of detachment. This is the secret of why philosophising, like the reading or witnessing of a tragedy, is felt to be a delightful occupation or activity.

In the second place, man has an urge to share the new forms of spiritual life, created or visualised by him, with others. This is the impulse behind our anxiety to defend the validity or value of our visions in art and philosophy.

Some existentialist thinkers seem inclined to call their philosophy metaphysics. While Edmund Husserl set forth the ideal of a presuppositionless philosophy, his successor, Martin Heidegger, declared philosophy to be pre-eminently concerned with being. Despite all the lengthy explanations and elucidations that Heidegger and his exponents have offered, 'being' remains a vague and elusive concept in the system of the German philosopher. Heidegger has written sympathetically about the Greek conception of philosophy. Philosophy, according to him, is in its nature Greek.[6] According to this eminent thinker there has been no philosophy outside the West and Europe. This may lead one to infer that Heidegger is opposed to the sort of religious philosophy that has been characteristic of some Eastern regions like India, but that does not seem to be true in view of the actual content of his philosophy. As an admirer of the Greeks, Heidegger refers approvingly to Aristotle's conception of philosophy (or metaphysics) as the study of 'the first principles and causes' (Ibid., p. 57). These first principles and causes, according to him, 'constitute the Being of beings'. This may be taken to mean that Being to is something inherent in man and constitutes the inner, driving force of his life. However, Heidegger also speaks of man's being open to Being, which seems to suggest that Being is something outside man. On the other hand, Heidegger speaks not only of the Being of Dasein or man but also of the Being of, e.g., a table. The capitalisation of the letter B in 'Being,' strongly suggests identification of Being with the First Cause or Ground of traditional philosophy. On the other hand, when we are told that the Being or Dasein is always at issue, Being seems to be made a synonym of the possibilities that may be realised by man.

In Heidegger's writings Dasein is characterised as a being who has the capacity to ask the question, what is Being? This ability of Dasein to question distinguishes him from mere things, and is a mark of his freedom. However, in his later writings, according to one interpreter, 'All the initiative is shifted to Being and Dasein is called upon only to "stay open" to Being.[7] Here again Being seems to be identifiable with the Ultimate Ground, or the Universe conceived as the expression of an Ultimate Principle such as Spinoza's Substance. In his *The Existentialist Prolegomena to a Future Metaphysics* (University of Chicago Press, Chicago, 1969) Prof. Frederick Sontag describes Being as 'an absolutely infinite set of possibilities' (p. 125). Whether so intended or not, the view may be taken to be an explication of Heidegger's concept of Being. In that case, however, it would not seem proper to speak of Being as if it were an object of reverential questioning or some other attitude like Godhead.

We do not consider it proper to go beyond man's conscious creative life while specifying the subject-matter of philosophy. Heidegger himself has not succeeded in saying anything significant about Being regarded as an ontological First Principle. Indeed, all his important pronouncements concerns Dasein. It is significant that his first major work, *Being and Time,* remained incomplete, and ended without tackling the problem of the relationship of Being and Time, as promised in the title of the work.

Still there are some significant similarities between Heideggerian view of philosophy and our own. Heidegger deprecates man's pre-occupation with 'being' or things of the world. His philosophical questioning, in fact, begins with the transcendence of the order of things. This transcendence constitutes man's freedom. On our view, too, man enters the realm of cultures by rising his attachment to the utilitarian order. The activities comprising the pursuit and production of non-utilitarian (or spiritual) meanings or values constitute the 'cultural self' of man; it is the business of philosophy to analyse and study this self with a view to contributing to its enrichment, growth and refinement.

Some Conclusions

We shall now attempt to highlight the main conclusions flowing from our discussion.

(1) Philosophy as distinguished from science, does not talk about entities or facts belonging to the empirical order of things. This order can be explored only by science. Nor does philosophy have any special instrument or organ at its disposal which may enable it to make contact with trans-phenomenal or transcendental entities, if any. On the other hand there is no intellectual discipline aiming at valid knowledge, which is without reference to some sort of experience. Philosophy deals with our experience relating to Spiritual Meanings or values whose incidence in the universe is relative to the peculiar structure of the human mind functioning creatively with the aid of language or symbolism.

(2) No presuppositions and assumptions having reference to speculative, trans-phenomenal entities or states of affairs, can be validly entertained in philosophy. Philosophers can legitimately and validly talk only about the order of spiritual meanings and the ways in which that order is related to other realms of meanings, e.g., the spheres of empirical and pragmatic meanings.

(3) Philosophers can or should talk only about shareable meanings or meaning-complexes, i.e., about the meaning-complexes embodied in public symbols.

(4) All philosophical statements refer to possibilities or possible facts about meanings or values. Any general statement in philosophy is but a proposal to view a relevant area of meanings or values in a particular light. Any such proposal justifies itself by presenting a connected and adequate picture of the meanings that

are considered important at a particular period in a particular cultural tradition.

Broadly speaking, philosophical statements may be of two kinds. There is a sense in which all philosophical statements may be taken to be general. However, when a philosophical statement is intended to be a statement of a 'particular' fact, it generally asserts a possibility of human response in a more or less isolate situation. Examples of such (supposedly) factual statements have already been quoted. A more significant class of philosophical statements seeks to indicate a general characteristic of an area of meanings. Such statements claim to embody important discoveries. This is not to say that the so-called factual statements may not be used by bold thinkers either in support of more important and more general statements, or in refutation of such statements.

Philosophical Discoveries

A philosophical discovery consists of a new observation, with far-reaching implications, about an area of meanings or meaningful spiritual life. Such a discovery draws out attention to an aspect of that life which is either intrinsically interesting or significantly related to something of intrinsic interest for us. Examples of such discoveries may be found in the writings of any important philosopher. Thus Plato discovered the need of unchanging referents for words having denotative meaning; and Kant made the momentous discovery that human subjects tend to experience or view phenomena under some definite modes of categories of knowing. In recent decades we owe some discoveries of great moment to several existentialist thinkers and to Wittgenstein, e.g., the intentionality of consciousness emphasised by Brentano, Husserl and others; the perception that human beings (largely) build up their own essence through acts of (free) choice; significant reflections concerning anxiety, boredom, authentic living etc.; emphasis on the multiple uses of language and reduction of the universal to family resemblance, etc. Recent philosophy has made considerable progress is the direction of clarifying the notions of evidence, proof, confirmation, falsification, explanation, etc. These notions of concepts belong to the region of the second order problems of philosophy. Even a wrong view or definition in philosophy

phy—i.e., a view or definition that is later on discredited—serves the important function of drawing our attention to some characteristics or oddities of a conceptual or spiritual situation which interests and/or is found intriguing by man. This is the secret of the perennial charm of philosophical questionings, problems and discussions. These contribute not only to the illumination of man's actual symbolic and spiritual life, but also to the extension and growth, both in richness and in complexity, of that life.

In the domain of philosophical discussion and controversy a new type of questioning or the raising of a new problem may lead to far-reaching consequences no less than a new perception, assertion or assumption concerning an area of shared symbolic life. Thus the logical positivists ushered in a revolutionary change in man's outlook on philosophy by declaring some sort of verifiability (or confirmability) to be an essential feature of meaningful discourse. The doctrine of the inentionality of consciousness is equally revolutionary in its implications; it provides an effective antidote to the theories of subjectivism and emotivism in ethics and the philosophy of art. One of the important implications of the view, presented here, that man lives not only in the world of physical objects or empirical and pragmatic meanings, but also with reference to the realms of spiritual meanings, is that, as one engaged in the enjoyment and production of the latter type of meanings, man behaves as a free agent. He also enjoys a measure of freedom in manipulating the physical (empirical) environment to serve his pragmatic ends.

Notes

1. G.J. Warnock, *English Philosophy since* 1900 (Oxford University Press, 1969), p. 118.
2. Delineating the philosophical aspects of Darwinism, Hans Jonas observes: 'In this new meaning of "origins" we observe a complete reversal of the older conception concerning the superiority of the originating principle over its effects. It has mostly been assumed that there must be not only more power but also more perfection in the cause than in the effect. Obviously this pattern is completely reversed in the kind of genetic deduction which modern theory inaugurated. The antecedent is here inferior to the effect, in terms of structural articulation. Thus generically as well as functionally, the primitive is called upon to account for order, becoming for being'. (*The phenomenon of life,* Dell Publishing Co. Inc., New York, 1968, pp. 40-1).

The Darwinian theory has made it unnecessary to posit a perfect First Principle as a source of our values.

3. *The Counter Revolution of Science*, The Free Press, Glencoe, Illinois 1952, pp. 26-7.

4. C. F. Waismann's paper on 'Verifiability' in *How I see Philosophy*, Macmillian, New York, 1968, pp. 60 ff.

5. Bernard Bosanquet, *Logic*, London: Oxford University Press, second edition, impression of 1931, Vol. II, p. 113.

6. Martin Heidegger, *What is Philosophy?*, Eng. Tr., London, Vision Press, 1968, p. 31.

7. See John d. Capute, 'The Rose is without Why', in *Philosophy Today*, Vol. 15, No. 1/47 Spring 1971, p. 10.

8

Metaphysical Models and Conflicting Cultural Patterns

G. MISRA

In this article, I propose to examine two metaphysical models of pure thought and pure action which have produced two conflicting cultural patterns. These conflicting cultural patterns have divided the present-day world into two opposing camps.

The question of the nature and relation of pure contemplation and pure action is a special case of the more general question of the nature and relation between body and mind. The human body and the human mind have been conceived as being entirely disparate in nature. The two are conceived in such a way that whatever forms an item in the one cannot form an item in the other. Mind is regarded to be non-extended and non-spatial, conscious and cogitative whereas the body is regarded to be spatial and extended, unconscious and non-thinking. The body moves and obeys the mechanical laws. It cannot initiate action; it is inert and lacks spontaneity, it moves only when it is moved; it can't plan and decide where to move and how to move. But the mind is regarded as being capable of initiating motion; it thinks and plans, decides which course to follow for attaining its goals.

My body moves only when my mind executes an act of will; my mind executes an act of will only when it has clear ideas of the goal to be achieved and the means for achieving it. In other words, my mind must tell my will what is the case, what kind of situation is existing around me, what kinds of objects and persons are around me whose existence I would take note of in case I decide to follow one course of action rather than another. And then my will, so informed and enlightened by my thought, decides what action is to be performed. And once a decision has been made by my will, my body moves in accordance with the plan and decision of my will. In this picture, the body is seen to be moving only when it is moved. The stone moves when it is kicked out or pushed out, similarly my body moves only when my will pushes it to move. But nothing pushes my mind or, if at all, only I, as a self-conscious being and agent, think and decide, and then give a kick to my body to move in a way that will help me to achieve my purpose.

This picture of self being the active agent which can start thinking and deciding and then producing changes in the world, is a more specific form of the world-picture of God who thinks of producing changes and brings about things to happen. He creates a world of things and persons in accordance with His decisions which are based upon the reasons known to Him. In the case of God, His thoughts are initiated by Him and then He decides or wills in accordance with His reasons to create a world. God's mind is completely active both in His thinking and in His willing. He is, in other words, *actus purus*. But in the case of man, it is believed that ideas and impressions are imposed upon him and he receives them passively and, once these materials are available, his mind can start thinking and reasoning about the situation and then his will decides what to do. God starts thinking without receiving ideas from outside; but man thinks only after he receives ideas. For man his situation is already defined in relation to which he can start thinking, and in which alone he can decide to bring about change; but in the case of God, there is no such thing at all. He only does what He thinks of doing. Thus there is a sense in which the concepts of 'pure thought' and 'pure action' apply only to God, and to nothing else. But man's thoughts and actions cannot be pure in this sense. In the case of man, pure thought and pure action is based upon another model. A thought is said to be pure if a self-conscious being performs it in his own private sphere of self-consciousness. An action is said to be pure if it happens to the body, uncontrolled by the mind, in a public world of physical objects in accordance with purely mechanical laws. Such a picture is the picture of an action not consciously willed and designed. Thus, an agent's thoughts and will are pure if they are spontaneously done and self-initiated and his action is pure if it is not consciously designed and not self-initiated. So the concepts of pure thought and pure action are different in the case of God from those that apply in the case of man. But in the course of what follows in this paper it will be clear that the two sets of concepts are muddled and unintelligible.

I will begin by examining the concepts of pure thought and pure action in the context of a human being who is born to a world which is already there. In this context pure thought belongs to the world of inner life, an inner theatre. Pure action belongs to the sphere of outer world, an outer theatre. One is completely private, the other is completely public though both are similar in being occurrences in a created world. And since both are created, there seems to be a point of identity; but since the two are completely different, there is no point of contact between the two. The ideas of identity and difference are conflicting ideas and therefore a problem arises as to how to explain away the difference or how to explain away the identity. The identity can be explained away if the difference is so accentuated that the thinking being, by a process of self-discipline, can stop its changing moods, thoughts and desires. At that time it will be at peace with itself, it will be an eternal life of pure consciousness—a conscious life of stillness and undisturbed peace. It is a life of liberation for the pure self. This is more or less represented in all philosophical systems where liberation is the only dominating goal to be attained. The self is identical with itself, withdrawn to itself and is at peace with itself. Similarly, the outer world of non-thinking bodies is pushed into its proper place where it obeys the mechanical laws which reign supreme. Unconscious nature goes on operating according to its own mechanical and natural laws undisturbed by the purposes and interests of a foreign conscious agent. The separation is complete on both sides. Such a world ceases to be a world created by God. Nature is God in its own sphere. It is purely mechanical. Its matter and energy are conserved within itself. God does not create it nor does He destroy it. Similarly, the conscious agent on the other side is withdrawn to itself. It has found its liberation. It is its own God or God himself. It is the *Brahman*.

But there can be another move, and we can use the picture in another way. We can accentuate the identity in such a manner that all differences would disappear. The conscious self can be pulled down to the unconscious nature, and allowed to be dissipated there. There is only mechanical activity everywhere. There are not two worlds of ghosts and machines, but only the world of machines. In this instance, man is merely, a machine, a mere body. His actions are no more than the behaviour of a machine. They obey the same mechanical laws. All his actions are strictly determined mechanically. There is nothing which an intelligent man does which a machine cannot do. Intelligent and deliberate actions are only more complicated types of mechanical actions. Reality is one and the same everywhere. All changes in it obey the same uniform laws. Such a world can go on forever, governed by its own laws, standing in need of no divine intervention. In such a world there is no place for God, because the idea of pure action with which we started to construct it, is completely different from the idea of pure action which is attributed to God. Ideas of pure action and pure thought, which are the frames of reference in the case of man and his surrounding world, being different from the ideas of pure thought and pure action in the case of God, necessarily leave us in a Godless world.

When these frames of references are seen clearly in their proper light we have no reason to wonder why philosophical thinking, whether in the East or in the West, became progressively Godless. Philosophers are bound to produce either two worlds each autonomous to itself or one world completely autonomous in itself. Philosophy asserts the autonomy of reason pure and simple, or it asserts the autonomy of reason which is the same thing as the autonomy of scientific knowledge. Philosophy produces the picture of two worlds autonomous in themselves. In one, spiritual progress, self-realisation and liberation of the soul seem to be possible whereas nothing can be achieved in the other world which is concurrent with it; or philosophy will produce a world where mechanical laws reign supreme and scientific knowledge is the only guide, where material prosperity can be achieved which is the same thing as where machines work more efficiently and drive man to degeneration and unbearable dullness, to a life of slavery and uncreativity. When the world-picture produced by philosophy is so disquieting that it creates either men of retiring temperament who are indifferent to bodily pleasures and pains and who are ascetic in temperament or it produces men who are mechanised, go on operating machines having no time to enjoy leisure, do not find occasions to engage in creative activity and are compelled to lead a life of drudgery—the cry comes to bring the ascetic down to the world and to relieve the machine-man of his burdens.

But the question is: how can this be done ? So long as we keep to the frames of references of pure thought and pure action there will be either ascetics or machine-men. In one tradition, man is left uncared for to himself; in another, man is compelled to work to whatever limits this compulsion can be conceived, and there is no limit to it. If I have a machine, its efficiency will lie in its output of work. The more a machine can work the more perfect it is as a machine. If the machine stops working at any time I am to effect repairs in it so that it can resume work at once. If man is a mere machine he can be put to work without restriction. If at any time he is found unable to work he has to be repaired, his health is to be examined, he is to be given better food, so that he can go on to work further. Eastern culture grew in one tradition. It accepted one type of philosophy and this philosophy produced ascetics. Planning is bound to fail in such a society, a society arranged in one philosophical tradition resulting from an exclusive notion of pure thought and pure action. Western society has accepted the other philosophical tradition.

This confusion of cultural patterns results from our sharply distinguishing between the mental and the physical in the case of the human individual. The picture of man's mind being extremely personal and private, is an absurd picture. Our thoughts and feelings, desires and emotions, hopes and wishes, decisions and intentions, are not occurrences in a private world. If they were such private items of a private world, they could not be intelligibly talked about. A private language referring to such items in a person's inner theatre, is logically impossible. If I use a word to stand for a private item which is in principle unobservable by others, my use of it cannot be checked by anybody else. Nobody can point out whether I am using the word correctly or incorrectly, since he has no means of knowing and identifying whether and when this item occurs in my private world. All that I am left with in this case is my personal subjective impression that I am using it rightly or wrongly. Where a subjective impression is the only thing that I can fall back upon, the distinction between appearance and reality, right and wrong, disappears. On this account no intelligible discourse about this supposedly private occurrence is possible; but the fact that we do talk about the thoughts and intentions of people rules out the possibility of such private occurrences. The supposition that such private occurrences might still be there even though we cannot talk about them in our language, is a contradictory supposition. The assertion that there are things about which we know nothing is an empty assertion. So the story of an inner chamber, the story that we have a private life in an ethereal world of nonphysical mental occurrences, a life of pure conscious existence, is less than a myth.

But rejection of the inner world does not mean that man is simply a body or a mere machine. The intelligent behaviour of a human being is different from that of a machine. A machine acts efficiently or inefficiently. It is perfectly in order or has gone out of order. But it cannot act intelligently or stupidly. A human being acts intelligently or stupidly, plans ahead and makes decisions, acts resolutely or loses interest and relaxes, feels interested or disinterested. But this is not what a machine can do. A machine cannot act stupidly and therefore cannot act intelligently either. It cannot lose interest and so cannot pick up interest either. It cannot refuse to act because it is not convinced about the rightness or wrongness of actions. It can clash against another machine, but cannot decide to go to war. It can stop work, but cannot hesitate, cannot doubt and cannot look for advice and counsel. It cannot raise legal issues and frame laws nor can it amend and repeal laws. This difference is supposed to be explained by the account that intelligent behaviour on the part of a man is due to the behaviour being caused by intelligence. Similarly, a man's intentional behaviour is supposed to be behaviour caused by a mental act of intention or will. His attentive behaviour is also supposed to be due to an inner act of attending preceding the behaviour and so on. His stupid behaviour is supposed to be, on this account, behaviour without intellection; it is behaviour which is mechanical. Similarly, willful behaviour is distinguished from unintentional behaviour by supposing that unintentional behaviour as such is purely mechanical behaviour. But since we have already pointed out that the machine's behaviour can neither be intelligent nor stupid, is neither intentional nor unintentional, the picture employed here is a misfit. A stupid behaviour of a human being is still a human behaviour and not a mechanical behaviour. We criticise a man for being stupid. We chastise him for not being mindful, we blame him for willfully doing a thing which is wrong. Nobody will think of rebuking a machine for a stupid action nor of scolding it for having done a wrong action willfully. The picture of assimilating human action to machine's behaviour is a wrong picture. Similarly, the question as to what makes a human behaviour intelligent or stupid, intentional or non-intentional is not a question asking for a causal explanation. When I ask what makes an action intelligent I am not looking for an operation, a thought, an act of intellection which, operating upon the bodily machine, makes it intelligent. Similarly, when I ask what makes a human action intentional, I am not asking for an identification of the little operator, the agent which has operated upon the human body and guided its course of action towards the goal intended by the agent.

'What makes human behaviour intelligent?' is a criteriological question. The word 'makes' in this question is a metaphor. We decide whether an action is intelligent or not, not by reference to the occurrence of a non-physical mental item. We decide whether a student is intelligent or not by comparing his performance with those of others. A man's action is judged to be intelligent by studying his behaviour and not because of an inner occurrence. We decide whether a man has willfully done it or not, not on account of the occurrence or non-occurrence of an act of will; we decide whether he has deliberately done it or not by examining the situation, taking note of his previous history, asking questions of people in his immediate surroundings or his close associates, searching for his personal correspondence and diary entries.

Similarly, when a patient is given anaesthesia, the doctor may ask the nurse whether the patient is still conscious or not. In asking this question he is not asking the nurse to open up the inner theatre of the man to get a peep into his non-physical mind to see whether the stream of consciousness is still flowing there. The doctor is asking the nurse to see whether the patient can count fingers, can identify persons and respond to questions. Whether a man is conscious or not is not a question as to whether the stream of consciousness is flowing in the person's non-physical mind. It is a question as to whether his behaviour has certain observable marks or not. Or, let us change the situation. Let us take the case of a parrot who has been trained to welcome visitors by uttering the sentence, 'Come, be thou seated'. We do not credit the parrot with any intelligent understanding of the meaning of the sentence, because it goes on mechanically repeating the sentence irrespective of the type of persons who come. It will utter the sentence not distinguishing between a beggar and a guest, a stranger or an inmate of the family. It will not ask for the identity and the purpose of the visitor and will not discriminate between who are to be welcomed and who are to be asked to stay out. But a human instructed to welcome guests will not admit visitors indiscriminately like the parrot. The characteristic behaviour of the man will show that he is intelligent while that of the parrot will show that he utters sentences mechanically.

The thoughts and intentions of a man are not occurring in a non-physical world which is perpetually screened off from public scrutiny. They are all there where his actions are. What thoughts prompt a man to embark upon a course of action will be known by studying his present behaviour as well as his past behaviour. A man is not a composite being of two sorts of things of an entirely different nature. He is not a soul and a body glued together somehow, so that when a separation takes place the soul will be wandering in a non-spatial, non-temporal world and his body will perish or continue in accordance with physical laws. A human individual is different from a machine not because it is composed of two types of materials of an entirely different character, whereas the machine is composed of elements of one type. A human individual is distinguished from a machine because of his characteristic patterns of activities distinguishable from those of the machine. A human individual is a unitary, not a composite, being.

A man's thoughts and actions do not develop independently and there is no logical necessity as to which one should be first. A man learns while doing and acts more efficiently because of his previous learning. A child, while exploring objects, learns how to behave towards them. It begins to know that fire is to be avoided and sweets are to be welcomed. While doing he learns to identify objects and because of his previous learning he knows how to react towards them. Because of what he knows his actions becomes directed and efficient. The more he succeeds in distinguishing and identifying objects and persons from one another, the more he begins to identify himself as one distinct individual among others. He takes care to keep himself away from certain things and persons and selects those with whom to work. Self-identification is possible in the course of identification of others and this double form of identification becomes more and more sharpened in the course of actions in varying situations. Self-identification is not possible in the case of a man who has not lived in society, and who has not been taught what to do and what not to do. Self-individuation and other individuation go together. If I do not discriminate others from me, I cannot discriminate myself from others. In order that this discrimination of things and persons might be done by me, I must have the means for identification. In other words, I must have a language consisting of both referring and descriptive words. I must be able to distinguish individuals from classes of individuals (either objects or persons) in relation to me. In such a language there must be referring words and descriptive words and also self-referring words. These are the minimum requirements of a language. The richer the language the sharper is the possibility of discrimination and identification and the more efficient are the people who act intelligently and efficiently which is the same thing as their discriminating and identifying the necessary details, assimilating and classifying by overlooking unnecessary details. Details become necessary or unnecessary according to the way they are or are not related to human purposes. No classification, therefore, is sacrosanct or ultimate, nor are there limits to man's power of discrimination.

Now it may be clear why the idea of a self-conscious God, reasoning and acting all by Himself and unrelated to any situation, gradually failed to gain human recognition. If my thoughts and actions are interdependent and if both are also dependent upon the institution of language, and since language by its very nature is bound to be public, the idea of a God thinking and acting by Himself and having no means of communication with others is patently an unintelligible idea. A God who has no means of formulating His ideas by means of language cannot think. Similarly, He cannot act as action must be aided by thought. He must know what to do. But if He acts without thinking and without deciding, He is no longer God, but an inanimate object in a world of other inanimate objects. He cannot bring about changes; changes only happen to Him. If again it be supposed that there are many gods who could develop their ideas in communication with one another, it becomes only an unnecessary duplication of the human world. Polytheism is unnecessary and monotheism is unintelligible.

Our talk about self-identification in the context of human beings may suggest the picture of a soul having a life of pure consciousness, bereft of the body which is its accidental outer form. People have tended to create this picture because of certain linguistic considerations. A person can be identified when one of his legs or hands is amputated. He may be identified even when both the legs or hands are amputated. In this sense, no one limb or a set of limbs is essential for the purpose of a person's identification. From this some philosophers have jumped to the conclusion that a person can be identified even when his entire body is gone. The concept of a soul which survives the death of the body is an unintelligible one which arose out of the misunderstanding of the functioning of our language. Another source of the concept of a self-conscious, self-luminous, eternal soul, is the peculiar role that the word 'I' plays in our language structure. It is an 'index word' like 'you' and 'he'; but this indexing, when it is directed to another person, takes as its referent different people at different times. But the word 'I' always refers, throughout the life-history of its user, to one unchanging, constant person. This creates the illusion of an eternal ego, a self. Since a man's discrimination of other things and persons is always done with reference to his own situations the self of the individual is regarded as occupying a central position in one's scheme of discrimination. This creates the illusion that the self which is the knower of all objects cannot itself be known. To attempt to know the knower would be to effect, what Professor A.C. Mukherjee calls, the 'transcendental dislocation of the self'. But there is nothing mysterious about it. As Prof. Ryle says, the index finger cannot point at itself; this does not mean that the other fingers cannot point at it. We can illustrate this linguistic fact in another way. Everything that can be said about me can be stated in the descriptive part of the first person declarative sentence. The 'I' which is the subject in such sentences, if pushed further and further to the border as all its descriptive contents are squeezed out more and more to the descriptive part, the contentless 'I' in this usage is seen to belong to the periphery of the language structure. It belongs to what Wittgenstein calls the limit of the language and is no part of the language. It is the pure syntactical 'I' having no semantic functions at all.

We can take another argument from Indian philosophy. It is argued that the objective experience of waking life changes into the subjective experience of the dreamer, and the dream experience also in its turn changes into dreamless sleep experience. Since the objective experience can change into the subjective experience which, in its turn, changes into the formless pure conscious state of the dreamless sleep, it is argued that the relation between the states of consciousness and consciousness itself is of a contingent nature. And therefore it is argued that pure, changeless, self-luminous consciousness is the nature of the self. This argument has another addendum to it. It is argued that since in waking up I can declare that I slept well and since this is a memory statement, it must be the reproduction of an original knowledge of self-consciousness of the period of dreamless sleep. To remember something is to remember that which was once known. If I have now the memory knowledge that I slept well, it is supposed to imply that I was conscious of myself during the state of deep sleep.

To take the first part of the argument, it has to be pointed out that the nature of necessary and contingent relations is conceived with the help of a picture. A thing necessarily related to another thing is pictured as the thing being inextricably bound up with the other. Similarly, the nature of a contingent relation is pictured as a kind of loose tie so that when the knot is untied each term of this relation will remain outside the other. On this analogy it is believed that subjective and objective experiences, being contingently related to consciousness, can be loosened away from it, and the self-luminous pure conscious ego can enjoy its life of eternal bliss. This is the life of complete freedom of self, a life of liberation in which the self is no longer driven hither or thither and is not tied to this or that, a bodiless soul or self-poised spirit. But these pictures are misfits to the occasion and create confusing illusions. There are no necessary connections, and for that matter no contingent relations even among items of furniture in the world. Necessary and contingent relations are significant only in the context of propositions and meanings. Propositions necessarily related are such that one of the propositions cannot be asserted when the other is denied. To assert the one and deny the other will involve self-contradiction and paralyse speech; but there is no such self-contradiction in the case of contingent relations. From this linguistic fact nothing about the world can be inferred at all. To say that something is red is to say that it is red and is coloured; but this does not mean that the existence of the coloured thing is necessary, that it could not be destroyed. To say that the activities in which I am engaged are not necessarily related to me is to say that I need not be conceived as doing the same thing all the time; but this does not imply that I would be eternally existing without doing anything and without being related to any situation or even without having a body at all. Similarly, to say that the amputation of my nose, or for that matter, of any particular limb of mine, is not necessarily related to me is not to say that I will continue to exist even when I have no loss of nose or no limbs at all. Or let us take another example. To say that something is a triangle is to say that it must be a figure, but to say that something is a figure is not to say that it must necessarily be a triangle. It could be any figure. But this never implies that it could still be a figure without being any one kind of figure at all. Similarly, consciousness need not necessarily be subjective or objective; but it would never be consciousness if it is not manifested in any of these forms. Hence the supposed idea of pure consciousness completely breaks down. From the necessary and contingent relation among propositions nothing can be inferred about things and their relations, nor about the existence and non-existence of things at all.

Now we come to the second part of the argument. It is true that to remember something is to have known the thing earlier. But is the statement that I slept well a memory-statement at all? To say that I slept well and that I do not remember any dream of that period is not to say that there was a consciousness concurrently going on during the period of sleep which I now remember. I only declared that I do not remember anything at all. But to say that I do not remember anything at all is not to say that there was a thing which I do not remember. To say that I know nothing is not to say that the nothing is the thing which I know.

We can now conclude that the model of pure thought and pure action pictures the human individual as a composite being of pure self and a mere body. This picture of pure soul and mere body is based upon linguistic confusions and bad logic. The Indian tradition, being lured by the possibility of a pure self, has created a culture of asceticism and indifference to worldly affairs. Similarly, abhorrence of the idea of the mystical has caused the human individual to be regarded as a pure body, a mere machine in the West. These conflicting cultural patterns have their deep roots in bad philosophical traditions based upon a misunderstanding of the logic of our language. Once these faulty philosophical bases of these conflicting cultural patterns are seen in their proper light the conflicting cultural patterns will dissipate. The philosophy which points out the logical errors in the metaphysical pictures of the past is the critical and analytical philosophy of the modern age. Its logic is without ontology, it does not indulge in creating different metaphysical traditions and consequently does not leave room for the emergence of clashing cultural patterns. In the darkness of logical errors and linguistic confusions there is no guarantee that all people should see things in the same way. Errors may take different forms and may create different cultural outlooks. Mutual checking and correcting lead to clear and uniform understanding. Clarity is the aim of this modern philosophy; logical analysis is its method; clearing away misunderstandings is the result which it achieves.

A philosophy which brings back man from this aerial existence on the one hand and slavery and forced labour on the other sees man as an individual, a person. It sees man as one individual having ambitions and wants, working under limitations and difficulties. Such a philosophy therefore is bound to be humanistic in its cultural outlook. When there is war in West Asia or suffering in Bangladesh, or racial discrimination in South Africa resulting in human suffering, the new cultural humanistic outlook does not allow for indifference and unconcern. This cultural outlook based upon a proper understanding about the nature of man does not allow a Lord Krishna to persuade an Arjuna to go to war to kill his own relations under the belief that in killing only the perishable body is destroyed while the eternal soul is neither created nor destroyed. Similarly, it does not also create the corresponding outlook of man being a mere machine which can be made to work and exploited. It does not work upon the analogy that, as a car is sent to the garage when it is out of order, a man who does not conform to the standard behaviour prescribed can be sent to the labour camps for correction and brain-washing. Because of the new philosophical outlook cultural isolation is disappearing fast. The releasing of international tensions and laying and securing the foundations of peace by negotiation and talks in conferences is the concern of the modern age, and helping to see the baselessness of clashing cultures is the role of modern philosophy. Deepening the human understanding is the role of modern linguistics and analytical philosophy and removing the clashing nature of cultural patterns is the result of deep understanding. Modern philosophy has brought man to his own original home and the man at his own home is engaged in a constructive programme of work in which the common interest of the human group is already prefigured.

9

Philosophy as Reflection on Experience

J. N. MOHANTY

Philosophy, in my view, consists of reflection on man's experience in relation to himself, to others and to the world. However, as a philosopher I find myself in a curiously ambivalent position. Being steeped in history, my reflection presupposes and proceeds on the foundation of the sedimented thoughts of other philosophers who either have preceded me in time or, though my contemporaries, have been able to exercise some significant influence on me. As a consequence, one may either say that my access to my own experience is mediated by the history of thought or that my experience itself is constituted by that history. And this history is not just the one history of human thought, but—to use a metaphor—consists in a series of concentric circles such that the closer the circle is to the centre the greater is its relevance for me. Thus, the history and tradition of Indian thought dominate my experience in a especially pre-eminent sense, but the history of European thought is also closer to that centre than many other histories (e.g., African and Latin American). There does not seem to be, for me, any major philosophical problem which I could think through without reference to this historical tradition. The most relevant of those problems, again, are those which relate me specifically to the tradition of Indian philosophical thought. Thus, philosophical reflection is inevitably historical, partly because my experience itself is permeated by history. At the same time, if philosophical reflection were merely historical then it could not have survived the passage of time, except in the form of sedimented memories of cultural achievements, it would not have been amenable to supra-historical logical assessment, scientific-objective questioning, it could not lay claim to truth.

In philosophy what matters most is not believing in a proposition, however historically relevant that proposition may be, but how precisely that belief has been grounded and is validated. This grounding or validating has to be based on principles that are not historical. Thus in the texture of philosophy, as in the texture of all experience, the historical and the supra-historical are inextricably woven together.

'Experience', reflection on which constitutes philosophy, should be understood in the widest possible sense. There is a common practice amongst philosophers to commit themselves, without saying so, to their most important philosophical decisions right at the beginning; they do so when they begin by delimiting experience, in an arbitrary manner, to some preferred mode or to some preferred type. Thus, for example, a great many philosophers want to mean by 'experiencing' something like 'sensing' and understand by the latter something like 'receiving impressions or data through one or more of the sense-organs'. In further analysis, experience so understood is neatly divided into momentary bits of sensings (of sense data). What escapes such an understanding of experience—often shared in common by empiricists and rationalists alike—is a whole range of other modes: experience of relations, of things in their complex setting, of cultural and aesthetic objects as such, of other persons, of oneself and also moral and religious experience. In order to remedy such one-sidedness of philosophical commitments, it has always seemed useful to me that philosophers keep the following statement of Whitehead in mind:

Nothing can be omitted, experience drunk and experience sober, experience sleeping and experience awake, experience drowsy and experience wide-awake, experience self-conscious and experience self-forgetful, experience intellectual and experience physical, experience religious and experience sceptical, experience anxious and experience care-free, experience anticipatory and experience retrospective, experience happy and experience grieving, experience dominated by emotions and experience under self-restraint, experience in the light and experience in the dark, experience normal and experience abnormal. (*Adventures of Ideas*, New York, Macmillan, 1933, pp. 290–1)

What does 'reflection' on experience mean? Just as a narrow
conception of experience arbitrarily restricts and distorts the data
to be reflected upon so also a false conception of reflection
misleads us as to what philosophy may have to do with these
data. Many philosophers understand by 'reflection' an attempt
to explain the data of experience or to account for them. Sometimes one also means by 'reflecting on experience' nothing but
'seeking to interpret experience'. As would be obvious, neither
explaining nor interpreting could, by themselves, fully characterise the
nature and goal of philosophical reflection, for there are other
kinds of thinking activity—the scientific for example—which
also want to explain and interpret experience. One then has to
seek for some distinctive feature of philosophical explanation
and philosophical interpretation. To this the usual answer is:
philosophical explanation and philosophical interpretation are
from the most comprehensive point of view, while the scientific
or religious explanations are from limited points of view. However,
this is a highly unsatisfactory answer. The answer no doubt
concedes that all explanations and interpretations are from some
point of view or other. It also covertly recognises that this choice
of a point of view has something arbitrary about it, and confers
a sort of subjectivity on the explanation or interpretation propounded. However, it entertains the hope, and gives us the
assurance, that once the most comprehensive point of view is
adopted somehow the alleged arbitrariness in the choice of a
point of view and the consequent subjectivity would be overcome,
and philosophical thinking would reach objective validity. Now
this hope and this assurance are but illusory. Either the most
comprehensive point of view is no point of view, but then it
makes no sense to say that the philosopher seeks to explain the
data of experience but from no point of view—for then he would
not be explaining or interpreting, if these activities require, by
their very nature, some point of view or other, some system,
model or framework. Or, the most comprehensive point of view
is a point of view, and then its claim to be the most comprehensive,
in fact the very sense of its comprehensiveness, would be in
question. Furthermore, what is the test of a point of view's
being the most comprehensive one? It seems to me that the
philosopher who wants to explain or account for the data of
experience is covertly operating with the idea of scientific explana-

tion but does not want to have his explanations suffer from the limitations which are methodologically necessary for scientific enquiry. This desire to have the cake and also eat it gives rise to a most embarrassing situation. What does, for example, 'explaining' mean in the philosophical context? In the context of scientific enquiry, a test of a good explanation is successful prediction. Philosophical explanation does not lay claim to this. And yet the philosophers do operate with the 'covering law model' of explanation.

It seems to me, therefore, that the proper task of philosophy is misconstrued when it is formulated in terms of explaining the data of experience. It is already a philosophical problem of the highest importance to ascertain what precisely those data of experience are. In the case of the sciences, each science lays down —implicitly or explicitly—what criteria are to be satisfied by its data in order to be accepted as data. In other words, the sciences are only obliquely concerned with the data of experience. They no doubt arise out of the problems and demands implicit in experience, but by the very nature of their undertaking they remove themselves from lived experience—not merely at the level of theory-construction but even at the primary level of data collection, for what sorts of things are to count as data are already pre-legislated by the demands of the theory. Thus there are no theory-neutral unidealised data in the context of the scientific endeavour.

For the psychology of the behaviourist, for example, only those forms of human behaviour which are quantifiable, as drained of all intentional and valuational significance, constitute the data. At least to begin with, by the very nature of the programme, it does not know of what we may call, by contrast, lived behaviour as contrasted with observed behaviour. Now it is precisely one of the tasks of philosophy to aim at the discovery and description of the structure of experience itself. This, by itself, is so difficult and engrossing a task that after this is done the further task of accounting for that structure would either wait till this is relatively well in progress or would lose much of its supposed theoretical attraction.

To be sure, a description of the structure of experience is no easy task, and possibly the philosopher could only asymptotically aim at satisfactorily performing it. Once we set aside the sort of reflection involved in efforts to provide a philosophical explanation for the way things are supposed to be, the other sense of 'reflection' comes to the forefront. This consists in trying to take an unprejudiced look at experience, to 'steal a glance' at it without disturbing it, to be able to watch it arise on the basis of past sedimentations of meaning and wither away leaving behind its own conceptual sedimentations, without forcing one's own concepts on it. This is not wishing to return to the childlike purity and innocence of a pre-conceptual immediate experience. That conception of experience as unstructured, non-conceptual immediate and pure—à la Bradley—is itself the result of a romantic desire for such, as much as the atomistic conception of experience as consisting in discrete bits of unrelated momentary sensations is the product of a large body of scientific theory. Experience, as we live through it, is not like any of these patterns. It is structured but not atomistic; it is lived, but not out and out sensationalistic; it is also conceptual but not idealised and exact. The concepts it lives behind and generates at the first instance are vague and fluid, inexact and lively. But again the experience to be reflected upon is not merely the pre-reflective, pre-judgmental encounter with the world of things and persons, natural and cultural objects, but also post-reflective, albeit predicative, judgments about whatever was so encountered. Furthermore, no reflection on experience is adequate unless it reflects on itself. Reflection is not radical unless it is aware of its own situation, its own movements and its own limitations and destiny. Such awareness is likely to limit the chances of an unbounded optimism (in the capabilities of reflection) and naive transcendentalism (which is unaware of its own situation in time and history).

One necessary pre-condition for philosophical reflection in this sense is the cultivation of a cautious watchfulness for the vitiating influence of unsuspected interpretations and prejudices. Various vitiating factors may be distinguished. There are, first, what may be called theoretical prejudices, deriving from either philosophical theories or scientific theories. There are practical prejudices deriving from one's valuational preferences and attitudes. There are also more deeply rooted interpretations which rest in the nature of the language one uses. It is in this last point, it seems to me, that the linguistic philosophers have made great contributions towards bringing to light persistent sources of misinterpretations of language. Linguistic analysis, both in this negative sense, and also in the positive sense of unravelling the multifarious ways in which words are used, is thus an indispensable aid to phenomenological description.

It seems to me that methodological monism, in philosophy, has to be rejected. At the most basic level, the philosopher's job consists in analysis (of concepts, meanings, uses of language) and description (of the essential structures of experience). We have now to see how, after the preliminary surveying of the terrain is fairly advanced, the philosopher may legitimately go ahead with the help of other methods. There are two such methods, in the use of which one has to exercise the utmost caution. One is metaphysical construction, and the other is dialectics. To consider the second first: I am using 'dialectics' not in the Hegelain sense of a progressive unfolding of concepts through a systematic use of contradictions and resolution of such contradictions through syntheses, but in the sense of a continuing process of arguments and counter-arguments. Allegedly wrong theories or false philosophical propositions are to be discarded either by demonstrating that they are untrue to facts, i.e., to some undeniable testimony of experience, or by bringing out some logical inconsistency in the theory or proposition concerned, or by both procedures. It is the second method of discarding a philosophical contention that requires dialectics. I should add that dialectics can at most prove a proposition to be false, but it cannot positively establish the truth of one. Positively establishing the truth of one would need either adequate phenomenological evidence or a sort of transcendental argument which appeals to the 'conditions of the possibility of experience being what it is'.

Philosophical thinking, it would seem, cannot avoid some kind of metaphysical construction or other. But one should be able to distinguish between metaphysical constructions that are speculative, in which thought is aided by flights of imagination, and metaphysical thinking that is solidly rooted in the descriptive soil. Nicolai Hartmann's dictum 'Minimum of Metaphysics' and Strawson's conception of a descriptive metaphysics appeal to me. If by 'metaphysics' be meant enquiry into the most general structures of experience, such enquiry—quite independent of the issues of realism and idealism—would require a minimum of transcendence of the attitude of description. It would be a metaphysics of experience in the true sense—neutral as between realism and transcendental idealism. Similarly, a metaphysics of subjectivity is a legitimate field of enquiry which would require a methodological suspension or *epoché* of the belief in, but not a denial of, the reality of a world transcending the life of consciousness. In the carrying out of these metaphysical programmes what the philospher needs most is: a profound respect for phenomena precisely as they present themselves, a refusal to deny phenomena to satisfy theory, a desire to search for simplicity combined with a willingness to distrust it, readiness to recognise diversities and 'gaps' as much as affinities and continuities according to how they show themselves, and an unwillingness to generalise, without caution, over the universal domain what has phenomenological 'backing' only within a restricted sub-domain.

These methodological principles may well be illustrated with the help of an example: the concept of intentionality. The descriptive metaphysician, once he recognises intentionality as an essential structure of conscious life, would refuse to deny it on *a priori* theoretical grounds (e.g., on the ground that consciousness, being self-revealing, cannot be, in reality, of an object), would recognise all the various modes of intentionality (bodily, mental; cognitive, affective, volitional; unconscious) without wanting to reduce them into any one, and would refuse to generalise the property of intentionality over the universal domain, i.e., to hold that all objects whatsoever are intentional (e.g., 'every actual entity prehends every other').

It is at this point that I should insist on the need for rejecting a conception of philosophy that has considerable influence on the Indian mind. Philosophy, I submit, is not a rational defence or clarification of the words of the scriptures. Interpretation, semantic or syntactical, of the scriptures is a different venture, and would constitute a part of the theology of the religion whose scriptures are under consideration. The belief, widely shared by classical Indian philosophers, that philosophy should accept the authority of the scriptures and rationally defend them is both supported by, and itself supports, the epistemological thesis that *śabda*, by itself, is a way, *sui generis*, of acquiring valid knowledge, a *pramāṇa*. I do not think this latter thesis is acceptable. On hearing a sentence being uttered by another person, one understands —if one 'knows' the language—its meaning, and in case one already trusts the reliability of the speaker one comes to believe in what he says. But neither the understanding of the meaning of a sentence nor the belief in its truth amounts to knowing that the facts are as stated. Knowing requires that mere understanding be supplemented by verificatory evidence, the grasping of the meaning-intention be fulfilled, the belief be supported by adequate evidence. Failure to distinguish between 'understanding', 'believing' and 'knowing' is at the root of the epistemological status accorded to *śabda*.

The only strong point in that thesis concerns the unique status of scriptural words with regard to giving us knowledge of what ought to be or ought not to be done. Other means of knowing— perception and inference being the most important of them— yield knowledge of what is the case. What ought or ought not to be done cannot be ascertained either by perception or by inference. Therefore, the argument runs, the unique, irreplaceable means of knowing about these matters are the words of the scriptures. No where there is no doubt an important element of truth in this argument, and it is this. In the case of an indicative sentence putatively stating a fact there is a distinction, as just pointed out, between understanding the meaning of the sentence and knowing that the fact is as stated. The latter requires some sort of verification. In the case of an imperative sentence, on the contrary, like 'One ought not to harm any living being', the question of verification, of ascertaining if one really ought not to harm any living being, is pointless, for an imperative does not say what is the case but tells us what ought to be done. It would seem then to follow that hearing an imperative being uttered and understanding its meaning would suffice for knowing that such and such action ought to be done—provided we have faith in the trustworthiness of the utterer. The argument, however, is faulty. One has to face the following alternatives: accepting an imperative as valid, as binding on me, as saying what really ought to be done may mean either choosing it and committing oneself to it on grounds other than theoretical (e.g., because it is emotionally satisfying); or accepting it as theoretically most satisfying. In the former case, hearing an imperative being uttered and understanding its meaning may lead to its acceptance but such acceptance would not amount to a knowledge that such and such action ought to be done. If it be replied that in cases of moral choices the question of knowledge does not arise, then it should be pointed out if that be so the argument sketched above would not prove that scriptural . utterances are means of knowing what ought to be done, they may at best be means of persuading men to make moral decisions. If one chooses the second alternative, i.e., holds that a moral injunction is accepted on theoretically satisfying grounds, then of course one should concede to the claim that one knows that such and such action ought to be done, but at the same time the original argument is defeated, for now something more than merely hearing and understanding is needed for knowing that such and such action ought to be done, and this something more, even if it cannot be a verificatory experience, can be rational argumentation of some sort or other. The point then in brief is this: if one can be said to know that such and such action ought to be done, then mere understanding of the meanings of scriptural imperatives cannot yield such knowledge; if one cannot be said to know such matters, then also the scriptures are not the means of their knowledge. My purpose has been not to question the usefulness, and even the importance and dignity, of the scriptures in man's ethical and religious life. My purpose has been to argue that they are not a unique source of knowledge, a *pramāṇa*.

It is also often held that supernormal experiences, not enjoyed by ordinary men, are embodied in the words of the scriptures, and if philosophy is to be reflection on experience then it cannot afford to close its eyes to the rarest, and yet the most valuable, of human experiences—e.g., the experiences of the mystics. There is a serious difficulty in accepting this contention. For although in principle a philosopher should not, as emphasised earlier, arbitrarily delimit the domain of experience or seek to level it down (or up) to one type, yet I cannot honestly make certain kinds of statements, or even investigations, about experiences I never have had. I can of course make hypothetical statements of the form 'If there were experiences of the said kind, then...'. I can certainly make internal statements ('internal' in Carnap's sense) which purport to characterise mystic experience as mystics would say they had. But I cannot make external statements ('external' also in Carnap's sense) categorically incorporating statements describing the structure of alleged supernormal experiences into my total philosophy of experience. For I do not know what it is to have those experiences. There are nevertheless several ways in which consideration of mystic experiences may be of relevance even to a philosophy of the sort I am here advocating. The logical possibility of such supernormal experiences would give me a sense of what is logically contingent, what is logically necessary and what is syntactically necessary in the structure of our normal modes of experience. Secondly, if the thought of such supernormal experiences be regarded as a demand of spiritual life, then it may be worthwhile to correlate such demands to the actual structure of our experience, without losing sight of the distinction between what is known to be the case and what is felt and appreciated as a demand.

No less misleading than the ones already discussed is the contention that the method of philosophy should be not intellectual but intuitive. The philosopher surely is not called upon to exercise any special cognitive faculty—a cognitive faculty that is not at the disposal of others. Perhaps it is unfair to the intuitionists to say that they want the philosopher to develop such a special uncommon faculty, and it may be that what they say is that many other people who are not philosophers—e.g., poets and scientists— also make use of the non-intellectual alogical cognitive faculty known as 'intuition'. But this would make the entire concept of intuition too vague to be of much use. This is not the place to go into the many different, often mutually incompatible, senses in which the word 'intuition' is used in philosophy. The one sense, if there is any such, that might be relevant in ascertaining the method of philosophy is that which, while retaining the core meaning of 'seeing', yet does not cut it asunder from that sustained, laborious intellectual effort which is involved in philosophical reflection. It is true that while many philosophers have constructed systems and theories, all philosophical reflection does not consist of such constructions. To say that philosophical activity is essentially intellectual is not to assert that it consists in constructing systems and theories; it is not also to deny that the great philosopher is one who acquires, validates and communicates genuine insights into the structure of experience. There is an important sense in which an essential structure has to be intuited or 'seen', but such intuiting is closer to what has been called Gestalt perception, and even to rational abstraction, than to the intuitions of the poet or the mystic.

It is of the utmost importance to note that having or living through an experience of whatever sort is not, by itself, to know. Philosophical activity itself is not to be a surrogate for any kind of pre-philosophical experience. Just as the philosopher's task is to reflect on experience and not to reproduce it, so also any one who lives through an experience unreflectively does not really know what it all is about. Knowledge, ordinary or philosophical, surely requires intuitive experience (direct sense-perception or any sort of appropriate verificatory experience), but such intuitive experience to count as knowledge should be playing the role of 'fulfilling' a prior meaning intention (e.g., verifying a hypothesis).

If philosophy is not a rational defence of religious faith or articulation of one's personal intuitions, it is also not a systematisation of scientific knowledge or a defence of scientific faith. One of the ideals of philosophical thinking is to be free from presuppositions by making every implicit presupposition explicit and subjecting it to critical examination. If this be so, neither religious nor scientific faith could provide it with that which is to be accepted in advance and subsequently defended. Certainly, it is one of the foremost tasks of modern philosophy to understand the structure of scientific thinking and its application, through technology, for both science and technology have added a new dimension to human experience. However, both science and technology presuppose pre-scientific experience, they arise out of it, they idealise the vague typicalities that characterise pre-scientific experience and transform them into exact concepts, they drain man's lived experience of its qualitative and valuational content and quantify whatever is left of it, they construct theories and theoretical models whose cognitive value is assessed by success in prediction, and then technology seeks to re-establish that contact with the lived world which had been lost through theorising. Saying all this is not meant to accuse the sciences of any moral or intellectual misdemeanour; it is not to say, e.g., that the sciences ought to have taken care of the concrete richness of lived experience. It is only to draw attention to the nature of scientific idealisation and to its genesis out of pre-scientific lived experience. The philosopher's prime concern is not with the sciences as such, but with the pre-scientific experience out of which the sciences arise and by which they continue to be supported. It is no wonder that 'perception' continues to be a

primary problem for philosophy. All thought aims at it and is
sustained by it.

II

Experience is not a merely immanent flow of subjective states
but, being incurably characterised by intentionality, is always of
something. Furthermore, just as bits of experience are not self-
contained atoms but are related to each other through primary
retention and secondary memory, primary protension and secondary
expectation, and the ubiquitous forms of associative synthesis,
thereby constituting one inner time-consciousness, so also their
intentional correlates, the objects of experience, are given not as
self-contained unities but always within a field or horizon which
again points beyond itself to larger and larger horizons. The
most comprehensive horizon within which any object of experience
whatsoever is experienced, is the world. In this sense, any experience is experience of the world, but in this sense alone. In other
words, the world is not an object of experience but the horizon
within which any object whatsoever is experienced.

The world, in this sense, is not the same as the physical world
or the world of physics. It is rather that of which the scientific
world is an idealisation. The pre-scientific perceived world is one
in which the natural and the human are blended together, in
which things have not only natural but also valuational qualities,
and in which persons are the centres of their worlds. The
objectifying theoretical interest has not yet come into play.
Within this larger horizon of the lived and perceived world, the
scientific achievements of man take their place both as cultural
achievements and as objectifying large segments of that world.
This is particularly clear in the case of one's own body, space
and time. The conception of my body, even of the other's body,
as a material object, subject to the laws of physics, chemistry and
molecular biology, is a later idealised construction. My body is
primarily, pre-theoretically, perceived by me as a set of motor
and cognitive abilities by which I, in a manner which is specifically
mine, explore the world in which I find myself. I do not locate
it in space as I locate other material objects, for all location in
space that I perform is with reference to my body as a 'zero'

point. Even when I perceive the other's body as a body, I ascribe to it thoughts and feelings as I would do to myself, so that the other's body is not given to me as a material object. Similarly, the originally perceived space is not the uniform mathematical space, it is rather qualitatively diversified with such distinctions as 'familiar' and 'strange', 'assuring' and 'threatening', profane' and 'sacred'. The time that is so perceived is not the uniform, measurable, therefore quantitative and one-dimensional series, but again is qualitatively diversified: diversified in respect of its 'flow' (compare 'an hour' spent in anxiety with 'an hour' spent in rapturous enjoyment) and in respect of direction (compare the linear time of profane existence with the 'cyclic' time of the experience of the sacred for which unique events like the birth of a god recur, to be celebrated and relived). To explain these diversities in experience of body, space and time as subjective —emotional, associative—interpretations of the objective body, mathematical space and mathematical time is to introduce a Cartesian distinction that is posterior to originary experience and an achievement of reflective thinking.

The theory of perception, as Merleau-Ponty has very ably shown, has suffered under the assumption that if the world is as physics supposes it to be, and if the human body is what physiology shows it to be, then our perception of the world must be the end-state of a long chain of physico-physiological processes and there must be a one-to-one correspondence between the elements (properties) of the object out there and the components of the perceptual experience itself. The latter then is decomposed into little bits of sensations (some of which we may not notice at all), each one of which corresponds to some property, aspect or component of the object that is being perceived. Onto this psychological atomism is then grafted a doctrine of 'construction', either in the form of associative synthesis or in the form of synthesis by the Kantian *a priori* categories. To perceive becomes to construct, perception being an intellectual process. Perception of the other person becomes an analogical inference, perception of aesthetic and cultural objects a subjective, or rather emotive, superimposition. As against this, two points need to be made: perception of material objects need not serve as the paradigmatic case of perception in terms of which all other perceptual claims (like those with regard to other minds and values) have to be assessed and, in the second place, perception of material objects itself need not be understood in terms of 'sensations' (and 'sense data') and 'construction'. The notion of 'sensation', far from being a descriptive concept, is rather the product of the scientific theories of classical physiological psychology. We do not have discrete bits of sensations—some of which we notice, others not. We perceive a meaningful complex structure within a field or setting—with its own 'inner' and 'outer' horizons, with intentional references to further possibilities of inner and outer explorations, to the 'other side' and to what is beyond, and so on. The material object is also perceived as that which others are able to perceive, which often has common inter-subjective significance, which others can manipulate or explore along with, and may be in opposition to, me. And my perception of the other minds is a genuine perception *sui generis*, it is not an analogical inference from the perception of the others' physical behaviour. The other's behaviour that I perceive is not a series of physical movements but has, right from the beginning, the significance of being 'pain', a 'smile', a 'warning', 'anger', a 'satisfaction' so that we need not analogically infer the presence of mental states behind and beyond them but, as it were, see the appropriate mental states through them as one sees colours through a transparent glass.

With this broadened conception of perception, a large part of my experienced, perceived world is the cultural world in which past history has been sedimented. No description of the structure of experience, then, can be complete without reference to the way cultural sedimentations constitute my world, or any world whatsoever. It is from this primitive point of view that, I suppose, philosophy of art or of aesthetic experience should begin. Otherwise, there is the risk of isolating aesthetic experience as an experience totally disconnected from ordinary perceptual experience, an experience which some people sometimes have in the presence of art objects while visiting museums or galleries. It would seem, however, that our ordinary perceptual experience has an aesthetic tinge; we perceive not mere men and women but beautiful and attractive faces, we perceive not mere patches of colour but colours that either attract or repel, not mere landscapes but ones which are perceived to be beautiful.

One could say the same of moral experience and also of logical thinking. The exclusive emphasis on the normative aspects of moral concepts, and on the notion of 'ought', has made moral philosophers blind to the fact that moral values are recognised as qualities of actual persons and their acts. Moral experience is not merely unconditional obedience to an imperative, an 'ought', but also perception of goodness, nobility, innocence, courage and other virtues in the lives and actions and persons of men and women around us. Systematic formalisation of logic certainly creates the impression that the logical is the product of a higher order abstract thinking, but it is at the same time also forgotten that there is a kind of 'proto-logic' imbedded in our experience of the world where we have the analogues and 'origins' of most of our higher order, defined, logical concepts like 'negation', 'disjunction', 'implication' and 'class'. The upshot of all this is not to 'reduce' the autonomy and distinctive traits of our higher aesthetic, moral and logical pursuits to lower level empirical terms—which is what empiricism is found guilty of—but to realise that our originative experience of the wo.ld is not as impoverished as empiricism, under the influence of scientific and epistemological prejudices, makes it out to be, but is rich and variegated enough to contain the 'origin' of all higher order developments out of it. This idea of 'origin' shall be so understood that it is compatible with a certain 'discontinuity' between the lived experience and the higher order concepts and significations that originate out of it.

III

I experience not only the world but also myself. My experience of myself is not a static, unidimensional phenomenon. In fact, however, I am aware of myself in many different dimensions: first, as a way of concretely existing as lived body, oriented towards the world and the others; then as a person who has a body, and finally as a subject who is objectively conscious of his body as also of the world and the others.

In the pre-reflective perception of, encounter with, wonder at and manipulation of the world, I am not conscious of myself as an 'I'. Here I concede to Sartre the truth that pre-reflective consciousness is non-egological. Our perceptions take the form

'Here comes the streetcar', our affections take the form 'This is lovable' and our volitions have the form 'This is to be done'. The distinctions between body and mind, outer and inner, are not there. I exist as one undivided being, intentionally directed towards the world, aware of my existence but not of *me* existing. I do not posit myself as a being over and above the world and others. My self-awareness is non-positional, non-thetic and non-egological, my awareness of the world is positing and thetic. I *am* my felt body.

How and why, i.e., on what sorts of occasions, this primary pre-reflective experience gives way to the reflective judgment 'I perceive the streetcar coming', 'I love her' and 'I ought to do this' need not concern us here. For our present purpose what is important is that reflection introduces the 'I' into my consciousness. As one who is still involved in the world and with others, who acts and manipulates, knows, loves and hates, I now experience myself as a person. The 'I' is now detached from my felt body, not however as a transcendental subject but as one who owns, wills and moves it. The body is still not one thing amongst others, but *mine* in a pre-eminent sense. But I am not my body. I have a body, and am aware of, intentions which I carry out but which I may not be able to actualise. My intending is not as such executing a bodily movement: hence the distinction, within my total person, between what is inner and what is outer.

It requires, however, a philosophical reflection of a special sort, or possibly a spiritual, voluntarily cultivated stance, to be aware of oneself as a subject of one's mental states as well as of one's own body, before whose gaze everything other than itself is crystallised into an object. From this point of view, the word 'I' designates me as a person, but symbolically refers to, but does not directly designate, the subject, the transcendental ego which surely is not corporeal, which literally does not possess the body, but which contemplates the body as an object amongst other objects. The Indian philosophical and spiritual tradition has concentrated on this form of self-consciousness and has built up systems of philosophy based on this stance. The Western tradition approaches it in its concept of transcendental ego, but at the same time ascribes to the transcendental ego the active function of constituting, through its synthetic functions, the world; and, in doing so, the Western tradition analogically ascribes to the transcendental ego functions that, more literally speaking, belong not to the subject but to the person.

The lived body then is not distinguished from me, nor is it explicitly affirmed as 'I'. I am both a person and a transcendental ego. This 'both...and' is not a conjunction, but an alternation which also contains an essential possibility. As a person, I am in the world, involved in time and history. As a transcendental ego, I am supramundane, reflecting on the world, time and history. I, as a philosopher, happen to be both. My philosophical activity moves, alternatively, on both levels. Hence the apparently paradoxical nature and also the pathos of responsible and honest philosophising.

10

God and Morality: A Conceptual Exploration

RAJENDRA PRASAD

I do not intend to discuss the omnibus question of the relationship between religion and morality, but the much more limited one of the relationship between the concept of God and that of morality. Though the two have sometimes been considered non-distinguishable from each other, they are different questions, since all religions do not accept the reality of God, and even in the context of a theistic religion the former is much larger than the latter. Nor do I want to discuss whether or not we can speak of God as capable of leading a moral life, of doing something that can be morally evaluated, though this is also an important philosophical question. It is not nonsense to conceive of God as totally transcendent to morality and limit morality to the human world. I do not even intend to discuss in an exhaustive or comprehensive manner all possible relationships which can be imagined to exist between the two concepts. My objective is a much humbler one: I intend to examine, from a purely philosophical, and not moral or religious, point of view, two specific types of relationships which have been claimed to exist between them. My reason for choosing them is the importance given to them in the philosophical tradition.

By 'God', in this paper, I shall mean all along the theistic God, a God who, in some sense, transcends the world of man, sustains it, and is personal, i.e., who can be responsive to man's approaches, or addressings, to Him. By 'religion' also I shall mean theistic religion. This is not to deny the existence or importance of non-theistic religions, but only to make the term suit the limited objective of this paper.

To discuss meaningfully the question I intend to tackle, it is not at all necessary that there is God, or that the discusser believes that there is God. All that is necessary for it is that there is a concept of God. That there is such a concept in our conceptual stock is too obvious a fact to be doubted or to require any argument.

I

Two propositions p and q are logically independent if it is possible to combine p with not–q and q with not–p without producing any self-contradiction or even logical oddity. 'A is a Hindu' and 'A is a teetotaller' are logically independent since it is neither self-contradictory, nor in any way logically odd, to assert either that A is a Hindu but not a teetotaller, or that A is a teetotaller but not a Hindu. p and q are logically dependent when they are not logically independent, i.e., when 'p but not–q', or 'q but not–p' (but not necessarily both) is self-contradictory or logically odd.

'p but not–q' or 'q but not–p' will be self-contradictory when p and q are synonymous, or when the meaning of either one is a part of the meaning of the other. For example, it is self-contradictory to say that A is not a widow though she has lost her husband and has not yet remarried, since 'A is a widow' means 'A has lost her husband and has not remarried after his death'. Similarly, 'x is red but not coloured' is also self-contradictory since the meaning of 'x is coloured' is a part of the meaning of 'x is red', though the two are not synonymous. What 'being coloured' means is a part of the meaning of 'being red', and not the whole of it; 'being red' means 'being coloured red', and not just 'being coloured'. This is the reason why 'x is red but not coloured' is, while 'x is coloured but not red' is not, self-contradictory. But since one of them is self-contradictory, 'x is red' and 'x is coloured' are logically dependent propositions. The earlier set of propositions, 'A is a widow' and 'A has lost her husband and not yet remarried' are also logically dependent, and since the two are synonymous, it is not possible to combine either one with the denial of the other without making the combination self-contradictory.

Logical oddity is a weaker notion than self-contradiction. 'p but not–q', or 'q but not–p', would be logically odd if, though it is not possible to establish it, by an appeal to any existing rule of language, in a definitive or conclusive way, the meaning-identity, full or even partial, between p and q, yet there is such a close semantic bond or link between the two that the combination 'p and $not-q$', or 'q and $not-p$' sounds logically discordant, or, to adapt a Russellian phrase, revolts against our robust sense of logic. A logically odd combination of two or more expressions hurts our logical (or linguistic) sensitivity, and signalises that something has gone wrong somewhere in putting them together.

The use of a self-contradictory expression breaks communication, but that of a logically odd one does not. Communication can still limp on. Rather, quite often logical oddities remain undetected and become sources of further oddities and confusions. It requires a greater analytic acumen to diagnose or give the etiology of a logical oddity than to diagnose or give the etiology of a self-contradiction. One needs a more sensitive and trained ear to detect the discordance in the sounds produced by a veena with a misplaced or loose string then one needs to detect the discordance in the sounds produced by one with a broken string. Logical oddities, therefore, provide extremely challenging materials for philosophical or logical analysis.

p and q would also be logically dependent when it is logically odd to combine 'p with $not-q$', or 'q with $not-p$'. For example, if I assent that today is Monday and then immediately add that I do not believe it, what I utter, 'Today is Monday but I do not believe it', would be a logically odd expression. So are the following: 'The picture on the wall is really good but I do not like it', 'He passed the examination though he did not appear at it', 'He stole his own pen', 'I cannot write even a single correct English sentence', etc. Some expressions conceal their logical oddities deep inside their bosoms. 'Existence is an essential attribute of God', 'Reality admits of degrees', 'Truth is God', 'Everything is illusory', 'The meaning of a word is the thing (or things) it applies to', 'Propositions are facts', 'Values reside in God', etc., can be mentioned as some respectable examples. With a little exercise one can find very interesting kinds of logical oddities in the history of philosophy, and the exercise will be as much rewarding as entertaining. To unearth the logical oddity concealed in an expression would be a real good philosophical excavation. Some such excavations have very ably been performed by some philosophers of this century.

Wittgenstein, in the *Tractatus*, defines the independence of propositions in terms of what he calls 'truth-arguments'. 'Propositions', he says, 'which have no truth-arguments in common with one another we call independent' (5.152). By 'truth-arguments' he means elementary propositions (5.01). Non-elementary propositions are the truth-functions of elementary propositions, and the latter are called the truth-arguments of the former. P and Q, and R and S will be thus logically independent, since they do not have any truth-argument in common. It is clear that this theory will apply only to a truth-functional language. Further, it also implies that any two elementary propositions will be independent since, even if we accept Wittgenstein's thesis that 'an elementary proposition is a truth-function of itself' (5.01), they will not have any truth-argument in common. The account of logical independence given in this paper, on the other hand, applies to both truth-functional and non-truth-functional languages, and also does not make by definition every two elementary propositions independent. The above observation, however, regarding Wittgenstein's position has now only a historical significance, since it does not represent his final or latest opinion.

The relation of conceptual independence (or dependence) can be analysed in terms of propositional independence (or dependence). For example, it can be said that the concepts C and D are logically independent if it is possible to conjoin p (which asserts that something is C) with the denial of q (which asserts that the something is D), and to conjoin q with not–p, without leading to any self-contradiction or logical oddity. C and D will be logically dependent when they are not logically independent, i.e., when at least one of 'X is C but not D', or 'X is D but not C' is self-consistent. For example, the concept of having been married to a person and that of living with him are logically independent, since there is no oddity in saying either that A is married to B but does not live with him, or in saying that A is not married to B but lives with him. On the other hand, the concept of being a widow and that of having been married are logically dependent concepts since it is self-contradictory to say that A is a widow but has never been married, though to say that A is married but not widowed is not. It is a logical truth that a woman can be a widow only after having first been married.

And that the death of her husband alone can make her a widow is also logically true. However greatly miserable she may become on account of the death of her lover, and however greatly relieved she may feel as a result of the death of her husband, it is only the latter, and not the former, which can bestow widowhood on her.

Two logically independent concepts may or may not be empirically related, i.e., there may or may not be an actual instance in which both are exemplified. For example, it is empirically possible to locate an *A* who is married to *B* and also lives with him, but she does not have to live with *B* in order that she may be related to him by the marriage relation, nor has she to be married to him in order to live with him. Similarly, whether or not *A* who lives with *B* is or is not also married to him can only be empirically, and not logically, determined.

What I have called the relation of logical independence or dependence among propositions or concepts has also been termed conceptual by many philosophers. There is nothing wrong in calling it conceptual, since it is a conceptual relation. I have used the term 'logical' instead of 'conceptual' only to avoid the apparent inelegance in such phrases as 'conceptually independent concepts', 'conceptually dependent concepts', etc. A conceptual relation is determined or ascertained not by means of empirical research, but by analysing the behaviour of the concepts concerned. If we can determine only by analysing the behaviour of *C*, or *D*, that it is not possible to affirm *C* of *X* and at the same time to deny *D* of it, or vice versa, in a consistent manner, then *C* and *D* will be logically dependent concepts.

II

In the case of any moral concepts, it is not obvious that there is a relation of logical dependence between it and a concept of God, or a conceptual complex involving a concept of God or of something else related to God. Attempts have been made to explicate such concepts as those of (moral) rightness, duty, goodness, etc., in terms which involve some reference to God. For example, it has been held by some that an action is right if and only if it is approved of by God. If this definition or explication is correct, or accepted, then it will be inconsistent to say of an action A that it is right but not approved of by God, and a tautology to say that it is right because it is approved of by God. But it is also obvious that, in the sense in which 'right' is ordinarily used, the former is not inconsistent, and the latter not tautologous. In fact one can maintain, without committing any inconsistency, that sometimes an action may be right though not approved of by God, or that it may not be right even if approved of by God. It is also quite sensible to consider it a genuine question whether an action is right because God approves of it, or God approves of it because it is right. All this would not be possible if 'being right' and 'being approved of by God' were logically dependent concepts.

In respect of its logic the situation will not alter if we replace 'being approved of by God' by any other concept or conceptual complex involving a reference to God, or if we replace 'being right' by any other moral concept. In fact, similar difficulties will arise when an attempt is made to explicate any moral concept in terms of a theistic concept. This point has very well been made in several recent writings and, therefore, I do not think it worthwhile to elaborate upon it.

It is because of the logical independence of moral and theistic concepts that it is not self-contradictory to say of someone that he leads a good moral life but does not believe that there is any God, or that he is a believer but has committed a moral sin. It is not nonsense to say of a theist that his moral evaluations are perverted, or that he has failed to fulfil his moral obligations, or that he does not always choose to do what is morally right. Examples are not lacking of such cases in which atheists have been admired for their moral excellence and theists accused of immorality. Rather, it is not difficult to find an example of what is considered to be an immoral action but has been done with a theistic motive, e.g., sacrificing one's son to please one's deity. The motive to please one's deity is, from the theistic point of view, a noble one, but the act of killing one's son, from the moral point of view, is an abominable sin.

It is true, however, that a reference to the concept of God is very often made in discussions about morality. Sometimes it is made with a view to procure a justification for morality, and sometimes to procure a motivation for it. In the former case it is claimed that the final or conclusive justification of the morality of an action, or that of the entire system of morality, i.e., the justification of moral life itself, cannot be had unless a reference to a theistic concept is made. In the latter case it is claimed that without such a reference the motivation for doing a moral action or leading a moral life cannot be adequately accounted for. It is the examination of the claims about these two relationships which, as stated on page 186, is the main objective of this paper. I shall first take up the claim about justification and then that about motivation.

III

When the morality of an action which has been done, or which is being proposed to be done, is not obvious, or is questioned, there arises a need for seeking or offering a justification for it. An attempt to justify the morality of an action consists in offering a set of reasons which would be considered conclusive if accepting them and questioning or doubting its morality becomes inconsistent or logically odd.

We quite often feel the need for justifying, or questioning the justification offered for, the morality of a certain action, and we do offer reasons, sometimes good, sometimes bad, in the defence of our claim that it is or is not morally right or obligatory. Almost everybody knows how to play this game. But some philosophers claim that the question of justification can also be raised on a much deeper or profounder level; i.e., it can be raised with regard to the entire system of morality as well. One may seek a justification not only for the morality of this or that particular action, but also for the entire system of morality. One may ask 'Why should I be moral?' in the sense of seeking justification for just leading a moral life.

We justify the morality of a particular action by appealing sometimes to a principle, sometimes to its actual or expected consequences, and sometimes even to an exemplar. For example, if someone turns his wife out of his house, he may, in order to justify what he has done, appeal to the principle 'Conjugal disloyalty ought not to be tolerated', in case he has turned her out on the ground that she has been disloyal to him, or to what he believes to be the felicific consequences to her of his turning her out. He may say that his action is going to make her more chaste and pure in character. Or, he may refer to the example of a similar action done by a mythical or historical person who is regarded as an exemplar of morality. In this particular case, he may claim to justify his action by reminding the questioner that Rama, who is accepted by many Hindus as an ideal person, a *puruṣottama*, also exiled his wife for a number of years. I am not saying that the principle, the set of consequences, or the example, referred to above, really justifies the action; I simply want to point out that these are the three important modes in which we in fact try to justify the morality of an action when required to. I am not also suggesting that they are three independent or irreducible modes, but the question of their inter-relationship cannot be taken up in this paper.

There is a very important difference between the attempt to justify the morality of a particular action, and that to justify the entire system of morality. When one does the former, one remains well within the boundary of the moral system; one accepts the morality of some principle, the moral value of a set of consequences, or someone as an exemplar of morality. But when one does the latter, the entire system of morality is made suspect. Now, in order to discuss its justifiability, one has to transcend the world of morality, just as one must transcend, must stand outside, the physical world if one wants to lift it up or to topple it.

Reference to the concept of God has been considered necessary in order to justify the morality of particular actions as well as to justify the entire system of morality. In fact, some theologians or theologically-minded people claim that justification, on either level, would not be final or conclusive unless such a reference is made. The logic of both the attempts, however, is the same. A particular action is moral, for example, the claim goes, because it is approved of or commanded by God, is going to please Him, etc., etc. Similarly, one may claim that we should lead a moral life because God wants us, or commands us, to lead a moral life, and so on.

When an attempt is made to justify the morality of an action on, for example, the ground that the doing of it is approved of by God, 'What God approves of ought to be done (or is at least right)' figures as an important premise in the chain of reasoning. But in any concrete case it can be effectively used as a premise only if it is empirically possible to ascertain whether or not the doing of the action in question meets with God's approval. It is needless to mention that this is (almost) an impossible task to perform. But even if this fact is ignored, and it is conceded that it is possible to ascertain God's approval, the argument using 'What God approves of...' as an ultimate premise can provide a conclusive or final justification only if 'What God approves of ...' is not itself in need of justification. But this is not the case. One can very reasonably ask for its justification. It is not obvious that what God approves of ought to be done, and it is at least as much in need of justification as any other moral judgement or principle could be.

It is true, however, that in almost all theological literature 'God' is quite often used as a moral term with the result that what God approves of becomes morally right or obligatory in a definitional sense. That is, it is taken to be a part of the meaning of 'God', that what God approves of ought to be done. If this be admitted, then 'What God approves of...' definitely would not stand in need of any justification. In fact it cannot be questioned as long as the moral sense of 'God' is not questioned. But such a move to render it unquestionable makes it a tautology, and therefore trivial. This means that it cannot function as a premise in a justificatory argument. A tautology cannot be used as a reason to justify the morality or otherwise of any action.

A theologian, to get out of this inconvenient situation, may try to retain the non-definitional character of 'What God approves of ...' and still urge that the question of its justifiability must not be raised on the ground that we have to stop somewhere in our search for justification. We have to accept some premise as unquestionable, otherwise we shall land in an infinite regress. All this is true since ethical reasoning to be effective, like any other reasoning, must stop somewhere. But then we can very well stop even with some non-theological premise as the last premise. In fact, other premises may be more obvious than premises involving a reference to God. There seems to be no special reason for the search for ethical justification to end only with a theological premise.

The attempt to justify the entire system of morality in terms of some reference to God is more ambitious. All the objections raised above against the corresponding attempt to justify the morality of a particular action apply unabatedly to it as well, and, in addition, it suffers from another very serious defect. To justify the morality of a particular action is to exhibit that it is right or obligatory to do it. Similarly, to justify the entire system of morality would amount to exhibiting the obligatoriness of just leading a moral life. But this would not mean justifying the entire system of morality, since it has to be in terms of the concept of obligation which is a part of the same moral system. One may try to get rid of this difficulty by attempting to justify the system of morality in terms of something which is not morally obligatory. But this would not really amount to justifying it. In fact, the very attempt to justify the entire sytem of morality is illegitimate. If one tries to justify it in terms of the concept of obligation, it would, if successful, amount to justifying the rest of the system in terms of a part of it (i.e., the concept of obligation) and therefore not to justifying the entire system. And, if one transcends the system of morality and tries to justify it in terms of something non-moral, an equally valid question about the justifiability of the latter can be raised. Therefore, the question 'Why should I lead a moral life?' cannot be asked if it is asked as a question seeking justification for the entire system of morality.[1]

What has been said above is true of all attempts to justify the entire system of morality, including the attempt to justify it in terms of the concept of God. For example, if it is said that I should be moral because God wants me to be moral, I can very well ask why should I do what God wants me to do. If doing what God wants me to do is said to be morally obligatory, then doing it is a part of being moral and hence it cannot be used as a reason for being moral. On the other hand, if it is not itself morally obligatory, it cannot be a reason for the obligatoriness of anything whatsoever, not to speak of being a reason for being moral.

Rashdall tries to link morality with God via its objectivity or absoluteness. Moral obligation, he says, is objective or absolute in the sense that its obligatoriness is independent of man's ideas and desires. If something is obligatory, it is obligatory irrespective of what people think of it, or of the desires they entertain about it. The reason for this, according to him, is the existence of the moral ideal in God. 'The belief in God... is the logical presupposition of an "objective" or absolute morality. A moral idea can exist nowhere and nohow but in a mind, an absolute moral ideal can exist only in a Mind from which all Reality is derived. Our moral ideal can only claim objective validity in so far as it can rationally be regarded as the revelation of a moral ideal eternally existing in the mind of God.'[2]

Rashdall has used this conception of the link between the absoluteness of morality and God as an argument for the belief in the existence of God. But one can also read in it an attempt to account for the absoluteness of morality. There is absoluteness in morality, according to him, because the moral ideal exists in God. If this is true, then a reference to the concept of God becomes necessary to at least explain or account for its absoluteness. But such an attempt at explanation is not unrelated to an attempt at justification. In Rashdall's scheme, I should do what is moral no matter whether it is in conflict or conformity with my thoughts and desires. This is what the absoluteness of morality means. But the reason for its absoluteness, i.e., the reason for my being unconditionally obligated to lead a moral life, is the fact that the moral ideal exists in God. Thus, one can interpret Rashdall's above argument for God's existence also as an implicit attempt at justifying the entire system of morality or the obligatoriness of moral obligation. Then, if Rashdall's reasoning is right, there is a sense in which a justification can be given for leading a moral life.

But Rashdall's argument is in no way less vulnerable than any other attempt at linking morality with God. First, it is not clear what is meant by saying that the moral ideal exists in God. Rashdall seems to be identifying the moral ideal with an empirical object— thereby committing a category mistake—since only then can the question of the former's existence arise. Second, it is also not at all clear what it means to regard the absoluteness of morality as the revelation of a moral ideal existent in God. Third, even if this difficulty is ignored, and it is admitted that the former can in some sense be derived from the fact that the moral ideal exists in God, this derivation, though it may bestow in some way absolutness on morality, will *ipso facto* convert morality into a matter of fact. This will amount to depriving it of its obligatoriness, or at least to making it questionable, since one can very well

question the obligatoriness of a moral rule even when granting that
its source lies in a (or the) moral ideal existing in God. 'Why
should I do what has its source in God?' is neither a trivial nor a
meaningless question. All this shows that Rashdall's argument,
when constructed as an attempt to justify morality, suffers from
the same logical difficulty from which other similar attempts
suffer.

A certain moral principle might have arisen in a theistic context, i.e., theism might have provided an occasion for its enuncia-
tion. But this would not imply that the reason for its being obligatory is also theistic; it may not owe its justification to anything
theistic. For example, the theistic belief that God is present in
every form of life might inspire one to enunciate as a moral rule
the principle of non-violence (*ahismsā*), i.e., the principle that 'one
ought not to do any injury to any living being'. But this would not
mean that the principle follows from theistic belief, nor that
it cannot be justified except in terms of the latter. It may be justi-
fiable on its own merit or on account of some non-theological
reason. It is not merely a matter of historical significance that
atheistic Jainas consider the principle of non-violence unexception-
able while theistic Śāktas consider certain types of killing sacred.

It may happen that a person identifies moral life with religious
life. He may say that moral life is worth living since it is also
religious life. But this move does not amount to answering why
one should lead a moral life, since a similar question 'Why should
I lead a religious life?' can now be asked. Moreover, the identity
of moral life with religious life is not at all obvious. It is not
illegitimate or meaningless to ask why one should consider reciting the names of God, religious meditation, or even being in the
company of God, a morally desirable or commendable thing.
Each one of the above is considered as carrying a lot of religious merit, but even if it is admitted that it does, it is not *ipso
facto* established that it also carries some moral merit.

To sum up, an attempt to justify the morality of a particular
action, or even the entire system of morality, in terms of God can
assume either of the following two forms. (1) It may claim that God
is the sanctioner of morality. The action A is morally right, or
the life L is morally worth living, because it has been sanctioned
by God. Or, (2) it may claim that God or something Godly is
the end or goal of morality. The action A is morally right, or the

life L morally worth living because it is a means, for example, to God-realisation. Both of these moves suffer from the same defect, since it is as legitimate to ask why I should do what God has sanctioned, as to ask why I should try to obtain God-realisation.

IV

The question of motivation can also be raised with regard to particular moral actions as well as with regard to the entire system of morality, and in both cases its logic is the same. In the motivational sense, one can ask 'Why should I pay back the money I borrowed from A?' as well as 'Why should I do anything moral?' Both these questions can be answered by providing an adequate motive. For example, 'You should pay back the money you borrowed, since doing so will establish your credibility with A' may be an appropriate answer to the first question, and 'You should do what is moral, since only then can you help to keep the society intact' an appropriate answer to the second. Similarly, one can say 'You should do what is moral (or this particular moral action), since doing so will please God'. There is no doubt that sometimes such theistic motives do work, or that the motives which work behind some moral actions of some people are theistic. But if it is claimed that theism alone can provide a satisfactory motivation for morality, the claim cannot be sustained.

Such a claim can assume two forms. (1) It may mean that, as a matter of empirical fact, whenever a moral action is done, or a person leads a moral life, the motive or motives behind it are invariably theistic. In this form the claim is obviously false because there is no dearth of examples of atheists leading morally commendable lives. Or, (2) it may mean that whenever there is a theistic motive, it always leads to some action or actions which are moral. This also has to be taken as an empirical proposition and not as a definition, otherwise it will be analytic and consequently trivial. Therefore, if it is true, it will be only contingently true; it would not be necessary that a theistic motive always leads to a moral action. For example, one who wants to please God (and therefore has a good theistic motive) may do something morally condemnable if one believes that by doing the latter one will be pleasing Him. Nay, a theist may feel encouraged to do what even he considers morally wrong and socially punishable hoping that by doing something else (reciting His names, performing a ritual, erecting a temple, etc.) he will procure His protection against social or governmental agencies. It is not difficult to find statements from religious scriptures to the effect that God forgives and protects even the meanest criminal who completely surrenders himself to Him, or even to the effect that however serious one's sins may be, one is saved by God if one reads a certain religious book, performs certain religious practices, etc. Therefore, a theistic motive may even lead to immorality.

Sometimes it is said that if one believes that a certain moral principle is a prescription or command issued by God, one will be more strongly motivated to act according to it than if one entertains a different belief about its source. This again is a claim which can be considered valid only if substantiated by adequate empirical evidence. It is not a valid claim *prima facie* and counter examples can very easily be produced. The above belief will work only if one wants to please God, and to please Him more than to please anyone else. But it would be very unrealistic to believe that all theists always want to please God more than they want to please anyone else. Such a desire may exist in some, but it would not be difficult to find others who feel more strongly motivated to obey the command of their boss or beloved than to obey what they consider to be a command of their God. It is not empirically true that a theistic motive is always more potent or successful than all other human motives for action. It can, therefore, be safely asserted that a theistic motive can be considered to be neither a necessary nor a sufficient condition, nor stronger or better, than every non-theistic motive, for doing a moral action, or for leading a moral life.

V

The conclusion of this paper can be stated briefly as follows: The concept of God and that of morality are logically independent concepts. It is neither necessary nor helpful to refer to the concept of God for formulating either an adequate theory of ethical justification or an adequate theory of ethical motivation.

Notes

1. Rajendra Prasad, 'The Concept of Moksa', *Philosophy, and Pheno-menological Research,* Vol. XXXI, No. 3, March 1971, pp. 381-93.
2. Hastings Rashdall, *The Theory of Good and Evil,* Vol. II (Oxford: Clarendon Press, 1924), p. 212.

11

Is Comparative Philosophy Possible

N. S. S. RAMAN

Although as everyone knows the Indian philosophical tradition is over three thousand years old, academic philosophy in our country, i.e., philosophy as is practised and taught in Indian universities, is just one hundred years old. Modern Indian universities are modelled on the European pattern, and philosophical activity in this country is also fashioned on familiar Western lines. The Indian student of philosophy is mostly familiar with English philosophical terminology, and perhaps even thinks in that language. The independence of the country has not made any difference so far to this tendency, except that Indians may in general be said to have become more conscious of the heritage of their land, and attempts are indeed being made to switch over to the Indian languages as media of instruction. A new philosophical terminology is being evolved, and, in most cases, Sanskrit is being used as the source.

Perhaps it is too early to say whether attempts are being made to re-orient our philosophical thinking. The influence of the West—particularly of the English-speaking countries—is too strong to be ignored. Many have taken to British ways of thinking. The influence of the European 'schools' of philosophy, like phenomenology and philosophy of existence, has not yet been fully felt. But with the shortening of physical distances, and with greater cultural contacts between East and West, the Indian student will no doubt show his awareness of these trends among many others. As India has tolerated many religions on its soil, it can also 'let many flowers bloom' in the field of philosophy. It is also too early to say whether inter-cultural understanding will contribute towards the development of a global, secular philosophy. It is this problem that will engage my attention in the succeeding pages. Inter-cultural philosophical understanding is indeed a fundamental problem for us, as we are attempting to build a new civilisation on the foundation of the old. India has always been a meeting ground for many religions, many cultures, many philosophical doctrines. She should also prove to be an ideal cultural region where studies in comparative philosophy may be pursued.

During the last four or five decades, what has been called comparative philosophy has come into prominence in certain philosophical circles in this country. The term in its loose connotation refers to comparing philosophical ideas in two or more different cultures with one another, with a view to bringing about a mutual understanding of peoples and their cultures. In a more strict sense, it involves a serious comparison of fundamental ideas, statements and whole systems with one another. Such comparisons (or for that matter, contrasts) may not be restricted to those of different cultures, but may be undertaken in respect of any two systems or individual thinkers belonging to the same cultural milieu. In the study of whole systems side by side, many of the intricacies of such systems may become understood in a better way. Thus, comparative philosophy has a purpose (or rather, may have a purpose) somewhat different from comparative religion, in so far as its aim is not merely to bring about a mutual understanding and achieve some kind of emotional bond; its aim can be purely academic in so far as it might result in the clarification of ideas. Comparative philosophy, as it has been pursued in this country, takes one of the following forms:

(1) Studies of alternate beliefs of man in various ages of human history. When Whitehead made the extravagant remark that the whole of the Western tradition is a footnote to Plato's teaching, he was attempting to interpret the ideas of various European thinkers through the same forms and content of thought which Plato had put forth.[1] A chronological history of a system or systems of thought (e.g., an account of the development of Kantian and neo-Kantian idealism in Germany, of the Vedānta in India, of empiricism in Britain) cannot however be classified under comparative philosophy, but a comparison within the history of a system would come under that head. For instance, a comparison of St. Augustine with Plato, and St. Thomas Aquinas with Aristotle may be a form of comparative philosophy. Again, the attempt

of the Marxists to interpret the whole history of philosophical ideas as progressively leading to dialectical materialism cannot be called comparative philosophy.

(2) One may take up just one mode of thinking (as Ewing does in his *Idealist Tradition*) and attempt to understand the various forms or types of such thinking. One may talk of 'Italian idealism', 'German idealism', British idealism', 'Indian idealism, etc. Here systems of thought have a direct reference to their cultural context, but still show a marked similarity with other systems in other cultural contexts. Such studies may be undertaken not only for mutual understanding of cultures, but may be made for their own sake for purely academic purposes. One of the leading contemporary comparative philosophers comments thus on this tendency:

There is real need now, however difficult and ambitious the task, to present both Eastern and Western philosophies together, not merely a few of their outstanding rounded-out systems but the traditions in their development and in their connections with life. This has to be done first, not as a fully detailed account, but as movements, trends, currents—which sometimes flowed parallel to each other, sometimes crossed each other, combining and separating, but always reflecting the widening and deepening outlook and ideals of life. One thus gets a bird's eye or aerial view, an overall picture, of the traditions as totalities, and can understand the peculiarities of their interests, standpoints and achievements.[2]

The above point of view is amplified in a more precise statement:

What is the subject-matter of comparative philosophy? 'The scope of comparative philosophy', says Masson-Oursel, 'is universal history and cosmos'.... And he declares that true philosophy is comparative philosophy. There is truth in this view. Philosophy has to explain man and his universe; the nature of man is expressed in history, and so the scope of philosophy is universal history and cosmos. Man has expressed himself in several ways in the different races and cultures and a true and comprehensive philosophy will be one based on a comparative estimate of the many ways of his expression. The scope of comparative philosophy is as wide as the universe.[3]

The declared aim of such writers as the above appears to be to effect some kind of close 'understanding' between if not 'synthesis' of various schools of philosophy in the world. It can certainly cement friendships between peoples or at least unite philosophers in an emotional bond. Philosophers from various parts of the world do exchange ideas in international journals, and even meet one another in international gatherings, and one has nothing at all against such an approach. They are as much necessary for philosophy as they are for physics, for instance. But the comparison between the two disciplines should stop there, because the disagreement between two physicists is not of the same order as the disagreement between two philosophers. While the physical sciences (which are classed among the so-called positive sciences) have a unified and universalised language, much of our philosophy is still culture-bound. And perhaps comparative philosophy has to assume this, otherwise there would be no point in trying to achieve 'mutual understanding'. The day is not near when we can talk of a culture-free, objective philosophical science, free from individual opinions, attitudes and outlooks. And for one who would attempt to reduce philosophy to a rigorous science (e.g., a positivist or a phenomenologist), there would be no need for comparative philosophy, as the differences in outlook and attitudes would all be smoothened out and a common realm of an ideal and unified language would make 'mutual understanding' wholly redundant. The responses to an objective reality would under such circumstances cease to be subjective.

But there is a dilemma here, for those who seek to make comparative philosophy itself into a rigorous discipline. If philosophy defies being reduced to a rigorous and universal science, then comparative philosophy too, being a part of the general philosophical discipline, will suffer the same fate. If, on the other hand, a rigorous science called philosophy is possible, then comparative philosophy would become redundant, as philosophy would become universalised.

Comparative philosophy has a secondary role, when the method of comparing or contrasting one idea or view in one culture with another in a different culture is done purely with a view to help to clarify certain issues in a philosophical system. Thus Europeans, more particularly English-speaking philosophers, would perhaps understand and appreciate in a more illuminating manner, the Buddhist theory doubting the reality of the self if one were to make it more intelligible by comparing it with a similar view in British philosophy: the view of David Hume regarding personal identity. Radhakrishnan, more than any other writer, is responsible for introducing this comparative approach in the interpretation of philosophical problems. His aim was to introduce Indian thought to the European public, and he employed English terminology to express some of the subtleties of Indian thought. He never deviated from his main purpose of interpreting Indian philosophy. A comparison of ideas was only a secondary purpose for him—at least in his book *Indian Philosophy*. In later works, however (e.g., in his *Eastern Religions and Western Thought*), he used the comparative method more thoroughly. Of course, Radhakrishnan, though a pioneer, was not the first to employ the comparative method. Paul Deussen had, in the nineteenth century, tried to interpret Vedānta in Kantian terms, and did make some headway in clarifying the complicated Vedānta philosophy to German students. Like Deussen, other European Indologists have also used a typically Western terminology to interpret various facets of Indian thought to the Western reader.

Other Indian writers (notably P.T. Raju) have followed in Radhakrishnan's footsteps. Raju's comparative method is even more rigorous than Radhakrishnan's. In his *Thought and Reality—Hegelianism and Advaita*, Raju compares the two idealistic systems on a logical level. In his *Idealistic Thought of India* this method of conceptual comparison is very admirably undertaken. Owing largely to such pioneers as Radhakrishnan and Raju, Western terminology is now used to interpret Indian thought. English language in this respect has had an important role to play; it would not therefore be wrong to say that, in spite of a rich philosophical heritage, Indian philosophers think in English as Sanskrit and Pali terminology does appear to be somewhat strange. With the increasing neglect of the study of Sanskrit, the Indian mind is becoming alien to its own tradition. In most Indian universities today, Indain philosophy is taught through the medium of English. It sounds as ludicrous as a contemporary Greek student of philosophy studying the works of Plato through Arabic or Persian! But there is a difference—the English language is well-suited to express contemporary modes of thinking because of its rich vocabulary. And it is a living language. Many leading thinkers of modern India—Radhakrishnan, K. C. Bhattacharya, Sri Aurobindo; and religious leaders—Swami Vivekananda and Tilak; and political thinkers—Gandhi and Nehru wrote in English. The immediate result of such preoccupation with the English language and English ways of thinking was the interest in English philosophy and, through English, in European philosophy. Thus Kant and Hegel are discussed in English in philosophical circles in India today. And comparative philosophy has come into prominence because of this reason, more in India than in any other country.

(3) Comparative philosophy as a method of conceptual analysis seems to involve us in a more serious venture. It has been pointed out that the confusions in philosophy are traceable to the wrong use of language. If we extend this remark to comparative philosophy, then we realise how difficult it is to compare two philosophical systems expressed in two different languages. The difficulty is twofold: (a) What goes under the name of 'comparative philosophy' is mostly comparative metaphysics, and if metaphysical statements are 'senseless' in the Wittgensteinian sense, then it follows that the comparative philosopher is engaged in the absurd task of comparing two senseless metaphysical systems. However, in spite of this implication, comparative philosophy does make sense, if the total sense of a system (e.g., Hegelianism) is compared with that of another system in another language (e.g., Advaita), although each single assertion in each of such systems may not make sense. But in a context where the possibility of metaphysics or its meaningfulness is denied, the value of a comparative study of the metaphysical systems of various cultures would indeed appear to us to be a futile endeavour, except when the objectives are purely historical; and, in general, it is not uncommon in India to confuse problems of the history of philosophy with the philosophical problems of the contemporary age. Or do we seriously believe that problems of philosophy are really perennial? In any case, philosophy in India (with the exception of early Buddhism) has always been divorced from the actual historical situation in which man finds himself; the emphasis has always been on a retreat from a situation than on an encounter with it. (b) The

question whether it would be possible to translate statements of one philosopher belonging to one culture, and expressing his notions in one linguistic system, into another system of language would of course side-step the first difficulty expressed above. Translatability may be one of the criteria of intelligibility; nevertheless, apart from the difficulty of finding the right equivalents of certain philosophical terms, there are other linguistic problems which pose a formidable obstacle in the way of the translator. For instance, the grammatical structures of different languages are not uniform, even if two languages fall into the same group or are otherwise near to one another. The aim of positivism is to make language as exact as possible, and the need to evolve such an exact language (even if it amounts to inventing an artificial language) is based on the desire to make terms exact and precise. But can one think in such 'artificial' languages if not trained from childhood to do so?

The aim to evolve an ideal language is perhaps too difficult to realise. Besides, it is based on a misconception of the structure of our languages. In one of their recent essays, Fodor and Katz remark:

> The situation in philosophy of language to-day is reminiscent of that in psychology near the end of the last century. In the latter case apriority led to sterility and conceptual confusion until the empirical constraints upon psychological theory were made explicit. In succeeding years, philosophical psychology came to take its proper role, viz., the analysis of concepts, theories and methodology of scientific psychology....What is needed is a theory of language developed on the basis of empirical methods. Given such a theory, the philosophy of language comes to take its proper role as the analysis of the concepts and methodology of that theory.[4]

In other words, the logical positivist is trying to evolve an ideal language without regard to the structure of 'natural' languages. On the other hand, the so-called ordinary language philosophers are naive in so far as they lack the necessary intellectual background of a sound linguistic theory. Recent contributions to the theories of grammar and to linguistics in general have brought out the inadequacies of both positivism and ordinary language philosophy. Positivists make the mistake of thinking that a natural language is similar or parallel to a logistic system and advocate that natural languages could be understood with the help of logistic systems. Ordinary language theorists accept the shortcomings of a logistic system in so far as the latter fails to express the variety and richness of a natural language, and so they attempt to study language by referring to each word and expression in a social context. The aim of both types of thinking is to achieve exactitude and to eliminate vagueness. But both fail to achieve the purpose.[5]

Philosophers (which also includes the class of comparative philosophers), in their anxiety to analyse concepts and meanings, fail to realise that 'language sets traps' for them to fall into. The philosopher therefore should not ignore the recent developments in linguistic theory, which have undertaken an exhaustive enquiry into the structure of languages. Such a scientific study of languages has served to expose not only the weaknesses of positivism and ordinary language philosophy which Indians try to imitate and apply to concepts of Indian philosophy, but also the flimsy foundations of comparative philosophy. There is need for philosophical enquiry to be more rigorous than it has been in the past few decades. Mere enquiry into meanings of terms and their relations is not enough. It is necessary to probe into the structure of languages in order to understand the structure of thought itself. Indeed, it has been aptly remarked that:

Structural linguistics might be of real importance to philosophy. And of course, if and when semantics is developed and integrated into structural linguistics along with grammer, the differences between the two sorts of enquiry in methods and status of conclusions, though not in ultimate aim, may well be reduced to the vanishing point.[6]

The comparative philosopher does not consider the linguistic problem inherent in the comparison of concepts or statements. If comparative philosophy is not to be reduced to platitudes and trite polemics, then we should properly investigate the problem of translation of philosohical texts from one language into the other—particularly when the two languages belong to different cultures or epochs.[7] This would involve a serious investigation into comparative structural linguistics and semantics. Then many of the weaknesses and shortcomings of comparative philosophy may come to light. Such a study, then, is not merely reduced to that of a use of terms, but extends into a more significant study of whether the structure of a language has a bearing on the expression of thoughts. For instance, the ideas and archetypes of religion in various parts of the world cannot be separated from the sacred texts, the myths and lore of religions. Just as such a systematic study of texts, etc., suggests a strict methodology to be evolved, similarly for comparative philosophy too, a rigorous methodological procedure has to be developed, in order that it may become more serious than what it is today. It is only then that translation from one 'natural language' to another might become easier. Even within a linguistic structure, there can be several forms, styles and orders of expression, which may defy transformation into simpler modes. This is particularly so, when we are dealing with ancient philosophy and its texts (like those of pre-Socratic philosophy, the Upaniṣads, the texts of early Buddhism, etc.). What the comparative philosopher should be interested in is a comparative interpretation of texts (which includes philosophical translation of texts), for which strict methodological procedures have to be laid down. Unfortunately, very few of the comparative philosophers (and a list of such thinkers would include Raju) have devoted much attention to this methodological problem. And for a serious and rigorous pursuit of comparative philosophy, such serious attention is indispensable.[8]

Neither positivism nor ordinary language philosophy is capable of putting forth a convincing procedure of philosophical interpretation. The history of philosophy, in the sense of an account of the various metaphysical or ethical systems of the past, has no meaning for them. The metaphysical constructs of both the philosophers of the West and of the East are, for them, unverifiable. For a country with a rich metaphysical tradition, this kind of analytical philosophy is rather out of place; what is even more surprising is the meeting on a common platform of both the positivist and the traditionally-oriented Indian philosopher. The latter practises comparative philosophy by attempting to fit in arbitrarily propositions of one system into another and forcing a conclusion which may be entirely unwarranted. Thus comparative philosophy becomes for him not only synthetic but also syncretic. Many Advaitins, for instance, assert that all points of view lead to Advaita. The linguistic analyst in India, on the other hand, does not want to ignore the past. He practises a different kind of comparative philosophy, by trying to analyse what he believes to be the characteristic statements of traditional Indian philosophy.

All this would not happen if proper criteria and purposes of such study had been laid down. Given such a rigorous procedure, there is no reason why comparative philosophy should not lead to fruitful results. This can also be said of comparative religion.

But if the future of Indian philosophy means anything to contemporary Indian thinkers, they should stop borrowing or echoing tendencies from the West. The analytical approach, for instance, cannot simply appreciate the power of the various types of philosophical expression in ancient Indian thought. No one but the foolish can subject the poetry of the Upaniṣads to fruitless analytical scrutiny. And in fields other than metaphysics, the emotivists would seem to imply that a comparative study of political and social beliefs would lack a sound conceptual foundation as all such beliefs would be based on 'emotive expressions'. Of course, in an ideologically-oriented world much of the so-called 'mutual understanding' has become very difficult indeed, not because of the failure of a meaningful comparative approach but because of the total lack of it.

For an Indian philosopher, who is used to many languages in his own native land, an inadequate orientation in linguistics is somewhat inexcusable. A study of classical languages has fallen into disuse. Sanskrit would undoubtedly have given him that necessary background to some of the philosophical problems. No philosopher in the world is so linguistically ill-equipped as the contemporary Indian philosopher; perhaps the political exigencies of the day delude one into thinking that a classical language is a remnant of a feudal age. Linguistic analysis imported from England adds to the ignorance. A noted English thinker criticises the English philosopher of today thus:

...philosophers given to talking about correct English seem to take little account of the existence of other languages whose structure and idiom are very different from English...but which seem equally if not more capable of engendering metaphysical confusion. Being, like their colleagues, concerned with conceptual matters, their protests against the misuse of English are not primarily motivated by a concern for correct *English* as opposed to a faultless Eskimo. The existence of other natural languages, whose structure, idiom and vocabulary are not completely congruent with those of our own, is philosophically relevant.[9]

It is further pointed out that the other natural languages are relevant in so far as they make us acquainted with concepts not available in the English language, besides enabling us to understand the different motive forces involved in the choice of words in different languages, and also introducing us to radically different logical characteristics of languages other than English. All this is true, and is particularly important for the contemporary Indian thinker oriented in analytical philosophy. He should not think of the propositional form only in the English language— or for that matter in his own language. The problem is more semantic than syntactical or grammatical. Would it be possible for Vedānta Zen Buddhism or even Heidegger's philosophy to be expressed in simple English prose? There are of course limitations to attempting to explain ideas expressed in one language in another language. But philosophy can grow only in communication between man and man and between one culture of the present or the past and another. Thus, comparative philosophy as such is not objected to, but only the loose and naive manner in which it is pursued is subjected here to close scrutiny. So also the study of the philosophical problems posed by another culture (say the British) is also here admitted to be quite useful. The ambition to evolve a synthetic philosophy is, however, too unrealistic, and is comparable to the attempt to synthesise all the great religions of the world in a universal system of religious beliefs. In fact, the religions of the world may perhaps be more easily synthesised than the various philosophical systems. For example, the emotional content of religious experience, the symbolism of religious language, religious ethics, etc., could very effectively be presented as a total perspective of all religions of the world. If ancient Indian thought (as is very often pointed out) is indistinguishable from religion, then Indian religious thought could indeed be interpreted sympathetically in the light of the ideas of other religons. (Of course, this is not the same as achieving a synthesis of religions.) But one very often confuses comparative religion with comparative philosophy. A religious bias is very much noticeable in almost all Indian thinkers. The Indian tradition has accepted *śruti* as an important source of knowledge. One is fond of pointing out that Indian thought is 'spiritualistic' (though there is no corresponding term in Sanskrit or in any of the Indian languages), perhaps because of the religious bias. Even if some heterodox systems do not accept scriptural testimony, they nevertheless accept 'liberation' as a primary aim of philosophical activity; this makes them religious, even if they do not accept the authority of a scripture or even do not accept the existence of God. For instance, even in Buddhism, which in general has more of a philosophical than a religious character, *nirvāṇa* has religious overtones. In spite of all these basic differences, attempts are still being made to evolve a global or even an inter-planetary philosophy:

> For our distant heirs there is reserved a still more intriguing task than any we confront to-day. When they make contact with the philosophers of Mars and face the challenge of developing a superworld philosophy—a way of thinking that could be shared by all minds inhabiting our solar system—they will doubtless find themselves in the presence of linguistic and methodological difficulties beside which those I have discussed will pale into insignificance. And when their distant heirs in turn establish communication with rational beings beyond our solar system a yet more breath-taking opportunity will open up—to build a galactic philosophy, harmoniously synthesizing ideas and ideals which have emerged throughout the entire precinct of stellar space which we inhabit.[10]

E.A. Burtt's fantastic vision is indeed far-reaching, but if we forget the flamboyant manner in which he expresses it, he still admits the many 'linguistic and methodological difficulties' that would stand in the way of global or interplanetary understanding. So Burtt tones down his dream-like ambition to a more down to earth objective:

> It is enough for us to-day to share the more modest challenge

and thrill of meeting this problem on a planetwide scale and of discovering a philosophic language adequate to express all the logical frames and all the criteria of fact and value that sincere enquiry on the surface of our little earth might need to employ.[11]

The challenge is unacceptable, as we have already seen, owing to the irreconcilability of the logical, linguistic and grammatical structures of various languages in which philosophical ideas have been expressed. Burtt indeed seems to recognise it, but he cannot give up his otherwise very laudable aims.

The discovery of the different nature of grammatical systems in various natural languages is rightly compared in its significance in the intellectual world, to the development of the non-Euclidean geometries in the last century. A philosophical synthesis is impossible to achieve in view of this, and whatever little 'understanding' that we may have succeeded in bringing about, would be dubious, lacking in depth and clarity. In all these ventures, we have confused a historical study of philosophy with the study of the problems themselves. Advaita Vedānta in India has always believed that the whole of the tradition preceding it necessarily leads to its own philosophy. All the preceding systems of philosophy are stated to be just various inadequate forms of Advaita. Carrying the argument further, the Advaitin regards even some of the aspects of Western thought as 'inferior' to Advaita. The refusal to grant independence to other views has led to dogmatism bordering on religious bigotry. There is only a little difference between the Advaitin and the early Christian missionaries, who devoted a great amount of attention to the study of the language, literature, art and religions of India, China and Japan (it is conceded here that the results of some of these undertakings have been outstanding), and came to the inevitable conclusion that however noteworthy the achievements of the 'pagans' might be, they were still inferior to Christianity. Perhaps Indology or Sinology, as sciences, owe their origin to the work of the missionary or the colonial administrator. But the dogmatism of the Christian missionaries had its reaction in the dogmatism of the opposite side; the colonial peoples have come to recognise the greatness of their own heritage, and some fanatics seek to establish the superiority of their own culture to all other cultures in various parts of the world. In philosophical circles, this has had a very destructive effect inasmuch as it shuts off any light from outside of one's own frame of thinking. By gloating over one's past philosophical glories, one refuses to learn more or to recognise the worth of other views. This is contrary to the avowed aim of comparative philosophy to bring about mutual understanding. The followers of the various schools of Vedānta unfortunately cannot defend themselves against the charge that they are too complacent about their heritage.[12]

Moreover, thinking and living too much in the past makes one inauthentic inasmuch as one is cut off from the situational context in which one finds oneself. The world of a historian of philosophy is very much like the world of a historian. He does not live in the present, and is a stranger even to the intellectual life of present-day society. If people in India today are dissatisfied with philosophy expounded by contemporary Indian thinkers (and this is amply reflected by the poor response to philosophy in Indian universities), it is because the contemporary Indian philosopher makes himself unintelligible in the contemporary context.

It would follow from the above discussion that there is an urgent need to re-orient philosophical thinking in this country. When such a task in indeed undertaken, then there would not arise any necessity to drop comparative philosophy altogether as a form of philosophical activity. It is only emphasised here that it should follow stricter patterns of enquiry. The following programme may be drawn up for such a purpose:

(1) An extensive programme of translation of Western philosophical texts directly from the language in which they are written into Indian languages. Similarly, translation of such ancient texts of Indian philosophy, which have not so far been translated, into European languages. The translation of texts would reveal the deeper layers of thought, which would not be noticed by a mere study of texts, however serious the latter may be.

(2) A comparative study, through close conceptual analysis, of the basic ideas of East and West can be extremely useful. It is here that some of the rigorous procedures of logical and linguistic analysis can be made use of. At present we have fallen into the habit of using English terms loosely while interpreting Indian thought through that medium. For instance, we apply the words, 'rational', 'spiritual', etc., to some aspects of Indian

thought, without realising that corresponding words do not exist. In Sanskrit and other Indian languages such terms are like the German term *Geist*, which does not find its exact equivalent either in English or in Romantic languages. One can go further than a logical analyst. The application of hermeneutical aims and procedures would enable us to discover the ultimate structures of our language and thought, which provide the true basis for a study of our cultural heritage.

(3) The need to orient oneself with current problems of linguistics may also be emphasised here. For a country with fifteen major languages, each having a rich literary tradition, the study of linguistics should come as a natural tendency. As logic is rightly regarded as a necessary adjunct to philosophy, so also linguistics may find a position similar to if not the same as logic.

(4) The study of ancient problems of philosophy has no doubt an important historical relevance, but a study of such problems of traditional Indian philosophy should not be confused with the study of problems with contemporary relevance. The new situation that has evolved after centuries of historical transition and the challenges posed by scientific and technological revolution have brought forth a set of new problems, so stupendous that they could not have been visualised by an ancient system such as Vedānta. The structure of philosophical concepts is by no means rigid and arbitrarily fixed, such that it may be valid for all times and places. Social and intellectual changes bring new ideas and problems to the fore. For instance, the birth of the Copernican-Galilean-Newtonian science (to borrow a phrase from E.A. Burtt in a different context) heralded new ideas in philosophy, and gave it a new frame of reference. So also much of the contemporary trends like Marxism and philosophies of existence are directly products of the age in which we live. No philosophy, no set of ideas, no values can claim to be perennial, when frames of reference undergo constant change. Indian philosophy therefore must abandon its indifference to human history, both social and intellectual. It has to show a concern for the situational contexts. Thus it may involve replacing such situationally irrelevant concepts as *mokṣa* or *nirvāṇa* by new ones having a social relevance. The caste-ridden ancient Indian society is undergoing a transformation, even if it is a slow transformation,

and intellectual activity is no longer confined to a small group or caste.

(5) Comparative philosophy would still be a valid form of intellectual activity, provided it can be made into a more rigorous method of studying alternate beliefs in parallel or different intellectual contexts, along lines already indicated above.

But, as I said earlier, philosophy is not based on team-work like science. It is not even a body of knowledge, but an individual activity. All the same, it can become meaningful and gain recognition only if rigorous methods are followed, and if it is related to an intellectual context where it can be intelligible and communicable. If a philosopher speaks a language of his own—a private and resricted language—then his impact on his contemporaries is not felt at all. On the other hand, if he speaks a language that is too universal and commonplace, repeating the already stale forms of thought, then he may fail to attract attention.

Notes

1. On the same analogy, the Vedāntin in general might argue that the whole of the Indian tradition is based on the philosophy of the Vedas and the Upaniṣads, which he calls under the general name, *śruti*. But just as Whitehead is indifferent to many thinkers and systems that have no relation to Plato, the Vedāntins also tend to explain away differences to their own standpoint. The Vedāntins are syncretic in this respect.

2. P.T. Raju: *An Introduction to Comparative Philosophy*, Lincoln, Nebraska, 1962, p. 6. In this work, Raju indeed attempts a bird's-eye view of the three traditions—Western, Chinese and Indian.

3. Ibid., p. 283.

4. J. Fodor and J.J. Katz: 'What's Wrong with the Philosophy of Language?' *Philosophy and Linguistics* edited by Colin Lyas, London, 1971, p. 280.

5. This is so because the positivist does no justice to the structure of 'natural languages' and the ordinary language philosopher lacks the necessary orientation in linguistics. Cf. Fodor and Katz, Ibid., p. 269. 'The unsuitability of the positivist's view of natural language has led many philosophers to reject this approach, and to turn instead to a careful study of the details of a natural language. But the approach known as ordinary-language philosophy has been rightly criticised by the positivists as lacking in systematicity and theoretical orientation.' Ordinary-language philosophers are perhaps equally correct

in their criticism of positivism that the positivists' logistic system fails to capture the variety and richness of a natural language.

6. W.P. Alston: 'Philosophical Analysis and Structural Linguistics' in Colin Lyas (ed.), op. cit., pp. 295-6.

7. N. S. S. Raman: 'The Problem of Philosophical Translation', *Indian Philosophical Annual,* Madras, 1971, Vol. VII.

8. I agree with my colleague N.K. Devaraja: 'One great benefit that an honest and sincere student of comparative philosophy in any of its forms, i.e., comparative ethics, comparative religion, etc., is likely to derive will consist in the detection of, and emancipation from, the uncritical assumptions lying behind his own cultural traditions. This may lead temporarily to unsettling and bewildering his mind. However, in the long run, it should result in the enrichment of his awareness of alternatives and in the sharpening of his methodological insight and critical tools. Such awareness and insights are likely to contribute to the efficiency, depth and comprehensiveness of his philosophising. 'Philosophy and Comparative Philosophy', *Philosophy East and West,* University of Hawaii, Honolulu, Vol. XVII, Nos. 1-4, p. 57.

9. A.G.N. Flew: 'Philosophy and Language', in Colin Lyas (ed.), op. cit., pp. 61-75. The passage quoted is on p. 63. Flew's essay is a review and sharply worded criticism of the trends in British philosophy since the Second World War.

10. E.A. Burtt: 'Problems in Harmonizing East and West', *Essays in East-West Philosophy,* edited by Charles A. Moore, University of Hawaii, Honolulu, 1951, pp. 122-3.

11. Ibid., p. 123.

12. The paradox of the present philosophical situation in India is that the student of philosophy is becoming increasingly divorced even from his own past owing to his inadequate linguistic orientation. Owing to faulty national policies, the Indian student is not well-equipped either in anyone of the foreign languages or even in the classical language of his country. He cannot read and understand the texts at first hand. Hence the quality of philosophical activity has regrettably suffered very much. One must wait for bold and far-reaching decisions regarding language policies at the national level.

12

Philosophy—Theory and Practice

SANTOSH SENGUPTA

The disagreement among philosophers on the nature of
philosophy is very much in evidence. What is all the more significant is the general acceptance among them of the disagreement.
The reason for this acceptance is the belief that philosophy,
unlike a simple *a priori* study or a mere empirical discipline, is
characterised by an indefiniteness or complexity in respect of
its scope and method. Philosophy, it is held, is not a field in
which one can look for plain proofs or simple solutions of problems.
Now the most important area of disagreement is the issue concerning the theoretical or practical character of philosophy. The
question is: Is philosophy a theoretical or a practical study?
There is no denying that it is in the sort of answer one gives to
this question that one's view of the nature of philosophy is
reflected. If it is said that to pose a question like this is pointless
as what we call a theoretical study admits practice and, inversely,
what is characterised as a practical discipline, presupposes theory
(i.e., there cannot be pure theory or mere practice), the obvious
answer is that the central point of the distinction between a
theoretical and a practical study is the nature of the relation
between theory and practice. We can say that while the former
considers theory as primal in relation to practice the latter
subordinates theory to practice. With this qualification of the
posture over the theoretical or the practical character of philosophy
it makes sense to make a distinction between theoretical and
practical philosophy. In this paper I shall (1) briefly illustrate
this distinction on the basis of a clear determination of the
meanings and scope of the 'theoretical' and the 'practical' and

(2) find out if philosophy is theoretical or practical in the light of independent investigations into the nature of philosophy.

There are some who characterise 'theory' and 'practice' in emotive terms. Expressions like, for instance, 'pure theory is idle or sterile', 'mere practice is blind or unenlightening', evince a con-feeling towards 'theory' and 'practice' respectively. Similarly, there are expressions which indicate a pro-feeling about the same. Naturally, the emotive meaning of the concepts in question is hardly of any interest to us. We are concerned with the descriptive or the cognitive meaning of 'theory' and 'practice'. Now, in respect of either, we can make a distinction between its loose and accepted usage. 'Theory' in its loose usage means conjecture or hypothesis. This usage does not conform to what I call the accepted meaning of the concept in question. 'Theory' in its accepted usage means a systematic statement of the principles of a field of enquiry. That is, we have a theory when there is a systematic or an organised account of what is enquired into. The systematic or organised account is in the form of elaboration of the principles underlying the nature or the function of what is studied for the obvious reason that predication-making is essential to a theory. Now, the organised or the systematised study is made with a view to yielding knowledge or understanding of the object under investigation, for its own sake. In a theoretical attitude, the subject concerned has as his sole object to discover or to find out the real, which means that he is in a receptive attitude. The meaning of this attitude is that the subject is not (as is the case in a conative attitude) aware of a distinction between what is there and what is to be attained or brought into existence. It follows that a study *qua* theoretical considers the knowledge or the discovering act as an end in itself. As contemplation is another name for the attitude of knowing for its own sake, a theoretical act is essentially contemplative. In respect of the concept of practice we can make a similar distinction between its loose and its accepted usage. 'Practice' in its loose usage means any interest in life or in what concerns life. This usage is not acceptable in view of its too wide range. It is, for instance, legitimate to say that in some cases the interest in life can be of a theoretical character, i.e., it can be directed to the understanding of what concerns life for its own sake. Practice in its accepted sense denotes action and as such it, unlike theory, naturally relates itself to the function or the operation of the will. The practical attitude *vis-à-vis* the the theoretical is one of bringing into existence what is not. What is essential is that the knowing act should be employed to effect into existence what is not there which amounts to the fulfilment of what is needed. It follows that such a fulfilment involves change in the present state of affairs. The change may naturally be in different directions, there being a correlation between the directions and the ends which need to be fulfilled. The range of the ends to be fulfilled is wide enough. It is wrong, for instance, to consider the material end as the only end and so to limit practicality to materiality. Practice, therefore, *qua* action or performance involves change. It is only natural that the upholders of practicality should defend it on the ground of dynamism which is inherent in it. The obverse of this defence is the attempted correlation of the theoretical with staticism. A practical study, therefore, is action or fulfilment-oriented. It admits knowledge but only as a means to the realisation or the fulfilment of the end sought. Inversely, a theoretical study is knowledge-centred. It requires practice or action only as a preparation for knowledge, considered as the intrinsic end or value. Thus the distinction between a theoretical and practical study represents a reversal of the means-end relationship. That is, what is a means in one is an end in the other. This relationship is different from the causal relation. That is, a theoretical study does not consider practice as the result or the offshoot of theory. Similarly, a practical discipline does not view a theory as the result of practice. There is no doubt that there are over-zealous practicalists who consider the relation between theory and practice as causal. Likewise, there are theory-centrists who consider everything other than theory as the function of theory. But the point is that the type of distinction between a theoretical and a practical study, which is relevant to the present enquiry, does not admit the causal relationship. This is particularly evident from the nature of motivation of a theoretical study or a practical discipline. The motive of what we call a theory-centred study is the acquisition of knowledge or understanding while the motivation of practice-oriented study is the attainment of an end or value that is sought. The theoretical attainment, in one case, is the intrinsic end and everything other than it is a means thereto. The practical attainment, in the other case, is the sole end and anything other than it can be admitted only as a preparation for it. Whether a study is theoretical or practical can be judged only in the light of the nature of the motive that gives rise to it. This is particularly evident from the nature of the distinction between what we call theory-centric philosophy and practice-oriented philosophy. The motivating factor behind the former is the promotion of knowledge for its own sake, while the motivation for the latter is action in the form of fulfilment of what is sought involving change in the present state of affairs. My present task is to illustrate the distinction between the two types of philosophy.

It may be stated without fear of controversy that the history of philosophy evidences the distinction between theory-centred and the practice-centred philosophy. Generally, philosophy in the West can be characterised as theoretical while philosophy in India can be called practical. I say 'generally' as there are philosophies in the West, e.g., Epicureanism, Stoicism and Marxism, which are practical. Similarly, some of heterodox Hindu systems are hardly practical. But the point is that they are only exceptions and the exceptions prove the rule. It seems to me that it is over the issue of theory and practice that we can profitably draw a distinction between Western philosophy and Indian philosophy. The attempted distinction between the two on the basis of some other issues is misleading. For instance, it is wrong to characterise Western philosophy as materialistic and Indian philosophy as spiritualistic. It is equally pointless to characterise Western philosophy as world-affirming and Indian philosophy as world-negating. In a paper entitled *On the Misrepresentation of Hinduism* which I presented at the department of Theology, University of Birmingham, recently, I tried to show that to view Hinduism in negatives is to misrepresent it. It is not wrong to say that it is on the issue theoretical *v.* practical rather than any other that Western philosophy can be contrasted with Indian philosophy.

Now to come to the essentially theoretical character of motivation to philosophy in the West. One cannot possibly determine the nature and the bias of philosophy in the West merely on the basis of the etymological meaning of the concept of philosophy. That is, it is superficial to say that philosophy is love of wisdom and, therefore, it is theoretical. It is patent that the etymological meaning of a subject does not always indicate its nature. For instance, *darśana*, the Sanskrit word for philosophy, means insight or apprehension. Now, this etymological meaning of *darśana* is contrary to the essentially practical motivation of philosophy in India. In judging if a study is theoretical or practical one needs to (1) enquire into the nature of the basic question or questions in which philosophy or philosophising originates and (2) to ascertain if one common motive is in evidence in the historical development of the philosophy in different periods. There is no doubt that the basic query which gives rise to philosophising in the West is of a theoretical character, involving as it does a demand for the attainment of knowledge of a comprehensive type. Thales, the founder of Western philosophy, sets himself to discover that which, when known, everything else can be known and this task was theoretical *par excellence*. It is legitimate to say that philosophy in the West originates in the sense of wonder as expressed in the demand for knowing fully and comprehensively.

To take up now the second criterion for determining the nature of philosophy. There is no doubt that an unambiguously theoretical motif is in evidence in the historical development of Western philosophy in all periods except the medieval one. But, significantly enough, the philosophy of the medieval period or the middle ages, has not gained recognition in the philosophical world of the West. That is, in the periods, ancient, modern and current, i.e., in those which are taken cognisance of in the West, the theoretical motif is dominant.

In the ancient period, the noted Greek philosophers were consistently moved by the desire to provide a stable and a clearly formulated system of knowledge of what is considered to be real. Socrates, as we know, had as his sole object the formulation of the cognitive basis of matters of practical interest. His thesis that virtue is knowledge is a case in point. Similarly, Plato's one principal object was to establish that only the philosophers can know and that they can be statesmen primarily because they know. If we come to the modern period we find the same urge of knowing. The rationalists of this period have as their principal aim to show that knowledge of the whole of reality can be modelled on mathematics and yield the same certitude which the latter claims and this is possible if one starts with *a priori* concepts and deduces conclusions thereon in a strict logical way. This is speculative philosophy *per excellence*. With the rise of empiricism there is a breakthrough or a new turning point. But what is significant is that with this change there is no weakening of the theoretical interest. The only change is in the direction of the restricting or the narrowing of the range of the theoretical interest to the extent that with the rise of the critical spirit the need or the demand is felt to know of less and to apprehend the conditions of knowing itself. Kant's primal philosophical enquiry—'Is *a priori* synthetic judgement or knowledge possible?'—has a pure theoretical interest. There is no doubt that Kant's principal contribution consists in the formula of the theoretical method of determining the conditions of knowing. With Hegel there is the revival of speculation. We can say that in the alternation between speculation and criticism the theoretical motif remains dominant.

In the philosophies of the current period, i.e., linguistic philosophy and existentialism, the same theoretical motivation is in evidence. In linguistic philosophy there has been a still further restriction of the range or the scope of the theoretical, the restriction being correlative to the narrowing of the scope and the function of philosophy itself. The task or the function of philosophy is limited to that of analysing statements of a certain kind, i.e., the scientific ones. The knowledge that analysis yields is essentially one of proper linguistic usage. The studies in values— aesthetic, ethical and spiritual—are admissible only as linguistic analyses of statements about values which are names for meta-aesthetics, meta-ethics, and meta-religion. The point is that a practical study like ethics is so treated that it is completely divested of its practical interest. That is why it is said that meta-ethics is not ethics at all.

Existentialism, too, is a theoretical philosophy. There are some who attribute practical motifs to existentialism on the ground of its primal concern for, or interest in, human existence. This attribution is wrong as the mere interest in that which concerns life or existence, as we have already noted, is practical only in its loose sense. Existentialism is characterised by the interest in the understanding or the knowledge of existence for its own sake, i.e., not for using it as a means to a change in existence itself. A programme of action or of effecting change in the way of existence through the fulfilment of end or ends is not known to existentialism, considered as a philosophy. For Sartre, or for that matter for a typical existentialist freedom, the highest ideal is not an ideal to be attained.

Rather, it is a fact to be encountered. It is a brute contingency that needs to be discovered or understood.

We referred to some exceptions to the theoretical tradition of Western philosophy. One exception, as we observed, is Marxism. There is no doubt that Marxism is a practice-centered philosophy and here there is a meeting point of Marxist philosophy and Indian philosophy. The two philosophies having opposed ontological commitments agree in admitting the primacy of the practical. Marx in conformity to dialectics speaks of the unity of theory and practice but in practice he admits the primacy of the latter. The basic question which moves Marx is essentially practical, viz., what needs to be done to bring about liberation? Marx throughout considers the task of pursuing knowledge for its own sake as fruitless. It is a luxury which a bourgeois can afford. Marx's classical utterance is: 'The philosophers have interpreted the world: the point now is to change it'. The liberation that is sought is material in character. It is in the nature of freedom from bondage to which the proletariats (the exploited class) are subject. In the words of Marx, 'philosophy cannot be made a reality without the abolition of the proletariats, the proletariats cannot be abolished without philosophy being a reality'. The point of Marx's exposure of Feurbach's materialism is, as we know, that it is not practice-oriented. Now, the epistemological or the ontological superstructure that Marx builds can be significant only in its directedness to the fulfilment of the task of liberation. Likewise, it is in the urge of the attainment of liberation that philosophy in India originates.

It can be stated without fear of controversy that the different systems of Indian philosophy except materialism are liberation-centered. There is, however, no denying that the practical motif of the attainment of liberation is made more explicit in some systems than in others. Now, the liberation which the Hindu philosophers seek, unlike the Marxists' goal of philosophical thinking, is not material. It has an essential spiritual content so far as it consists in self-realisation, the realisation being in the form of the fulfilment of the self's transcendent or real state, as it is in the Sāṇkhya system, or of the state of union or identity with the Infinite, as is in evidence in the other orthodox systems. Now, the liberation or the state of self-realisation is essentially practical and that for three reasons: (1) It is in the nature of bliss, (2) It has a transforming effect on the conduct or the living of the person seeking liberation or realisation. One who attains liberation in this life (*jīvan -mukti*) is really different from the one who is not a *jīvan-mukta*. (3) The discipline of the will involving ascetic and altruistic conduct is a necessary condition for the attainment of liberation. The emphasis on the release from suffering is in evidence particularly in Buddhism and the Sāṅkhya. Some object to the characterisation of philosophy in India as practical on the ground that at least two influential systems, Nyāya and Advaita Vedānta, have a predominantly theoretical interest in view of their logical and metaphysical character respectively. The obvious rejoinder to the objection is that both the systems are practice-centered in so far as they are oriented to the fulfilment of the ideal of liberation.

The practical bias of the Nyāya school is in evidence in the *Nyāya-Sūtras*. To quote from the *Sūtras*: Pain, birth, activity, fault, misapprehension—on the successive annihilation of these in the reverse order there follows the release. Release which consists in the soul's getting rid of the world is the condition of supreme felicity marked by perfect tranquility and not touched by any defilement. A person by the true knowledge of the sixteen categories is able to remove his misapprehension (*Nyāya Sūtra*, 1:2 with commentary, *Sacred Books of the Hindus*, translated by M.S.C. Vidyabhusana). Similarly, the systematically worked out metaphysics of Advaita Vedānta can be considered to have a practical character for the following reasons: (1) Brahman—the ultimate Reality which the Advaita Vedānta enquires into—is of the nature of bliss. (2) The knowledge of what liberation is, has a transforming effect on one who is liberated. (3) *Karma* or action is admitted as a necessary preparation for the attainment of the goal. To elaborate the last two reasons, Śaṅkara, the most noted exponent of Advaita Vedānta, consistently upholds that the discovery of the knowledge of the real which liberates the seeker concerned means a new way of life for him. This is evident from Śaṅkara's description of the mode of life of a *jīvan-mukta*. For a *jīvan-mukta*, for instance, the virtuous way of life is natural or spontaneous. It is, therefore, wrong to attribute a theoretical motif to the Advaita pursuit of knowledge. To come to the third reason. It is misleading to maintain that Śaṅkara does not have a place for action in his account of the mode of attainment of liberation. He maintains throughout that a rigid cultivation of the will in the form of the withdrawal from the ego or from passion prepares one for the discovery or the apprehension of the Real. There is no reason to believe that Śaṅkara is anti-action. The objection to the characterisation of Indian philosophy as practical on the ground of the indifference of the Hindus to materiality has no point as the scope or the range of practicality cannot be limited or restricted to materiality. It may be stated in this connection that the Gītā, which is the Bible of the Hindus, is action-centred.

We have given a brief exposition of two views of philosophy— one theory-centric and the other practice-oriented—the views as associated with two philosophical traditions, the Western and the Indian respectively. Marxism is one of the exceptions to the Western philosophy and in this sharing we have a meeting of the extremes. My task in the constructive part of the paper is to find out if philosophy is theoretical or practical on the basis of independent investigations into its nature. The thesis that I shall try to uphold is that philosophy is theory but the theory that philosophy is, vis-à-vis scientific theory, has what I may call, practical implications. By 'practical implications' I mean the internality of practice as a means to theory. Now, as the practice which is internal to theory is not what philosophy seeks as an end, we cannot say that philosophy is practical. In the discussion on the nature and the scope of the meaning of 'theory' and 'practice' I observed that one can judge a study as theoretical or practical in the light of its motivation. The essential motivation of philosophising is the pursuit of knowledge. The elaboration of the thesis is possible through a discussion of the nature of philosophy.

Philosophy is an autonomous discipline in so far as it has, for its subject-matter, that which cannot be fully determined, and cannot be apprehended through the epistemic method as it is in evidence in an ordinary empirical study or a pure logical discipline. That is why philosophy cannot be modelled on a completely determinate study having a definite method of answering completely well-defined questions. It is not wrong to say that the autonomy of philosophy consists in its indeterminateness and openness which, it may be observed, have their source in its (philosophy's) subject-matter. The subject-matter may be characterised as being. Philosophy is primarily ontology in so far as it seeks knowledge of

being. Being (which is plural) is beyond, which, by the nature of
the case, cannot be fully determined in an empirical and logical
way, which means that it (being) is indeterminate. The approach
to being—the beyond—can be called mystical—mystical, as we shall
observe later, in what I call its deeper meaning. Being—the beyond—is a mystery and like the latter it is both manifest and hidden.
A mystery, as we know, in its complete disclosure loses its mysterious character. This is also true of being. Heidegger, in his
characterisation of what he calls Being, refers to its irreducible
concealment. The Being, in its complete manifestation, loses its
distinctive character. My difference with Heidegger is that in my
view being—the inescapable beyond or mystery—is plural. Philosophy thus seeks knowledge of the plural beyond or mystery.
Now, the starting-point of the enquiry into the nature of being—
the beyond—is one's awareness which is indubitable. Descartes'
insight that one should not in one's philosophical enquiry start with
a posited entity but with what he cannot escape admitting is indeed valuable.

Broadly speaking, there are three different kinds of awareness:
(1) object-awareness, (2) self-awareness and, (3) value-awareness.
The phenomenological description of each type of awareness indicates its intentionality which consists in its directedness or reference
to something that is beyond the data. The point of the transcendence of the states in question is that the characteristics or the
facts about the data cannot be explained on the basis thereof.
It is only on the presupposition of something beyond the data
that we can make the characteristics or the facts in question intelligible. The referent of the data concerned, which is the source
of the characteristics thereof, is a persistent beyond and as such it
cannot be completely disclosed as any such disclosure amounts
to its reduction to the status of data with all the difficulties of the
explanation of what is given. Thus, the referent of the given discloses itself into the given, and yet it remains concealed or hidden
like a mystery. Corresponding to the data of each type of awareness, therefore, there is a mystery. Now, the thesis or the rationale
of the transcendence of the given to mystery can be explained with
reference to each of the three types of awareness.

The object-awareness, which is characterised by an impression
of externality, has for its data sense-data. Now the dual characteristics of sense-data—viz., (1) variation, and (2) uniformity—cannot be

explained on the basis of the data themselves. To take up the first, we see blood as red, milk as white, taste sugar as sweet and pickle as hot. We apprehend a sofa as soft and a stone as hard. Now the difference in sense-apprehension cannot be explained on the basis of data. It can have its source in the nature of the objects which are apprehended. That is, its objects being what they are, we have different sense-data. The other fact about sense-data, viz., uniformity, likewise cannot have its source in what is given, the sense-data. The normal subjects apprehend the same objects in a similar way under similar circumstances. It is the uniformity in sensory apprehension that makes the ordinary social communication possible. If normal subjects respond differently to the same objects we would have been in a very confused state. Now this basic fact about sensory apprehension cannot be explained on the level of sense-data, the reason being that they *qua* data are in the nature of private states, i.e., the states as experienced by this or that subject. The uniformity, therefore, has its source in what may be called the object-being which is intelligible as that what is beyond the data.

The object-being which is characterised by externality is the natural referent of the data. The being is in the nature of a mystery as it cannot be completely manifested in the data as the total disclosure of the being amounts to its reduction to the given—the data; and as the data *qua* data are not self-explicable, we face the predicament of the persistent postponement of explanation thereof. The realist's insight into the non-reducibility of an object-being into mere data is indeed sound. Phenomenalism seeks to avoid the predicament referred to through the false attribution to sense-data of certain properties which do not belong to them at all. What is characteristic of modern empiricism is that it represents a reconciliation between the realists' insight and the phenomenalists' reductionism. This reconciliation is pointless as it is only obvious, and some of the modern empiricists are realising this, that the external object, in its beingness, is something other than the data. It is in the nature of a beyond, a mystery.

The range of the external object is wide enough, extending as it does from the paper I am writing on to a distant star. There is no denying that the mystery-element varies from one external object to another. Now to come to the second type of awareness, viz., self-awareness. This awareness likewise is transcendental as

it refers to beyond itself and its data to a being which, by the
nature of the case, resists reduction to data. The data of
self-awareness are the states. The states are not self-explicable as
certain facts about the given, i.e., the self as presented, are explicable
only on the presupposition of what I call the self-being. These
facts or characteristics are identity and unity. The self as presented means, as we know, identity and unity. As the identity is not
of each of the successive states of the self but is of the self as a
whole; it implies unity. Now the two inter-related characteristics
of the self as presented or given cannot be explained on the basis
of the states which are plural and successive. We are, therefore,
referred to something which can be called the self-being which
makes the identity and the unity of self-experience possible. This
something is, by the nature of the case, that which is beyond the given—
the states. It discloses itself to the states but not totally, as any such
disclosure would mean its reduction to the states with the inherent
predicament as referred to. There are, besides identity and unity,
experiences of harmony, depth, etc., which point to the self-being
or mystery as the ground thereof. It is evident that the transcendence as involved in the self-awareness and its data, and the
mystery as correlative to the transcendence, are different from
the transcendence and the mystery as involved in object-
awareness.

The correlation between transcendence and being is evident also
in the third type of awareness, viz., value-awareness. Value-
awareness is likewise transcendental, i.e., it points to value-being, the
being which is other than the data concerned. Broadly speaking,
value-awareness is two-fold corresponding to two types of value,
ethical and aesthetic, good and beauty. Good-awareness and beauty-
awareness have correspondingly different types of data. The
former has as its datum the presentation of something as commanded or approved (the something, in this case, being action); while
the latter has as its datum the presentation of something as appreciated (the something, in this case, being an object, the range
whereof is wide enough). Now the good as being is more than the
state of being approved. One obvious fact about ethical
responses, viz., uniformity, cannot be explained on the basis of the
states in question in view of their private character. That is, there
is something about ethical value—good—which cannot exhaust
itself into the given. Similarly, beauty—the aesthetic value—is more

than the state of appreciation. The state of appreciation is not self-explanatory as the fact of uniformity about it cannot be accounted for on the basis thereof. It can have its source in beauty-being. This being cannot exhaust itself into the given. Thus, the value of either type is a beyond, a mystery. An enquiry into the nature of the different types of awareness thus leads to an insight into the nature of being-mystery. We observed that the mystery— the being—is plural, the difference between one mystery and an-other being correlative to the difference in the nature of the tran-scendence involved. The view that God, or for that matter the One alone, is the mystery involves an arbitrary delimitation of the range of mystery. In my view there is no reason to affirm being in the singular in the manner of Heidegger.

We have now an idea of the ontology which philosophy is. The ontology is, as we have seen, metaphysical in view of the correla-tion between transcendence and being and the transcendence or the beyond-character of the latter. It follows that the knowledge which philosophy seeks is such that it cannot be modelled on ordinary knowledge, *a priori* or empirical, as, unlike the former, it cannot be complete or final and, unlike the latter, it cannot be determined in a direct or simple way. What then is the nature of the knowledge which philosophy seeks?

In answer we can say that the knowledge is mystical not in its traditional usage but in what I call its deeper meaning. (I have developed my view of the deeper meaning of the mystical in my book entitled *Transcendence, Mystery and Māyā*.) The 'mystical' in its deeper significance denotes an experience of participation in being-mystery. The mystery, on the deeper view of the mystical, is not the one spiritual Being (as it is on the traditional view). It is, as we have seen, plural. The experience of the mystery, the being, is one of participation in and not of complete identity with the being encountered; what is distinctive of what I call the ex-perience of participation is its irreducible awareness of the difference with the object of experience. This awareness is inevitable in view of the persistently transcendent character of the being in question. The point is that the experience of being is dual in charac-ter, so far as it is one of participation in an awareness of difference from what is apprehended as real.

Now the knowledge through participation, i.e., the type of know-ledge which philosophy seeks, is different from the type of knowledge which science (pure science) aims at. The distinction between two types of knowledge can be best understood in the light of the difference between a problem and a mystery. We can say that philosophy and science belong to the realm of mystery and the sphere of problem respectively. A problem is that which is clearly determinate and awaiting a complete solution thereof. What is distinctive of a problem is that with its solution the immediate task of a scientist is finished and this is so because of the externalistic character of a problem. It (the problem) appears as something external to one who encounters it.

A mystery has characteristics which are opposed to those of a problem, and it is characterised by its indeterminateness. It is also such that it cannot be fully resolved. Besides, it is that in which the subject in question is involved. The demands which a problem and a mystery respectively represent, therefore, are essentially different. It is possible to consider a mystery in the light of the characteristics of a problem. But such a view of it involves its reduction or degradation to the status of a problem. A degradation of this kind is in evidence in the extension of the scientific or the externalistic attitude to the sphere of mystery to which it does not apply. The externalistic character of problem-centred scientific knowledge is equally evident in the case of the scientific treatment of, say, life and mind. The sciences of life and mind treat the phenomenon in question on the model of an external object. Now, the distinction between knowledge through participation and externalistic knowledge helps us to determine the nature of philosophy in respect of the issue concerning theory and practice. This brief discussion of the nature of philosophy clearly indicates that philosophy as ontology has as its primary function the pursuit of knowledge, and as such it is primarily theoretical. What is significant is that the knowledge in question is viewed as an end and not as a means to the fulfilment of this or that need. That is, philosophical inquiry does not seek the utilisation, material or otherwise, of the knowledge concerned.

Heidegger, in his emphasis on the theoretical character of ontology, refers to the risk of the adoption of the use-attitude to the knowledge of being. Such an adoption, in his view, involves distortion and degradation of ontology, and, for that matter, of philosophy. There is much in Heidegger's insight into the essentially theoretical character of philosophy. But the important point is (the point which Heidegger does not admit) that from the fact that one should be free from the use-attitude to the knowledge that philosophy seeks, it does not follow that the knowledge concerned cannot have practical implications. 'Practical implications', as I have already observed, denotes the internality of practice as a means to knowledge, the intrinsic end. This implication is, however, a matter of degree. For instance, it is more extended in cases of self-knowledge and value-knowledge. Now the practice viewed as internal to the type of knowledge that philosophy seeks involves a change in the mode of willing. This change is not merely appropriate, but is also essential to philosophical or metaphysical knowledge, and this is so for (1) the latter's character of participation or involvement in the object concerned, and (2) the beyond-character of the object in question. By the same token its practical demand on will as referred to is absent in scientific or externalistic knowledge.

The change in the mode of willing consists in the attainment of the states of detachment and humility which are interrelated. This practical attainment is not required of scientific knowledge. Detachment, it may be pointed out, is not a mere negative state of withdrawal from the needs to be overcome. But it is a positive state of freedom, freedom from two-fold domination—one of the way of the ego and the other of the interest of what is ordinary or commonplace. The way of ordinary existence is one of two-fold domination. Similarly, humility which is related to deteachment is a state of freedom from the claim to exclusiveness or aggressiveness which, it may be pointed out, is a reflection of the expression of the first type of domination. Now, both detachment and humility are necessary to the knowledge which is in the nature of involvement or participation in the beyond or the mystery.

The opening to being, which is beyond, is possible in the state of freedom from the way of the ego. The function of the ego, as we know, is one of narrowing or obstructing the expansion of consciousness which an insight into the beyond requires. This expansion is all the more required in the case of involvement or participation in the object concerned. It may be said that the degree of involvement (involvement is a matter of degree) is correlative to the extent of detachment or freedom from what we have called the domination of the ego. The release from the domination of 'everydayness' is not that there should be a temporary withdrawal from the total or the exclusive demand of what is ordinary or commonplace. What is required is that the attitude of withdrawal should be dispositional. Now, one who is involved in the beyond is disposed to behave in a way that what belongs to the sphere of what is commonplace or ordinary has a subordinate or secondary role. He adopts the role of being a spectator or witness to the matters of ordinary interest (Heidegger himself admits that the adoption of such an attitude constitutes what he calls 'ontological freedom'). The state of humility is likewise natural to the disposition that is essential to an opening to the mystery, i.e., we have observed that the being is such it cannot be completely known and the mystery, which the being is, cannot be fully resolved. The attitude of admission of the non-finality and the incompleteness of the knowledge of being is another name for humility.

Humility is not humiliation as it is in the recognition of the inherent limitations of human knowledge, and it is in the consequential opening to mystery that one discovers a meaning or purpsoe of existence. Now the practical demand which is implied in philosophical or metaphysical knowledge is not in evidence in scientific knowledge in view of the fact that it is externalistic. Scientific knowledge, we have noted, is externalistic in so far as it is in the nature of solutions to the problems wherein willing is involved.

I shall now show this with brief reference to the nature of self-knowledge. (I shall undertake a treatment of the nature of value-knowledge in a subsequent paper.) Self-knowledge is involvement or participation in the inner reality or the mystery, and as such it has a greater relatedness to willing than the participation in the outer or the external mystery. The involvement in the self-mystery is, as we have seen, in the transcendence of a given complex of states, the important components whereof are desires, emotions, passions, etc. Now, the transcendence of the given subcomplex of desires, emotions, passions, etc., naturally relates itself to the function of willing to the extent so far as the freedom from the absorption into the complex in question is another name for self-control. It follows that self-control is internal as a means to the insight into the mystery of the self. If it is pointed out by way of objection that it is self-knowledge which yields self-control and that, therefore, it cannot be conditioned by the latter, the obvious reply is that self-control can both be a means to, and the result of, self-knowledge. There is no contradication here as the self-control which conditions self-knowledge is not the same as the self-control which results therefrom. The point is that it is in an attitude of control of what is given that one can have an experience of the involvement in the mystery of the self. The emphasis on the connection between self-control and meditation on the nature of the self which is much in evidence in Hindu thought has its obvious point. Self-control is not at all essential to the treatment of the self on the model of an external object—the treatment that is typical of the scientific approach to the inner life of man. We have so far tried to give an exposition and a justification of the practical implications, in its general and extended form, of the nature of the knowledge that philosophy seeks *vis-à-vis* scientific knowledge by way of showing the distinction between scientific knowledge and philosophical knowledge.

It does not follow, as I have stressed, from the thesis of the practical implications of philosophical knowledge that philosophy is practical. I have tried to show that philosophy, as ontology, seeks knowledge as an end and so far it is primarily theory. But the theory that philosophy is, unlike scientific theory, is characterised by what I have called practical involvement, the involvement which is in evidence in the pursuit of knowledge as an end. It is in this pursuit that the autonomy and the distinctiveness of philosophy consist.

13

Philosophy and the Human Predicament

RAMAKANT SINARI

The Philosophical Activity

There is no inquiry more fundamental, more wholesome, and more difficult than the inquiry into man's consciousness and his experience of being in the world. In some form or the other this inquiry has occupied the minds of philosophers of all times. To a person absorbed by the rigmarole of daily life the world does not posit itself as a problem; but to a reflective mind everything concerning its experience requires an explanation, an apprehensible setting, a place in some intellectual system. Philosophy has undoubtedly originated in the encounter of consciousness with itself and with the world. It embodies man's attempt to know the nature of the universe and the meaning of his being in it.

Not merely as conducts of inquiry, but even in respect of their aim, philosophy and science are distinguishable from each other. While in the scientific study of man and the universe one concentrates on the causes and laws of various phenomena, in philosophy one is concerned with the very significance of existence, that is, the worldliness of the world *vis-à-vis* man's consciousness and being. Therefore, whereas it is possible for science to reach some sort of solution to its problems—explanations specifying why and how phenomena of different classes take place—it is impossible for philosophy to 'solve' anything. My idea of philosophy springs from this apparently negative result of the philosophical activity— an activity for which it is impossible to obtain what in the language of science we call explanations.

Philosophy is an act of inquiry without any terminus. Along this act there are indeed knowledge stages, points of 'transparence', 'discernments', 'seeings', 'certainties', but they are found to be fragmentary when considered from a comprehensive outlook or with a view to coordinating them to form the ultimate truth. No single system or discovery in philosophy is so complete that it is able to embrace answers to all questions. Just as there is incessant querying and diversely constructed and reconstructed issues in philosophy, there are in it 'illuminations' too; but none of these illuminations would be, in the ultimate analysis, apodictic to all. Those who examine any one of them from outside—that is, on the basis of a different illumination—are likely to question its validity. As a matter of fact, most of the conflicts and disputes among philosophers in the world can finally be traced to the diversity of their illuminations. One of the specific concerns of philosophy should be to account for this diversity, to make intelligible the meaning of the illuminations, to interpret their assumptive functions in various thought-systems.

The business of philosophy is to understand the fundamentals of experience: space, time, and the world as we live them; the sense of being a 'human' among humans; the fact of my being a conscious and self-knowing being, of having a body and a mind, of being an I-locus. These fundamentals are perpetual mysteries to human intellect. And it is their presence that justifies the philosopher's search. The philosophical activity is an ever-incomplete truth-unfolding process—critical; analytical, rigorous, interpretative, and essential.

As one reads the works of different philosophers—from logical positivists and linguistic analysts to phenomenologists, existentialists, and Vedāntins—one might wonder what knowledge or truth the philosophical discipline tries to achieve. What are the aims of philosophy?

When one philosophises one is inside a uniquely trance-like state of mind—one thinks from behind the given so to say, breaks through the appearance in order to grasp reality, transcends what is ordinarily and 'naturally' offered to consciousness. Philosophical thinking has to be an incisive activity whichever problem it may be directed to. Philosophers have always sought to understand the meaning of the world, whether the world is as it appears to our senses, what the act of knowing is, how experience and language are related to each other, what the destiny of man's existence is, and why and how we are essentially self-transcending beings. The human mind never withdraws so much from the domain of commonsense and scans its own interior as it does when it is engaged in philosophical reflection. The philosopher has to probe what can be called the geometry of human consciousness, introspect and see what 'happens' to consciousness as it perceives the world, grasp how the meaning of existence emerges in us. As a seeker of the ultimate truth of things he is persistent in his inquiry. The demands of a philosophical mind are not easily satisfied. Its investigation would not end unless intuitions dawn on it that make any further interrogations superfluous.

Doubt and 'Seeing'

The not much explicitly emphasised feature of philosophical thinking is doubt. Doubting is an attitude of mind to which the world, as it is given in perceptions, is not an ultimate reality. The phenomenal world, within and without the knowing mind, has a transcendental foundation or a trans-empirical background without whose comprehension it would remain basically an enigma. Nāgārjuna and Śaṅkara, no less than Descartes and Edmund Husserl, are eminent representatives of the doubting attitude. It would be normal if a philosopher suspects the 'reality' of the universe, thinks, for instance, that perhaps the universe is not exactly the same as that which we perceive, that perhaps external objects and their impressions in us are a kind of secretion of our mind, that perhaps the categories and the frames of thought and language are arbitrary conditions concealing the primordial nature of consciousness and its objects. I cannot conceive of a philosophical school whose rigour and search is not enhanced by the sceptical disposition at its centre. And if it is said that doubting is only an initial step in the philosophical method that must be abandoned as soon as one's reflection reaches *a priori* truths, I would suppose that even such truths are not totally immune to metaphysical questioning. Just as there can be no philosophical inquiry if our interests are wholly anchored in the practical view of things, the philosophical activity would not be sufficiently radical if it terminates in the so-called self-evident propositions. Philosophical thought has to be presuppositionless, self-corrective and self-questioning, persistent, and open.

The aim of philosophy is not to furnish conclusive answers to questions. Why does the world exist? What is consciousness? How does the mind reach out to reality? What is the meaning of our being in the world? Who or what am I? What is the ultimate design of existence? Philosophies of all times have handled these questions but provided no final solutions to them. During the process of his reflection it is improbable that the philosopher does not discover that his thought-system is founded on certain assumptions about the real. Philosophies are edifices of ideas built on the foundation of assumptions. Particular assumptions are intuited or 'seen' by particular philosophers. If the assumptions are doubted, the entire edifice of ideas based on them would also be doubted. Therefore, even when a philosopher grapples with a philosophical question he views its implications in a certain way and takes it in and according to the light of his experience. The very raising and understanding of a philosophical question, like the attempt of replying to it, is governed by one's assumptions.

Take, for instance, the thoughts of the two most original philosophers of our own time whose primal assumptions are opposed to each other: Ludwig Wittgenstein and Martin Heidegger.

Wittgenstein takes philosophy to be the analysis of language, a kind of purification of different organs of language. For him the concepts of meaning, of logical form, of understanding, the grammatical structure of language, the foundations of mathematics, states of consciousness, the forms of different kinds of statements, etc., are the only concerns of philosophy.[1] Underlying his entire philosophical endeavour is the assumption that the logic of language is the same as that of the world. To discover the 'form' of language, therefore, is to discover the foundation of the world itself. Wittgenstein's famous picture theory presupposes that since language is the sum-total of propositions and propositions are capable of mirroring our experience of the world, language (provided it is scientifically constructed) would present a 'picture' of the reality of the world.

Heidegger, on the other hand, is mainly interested in ontological questions. What is Being—Being as it is intuited and 'lived' by man-in-the-world? He tells us that the central purpose of his philosophy is to unfold the structure of Being and to understand the relationship of man with this structure.[2] He repudiates the rationalist attempt to define Being logically or to objectify it by reducing it to 'beings'. By assuming that man's (*Dasein's*) immanence is in Being, he tries to show how through his act of existing man unfolds Being. Unlike other entities in the world, Heidegger says, man 'stands out' and 'is there' in the world. For the author of *Sein und Zeit* our state of 'thrownness' in the world, our metaphysical homesickness, our self-transcending and self-nihilating essence, and our ontological grounding in anguish, death, and Nothing constitute the structure of our lives. The task of a philosopher is to understand this structure.

What is interesting is that Wittgenstein and Heidegger do not 'feel' the same problems. They start from definite experience-areas, take definite positions on fundamental questions, assume specific standpoints and choose relevancies to suit those, and organise the linguistic presentation of their concepts to produce maximum effect. Although they follow predominantly descriptive methods, their portrayals of the composition of human consciousness are deeply rooted in their peculiar insights into their own being. Such insights are the ontological support of great philosophies. They figure as the vantage points from which philosophers try to encompass the meaning of life and reality.

A total detachment of the philosopher from his 'seeing' of his own existence, from his grasp of his own situation, is impossible. A philosopher cannot analyse himself as if he were an object. Indeed, while Wittgenstein carries his analysis-of-experience-via-language method to its extreme limit and apparently discloses no ontological assumption of his thought within the body of his philosophy, Heidegger begins with an elucidation of the trans-linguistic foundation of things—the *Sein* and the *Dasein*—and is committed to it all through his writings. Therefore, although doubting is intrinsic to the very discipline of philosophical thinking, once a philosopher intuits certain primordial conceptual relations he undergoes some sort of intellectual metamorphosis and considers doubting as preposterous. The insights in Wittgenstein's and Heidegger's philosophies may be questioned from the basis of some alien insights, but to Wittgenstein and Heidegger themselves they constitute their distinct visions of Being.

When I read Wittgenstein and Heidegger I find them throwing open before me multiple horizons of human reality by introducing original and powerfully expressive categories. According to

Wittgenstein, the sole function of philosophy is to clarify statements by means of statements since clear and logical statements reflect the logic of the universe itself. Once the statements have completed the job of clarification they can be discarded as useless. Thus to Wittgenstein philosophy is virtually a critique of language. But while he conceives the activity of philosophy in this way he looks at language and reality from a certain range of intuitions, which cannot be subjected to any further questioning. For instance, the concept of 'form' is one of the most fertile and perhaps never otherwise construeable concepts in him. One has to 'see' its characteristic nuance— that which its author has injected into it—in order to understand the whole picture theory erected on it.

The way of seeing philosophy embodied in the writings of logical positivists, linguistic analysts, and ordinary language philosophers today is committed to Wittgenstein's vision of the world. To this vision the world is a structure of logical entities encompassable by scientifically founded language.

Heidegger's existentialist theory, on the other hand, views man and the universe as ontological realities. Man is an act, an eternally manifesting Being. The world is not an abode of colourless and arid logical atoms to be mapped within propositions. It is a living energy bouncing in and out of man, who himself is an expression of it. Man is 'flung' into the expanse of this energy—isolated, helpless, heading toward death, anguished. He is in search of his 'roots' and a 'home' for himself. Anxiety perpetually gnawing him unto pain and fatigue, his only urge is to transcend his natural fate, to liberate himself from the inane, to explore his destiny. But according to Heidegger man's destiny is Nothing.

The categories of human existence which are so transparent to Heidegger and other existentialists have no place in the clean logical picture of reality that Wittgenstein and the language philosophers are intent on constructing. It is ultimately the philosopher's perspective and purpose, the direction of his interests, that underlies his speculation. Man's being *in* and, at the same time, being *beyond* the world, his desire for the assertion of his freedom, his sense of being an alien along with his quest for a unity with others, his concern with his inevitable end in death, his perpetual journey through situations that have no tangible beginning or end are typical existential enigmas. They are the very *raison d'être* of existentialists' philosophising. Existentialists feel that it is man as 'existing' rather than man as 'thinking' that is the sole mystery for philosophy to unravel.

Thus philosophical reflections are fundamentally governed by the ontological intuitions or seeings behind them. To the intuitions of this type philosophers are committed 'instinctively'. It is an absolutely free commitment, because these intuitions motivate one's entire style of thinking almost like revealed truths. Moreover, they form the ground of justification—the final point of reference—of philosophers' thought-structures, the evidence of their systems and methods. They, as I said before, might be doubted from 'outside' but not from within the conceptual framework emanating from them. They are the self-fulfilling meanings in the inner space of one's being and hence the limit of one's doubt.

The Ontological Intuition and Language

A philosopher's task becomes infinitely complicated when he inquires into the nature of the ontological intuitions of other philosophers' thought-structures and estimates the adequacy of their idiom to transmit these to others. One cannot look for a proof, an indisputable conclusion, in a philosophical work. What it contains is food for thought, an individual percipient's endeavour to figure out the meaning of the universe and to express it through logic and language. A philosopher, like a scientist, generalises his vision of reality.

The job of a critic in philosophy should not be different from that of an open-minded interpreter of the primordial assumptions of different thought-structures. He must delineate the philosopher's range of intuitions and find out how the particular edifice of ideas founded on them reflects the perennial meaning of human existence. However, this is a complex work and involves, directly or indirectly, the critic's examination of his own postulates.

Now we must draw a distinction between those philosophers who are concerned mainly with the setting of the distinctive method for philosophy and those who establish systems of experience. For instance, while logical positivism, analytic philosophy, and phenomenology are primarily methods of doing philosophy, subjective idealism, dialectical materialism, and existentialism are systems for explaining experience. A method-builder's interest is strictly epistemological—that is, to doubt and perhaps to cancel the ordinary ways of knowledge, and to institute 'new' ones. To him the mechanism of knowledge is more important than its contents. He is a logician, a kind of archaeologist of mind, an investigator of knowledge forms and rules. He has to cast and recast his propositions regarding the act of knowing, regarding experience, interpretation, understanding, the categorial suppositions, the inductive-deductive procedure, etc. His thinking is methodogenic.[3]

Methodogenic thinking is today a type of philosophical activity in no way less important than the job of system construction. Any thoroughgoing philosophy has to analyse its 'morphology', the constituent principles of its method, and, unlike the positive sciences, reconstruct the foundations of knowledge.

A system constructor therefore cannot entirely do away with methodogenic questions, for while explicating his system or working out its internal relations he must be vigilant of the norms that regulate it. The study of what can be called the geometry of the thought-forms of a system is an essential part of philosophy. Many a time system constructors, because of their contempt toward an inquiry into their methodology, turn out to be dogmatists. It is difficult, however, for a philosopher to be both simultaneously and equally effectively a method-builder and a system-maker. This is why pure method-philosophers like Wittgenstein, Husserl, J.L. Austin, and Carnap devoted their abilities to the work of overhauling the principles of knowledge, and consequently could not produce theories of the universe. But whether a philosopher is a method-builder or a system-maker, his philosophisation is a sort of explicitation—almost a justification—of the ontological intuitions to which he is committed.

Just as it is not necessary for an ontological intuition to be either true or false, it is not a part of its assumptive function to be fully linguistically expressible. An ontological intuition is born with a dizzy inarticulate meaning, is pre-logical and subject to different interpretations, and above all else lies underneath thought as something absolutely certain. Once you accept the ontological intuition of a philosophy, therefore, the disagreement about everything else is taken care of by logical reasoning.[4]

An ontological intuition has also a persuasive character—that is, a character by which when it is transmitted by one mind to the other, it works, whenever it works, by causing some sort of metamorphosis in the latter's *Weltanschauung* and establishing its obviousness. When this happens as a matter of fact, the assumption gains in the degree of necessity and universality, is regarded as apodictic in the corpus of a particular thought-structure whose entire logic appears to be remotely anchored in it and at the same time to confirm it. The assumption, in other words, becomes the beginning and the end, and indeed the central motive of the philosopher's intellectual process.

Today we often speak of the assumptive commitments of different philosophies in the world. Any claim that philosophy might make for being totally without any ontological intuition would be found as hollow the moment it is shown—and it can be shown almost in every case—that the foundation of that philosophy consists of a pre-reflective knowledge, an intuitively grasped logos, a trans-intellectual flash as it were, a *darśana*. This could even imply that there is simply no criterion for establishing the validity or otherwise of a philosophy. All ontological intuitions are immune to judgement or proof. If there is too much precision and clarity in a philosopher's language it is largely the result of his exercised discipline not to allow the blurred pre-reflective intuitions to interfere with his articulation. But, on the other hand, highly condensed metaphors, equivocations, and poetry in a thinker do not always signify very profound insights below. Thus when Wittgenstein, the founder of the language philosophies, said that '*the limits of my language* mean the limits of my world'[5] and 'what we cannot speak about we must consign to silence',[6] he could not have failed to notice that it is that which one consigns to silence that is the *sine qua non* for the complete understanding of what is spoken about. And when D. T. Suzuki, the highly insightful Zen thinker, referred to the Bodhidharma's symbolic 'gazing at the wall' as an expression of his most lucid inner state where thoughts cease to operate, he could not certainly be unaware of the necessity of clarity and precision in the linguistic communication in philosophy. There is something inherently transcendental about the ontological assumptions of philosophical constructions. They escape thought and words because they are closely intertwined with pure consciousness itself.

So whether a philosopher's language is clear or poetic, whether his organisation of ideas is logically coherent or studded with metaphysical terms and paradigms, his aim is to grasp within it a certain pre-reflective and pre-linguistic area. This area constantly glides beyond rational thought, and appears to fade into an infinite expanse of Being and tranquility.

Ordinarily it is not the method-builders' concern to define the exact role of the ontological assumptions in philosophies. Often a methodologist is so deeply involved in the rules of the formal validity of experience that he refuses to allude to factors beyond thought. Besides, certain methods, such as logical positivism and linguistic analysis, are positively anti-metaphysical and hence too rigid to permit an investigation of the transcendental basis of reflection. As a rule, the greater the method-oriented interest of a philosopher the greater is his confinement to the logical and epistemological subtleties, and further the stronger is his anti-metaphysical bias.

The plan of a comprehensive intellectual system should be not only to weave all the elements of our total experience into a consistent pattern but also to show that the foundation of this experience lies in the sphere of pure consciousness or Being. It is in this sphere that the meaning of experiences originates. The ultimate goal of metaphysics is to comprehend Being. That is why the creation of new patterns of language is very often necessary in metaphysics. Something is intuited as the sense of experiencing the world, and language is employed to say it. When a philosopher strictly adheres to the rules of language— the logical, the grammatical, and the syntactical—he misses the essence of what is sought to be expressed. Being cannot be made to descend in all its originality inside a given linguistic scheme. What Wittgenstein calls the 'language games' are in a sense an essential aspect of the philosophical activity. The language game played by any original philosopher is one in which word patterns are used to approximate to the world of essences in his mind. In a complete philosophical enterprise, the apparently illusive field of Being on which all intuitions 'float' must be contained within the mechanism of verbal communication.

Transcendence : Being or God?

What I have indicated so far is that philosophy as the most rigorous intellectual activity must endeavour to bring out the connection between what is experienced on the plane of reflection and what remains behind as ontological or pre-reflective. The line of separation between the reflective and the pre-reflective is always unclear. Just as the act of reflection is grounded in the person's ontological intuitions, which are its very meaning-giving background, the ontological intuitions themselves extend across the notably indecipherable sphere of pure consciousness or Being. To feel and to understand, to interpret, and to verbalise this sphere is the function of philosophy.

Now there is another way in which the whole pre-reflective basis of our world-consciousness can be looked at. Pure consciousness or Being has some affinity with the mystical in religion. In different theologies in the world it has been given a God-referring import. Theistic existentialists like Kierkegaard, Karl Jaspers, and Paul Tillich, for instance, have equated Being with the realm of spiritual reality and explained man's being-in-the-world as the state of his dislocation from it. In fact there is something volatile about the notion of the pre-reflective in the theists' writings. Here the pre-reflective is deified. It is looked upon as a limitless Will—the infinite Truth-Goodness-Beauty unison—from which man has fallen.

Religion personifies Being. Being—that is, the transcendental in metaphysics—has become God in religion. Man, according to religious thinkers, tends to think of God, and seeks His bliss in his progress toward his destiny. The human conscience reflects the divine conscience on earth; its essential voice is the voice of God.

One of the unique features of the interpretation of pure consciousness or Being as God is found in Hinduism. In Hinduism, God is recognised as the author of the imperishable Word (Śabda) of the Vedas, whose validity is believed to be beyond the judgement of man. Being has communicated with man through the Word. Under the consoling shelter of the Word, Hindus have invariably lived a life of resignation and hope, suffering and indulgence, bondage and freedom. It is largely people's faith that bestowed meaning on the Word, although it

must have been originally revealed only to a few. The sublime
and subdued mood of the Āryans of ancient times discovered in
it the very essence of the universe.

Not only did the Word guide the Hindu way of living, it was
also propagated by them as the most sacred and the only infallible
instruction ever transmitted to man by God. Besides, it was
employed to achieve various mundane and extra-mundane
purposes. It was used to initiate children into a self-restrained
adulthood; it was hurled at fire, water, sky, air, and earth to
temper their fury; it had the power of mesmerising the young
Brahmins, and of opening up to them the ultimate secret of all
human life. It was thrown at the dead to salvage their spirit,
at the enemies to clear the path of their destruction, at deities
to win their favour, at one's own self to bring about its fusion with
Being. One must go through the most devoutly composed pages
of the Vedas to realise what the faith in the power of the revealed
Word can psychologically amount to.

For Hindus every Vedic expression possesses an inherent
trans-worldly nuance. After creating the Word, God radiated
it so to say to the ancient *rishis* who spoke it and left it like
an immortal sound in the atmosphere. The Word springs up in
the guru's intuition and is conveyed to the disciple, who has no
right to doubt it. It has determined the course of the Hindu
ethos through centuries. Just as it has always been the basic
motivation of the transcendentalist philosophies its blind following
by millions has generated wide-spread obscurantism and regression
in India's history. The function of the Vedic Word and Vedic
sentence (*vākya*) is supposed to be to convey eternal truths to man
for his benefaction and ultimate salvation.

Linguistically speaking, the theory of the revealed Word in
Hinduism is as abstruse (notwithstanding its subtleties in the
analysis of transcendental knowledge) as the Pythagorean theory
that numbers or figures are the essences of reality and, as such,
gleam through human minds from the celestial music. Apart
from the variations in the Hindus' views regarding the exact
source of the meaning of the Vedic Word, what is central to all of
them is the belief that the vision embodied in the Word is to be
intuited and not discussed. It is the Nyāya and the Mimāṁsa
thinkers more than others who focused their attention on this
belief and extensively explained the relation between meaning

and word. The Vedic expressions, the Nyāya and the Mimāṁsa schools hold, have an intrinsic and supersensible authority.

That the divine voice is heard by a few chosen seers among the entire mankind, who also have the obligation to propagate it for the enlightenment of others, is one of the fundamental beliefs in the world's theologies. This belief centres around another analogous belief that God reveals truth to man like a flash. However, history has shown that all that is regarded as God-oriented in the scriptural heritage of different communities is not conducive to their spiritual advancement. In India, dangerous social schisms have resulted from the observance of the *varnāshramadharma*—one of the institutions in the Hindu society supported by the Vedic Word.[7] The Word testimony is largely a matter of faith; it makes no sense to one who doubts the existence of God.

The experience of God pronounced by theists, however, could be taken as one of transcendence, infinitude, absolute harmony, and joy. The religious people cannot but conceive a supernatural being, a complete person, as the source of this experience. Saints, mystics, and prophets have claimed to be in communion with God, to realise a fusion with His person, to feel Him within their own heart. Religious experience is a form of introvertive feeling having for its goal a total 'melting' of one's own subject in the infinite being of God.

But whether it is Being or God, our state in the world has put us at a distance from it. Man's destiny is not to be consumed by the world. He yearns for a total encompassing of his self. His life in the world and at the same time his longing for the beyond are the perennial character of his metaphysical reality. Man has always lived as a tension between what he is here and now and what he is as a metaphysical possibility. This tension has been the momentum behind the making of human history. Religion has sought an escape from this tension by teaching man to keep faith in the goodness of God and in his ultimate salvation with His succour. When Being is deified, it becomes a super-person—omnipotent, omniscient, and omnipresent—with unlimited benevolence toward his creation. Through practices like prayer, sacrifice, meditation, worship, and devotion, a religious man entreats God to salvage him from the world. To him no other path is more certain for his own and others' final deliverance than the path of total surrender to God.

While the theists' experience of a supernatural being governing the affairs of the universe could be regarded as the manifestation of a peculiar mentality which need not indicate the actual
existence of such a being, there is no doubt that the experience itself
leads them to maintain a certain mental equipoise toward things,
to look upon the world and their own station in it with justification. And yet philosophy must seek to account for the experience
of God from the standpoint of the constitution of the theist's
subjectivity. One has to study what transcendental import the religious person derives from his experience. A phenomenological
research into the phenomenon of revelation, the prophetic insights,
the vision of God, the process of psychic conversion, etc., would
be essential to bring out the essence of man's religiosity. In a
religious person, his faith does not offer itself to the criticism from
his reason. To understand religious consciousness is therefore
to demarcate the boundaries of faith and reason, to define the
various psychological and ontological factors involved in the consciousness's tendency toward the divine spirit, to see what happens
to one when one enters into the so-called fellowship with God.

The Human Predicament

It is the *Rg Veda* that for the first time in the history of speculative literature touched upon the greatest mystery of all: 'What
thing I truly am I know not.'[8] Perhaps ironically, philosophical
thought (and metaphysics in particular) over the centuries is a
record of man's attempt to unfold this mystery about himself.
Even through science, arts, culture, civilisation and technology
one finds an expression of man's age-old urge to encompass himself and his environment, to live in absolute freedom, to create a
perfect state of consciousness for himself. Man is the only being
who can locate himself as a mystery and direct his inquiry towards
solving it.

Any search for the essence of man must begin with a study of
man as he is in the world. The most unique characteristic of
human reality, however, is its ambiguity: it is in the world and
yet not wholly absorbed by it; it surpasses itself; it oscillates
between its 'givenness' and its pre-reflective void-like background.
Nothing can posit itself as rigid on the field of human conscious-

ness. We 'fly' beyond the realised freedom, beyond the fulfilled state of being, and beyond all that we are at any given point of time. The ambiguity of man consists in his being born in the world as one among many and still not being a 'native' in this habitat.

The famous Indian doctrine of man's bondage, which basically implies that by being born in the world man is alienated from his transcendental origin in Being for whose recovery he perpetually longs, contains one of the most insightful observations concerning human fate. Our bondage is made of our finitude. We are netted in a spatio-temporal domain in which situations emerge rarely to our liking. The state of bondage would not mean anything unless it is viewed in opposition to a state of harmony and freedom. What we desire is this latter state of permanent fearlessness, inner composure, spiritual indigenousness, and security. The fundamental direction of human activity has always been towards seeking a re-creation of the world. The more remote we feel from the aspired end, the greater is the tension we undergo between our worldly being and our longing for the transcendental.

Deep down in human self there is a vast hollowness that should be of immense interest to a metaphysician. Just as, as we have seen, different ontological intuitions governing our reflection are finally traceable back to this hollowness, our very sense of being present in the universe springs up somewhere here. Our sense of having a body, our awareness of the existence of other persons like ourselves, our compulsive realisation that we are in the world, our ego-awareness, are the dimensions of this hollowness.

There is nothing in our ordinary experience about which we are so certain as the fact that we are present to ourselves. We perceive ourselves as being in the bodies (we *are* our bodies) and in the world. Unless, therefore, by means of some arduous psychic process one were to disconnect oneself from everything that constitutes one's worldliness, one's being given to one's self would remain the most fundamental phenomenon of all. When considered from this angle, the eminent Cartesian thesis that *cogito ergo sum* is 'the first and most certain knowledge that occurs to one who philosophises in an ordinary manner' seems to have assumed something which no argument is able to demonstrate. Man's existence involves his immediate awareness of being amidst objects and persons, his discovery that he is a 'presence' amidst presences. Human consciousness continuously breaks the line that divides presence from absence. To an introspective act directed towards ascertaining from what basis we emerge as presences, what generates the content and meaning of our sense-data and thoughts, what posits us in the world as experiencing beings, the area of presence gradually fades out into a primitive absence. When the mind's external and internal preoccupations are cancelled, and it is drawn in toward the source of all beings so to say, the sense-data and all those principles which cause their blending crumble like sandcastles. One would thus be almost at the point from where the whole phenomenon of existence must have begun. This is the end of one's tether. If one ventures to go further, one would be lost in an abyss of Nothing, a boundless silence, death. An understanding of the consciousness's journey in this direction is the business of a philosopher.

However, what we cannot ignore is the reality of the world. Our commitment to the world is both the beginning and the end of our inward search. For the world is not an inert 'solid' object but a moving human force evincing the skills, the programmes, and the purposes of others like myself. The pen and the paper I use for writing, the books I read or write, the buildings, the roads, the vehicles I see around, touch my consciousness as the creation of man. And, rather more fundamentally, the body I possess, the language I use, and for that matter the entire culture and civilisation that has become the essence of my life in society, strike me immediately as the products of others—parents, educators, community, the state, etc. We are surrounded by other consciousnesses every moment, in so far as we employ things made by others and others employ things made by us and in so far as we are genetically accountable systems.

There is another aspect of the human world which we cannot afford to miss. While admiring or condemning art—music, paintings, statues, and so on—while approving or disapproving a technological device (say, a razor), or while supporting or rejecting a judgement, my judging consciousness, besides being directed to some object, is directed also to other judging consciousnesses. In moral evaluation this phenomenon becomes much more evident. No moral judgement is strictly limited to or ends in its object. It has dimensions reaching other persons, others' frames of values. When I judge something as right, when I posit a value, I anticipate a response from others as my moral counterparts. One's ethical awareness has an intrinsic range over similar awarenesses in others.

Our journey into the pre-reflective void-like background of our ordinary consciousness, therefore, is not a journey of no return. To complete the circle so to say, the consciousness withdrawn from the reality of the world and probing its roots within the 'subterranean' expanse of Being must be brought back to the world. It is the world that forms the anchorage of human life. It is here that man is born as a force, a volume of possibilities, a source of history and praxis. The domain of Being verging on the unencompassable Nothing cannot be an eternal abode for man. And yet it is the only experience by which he can unlearn the elements history has thrust on him. The domain of Being 'purifies' one's view of the universe. It enables one to touch the very genesis of one's world-consciousness. There are no marked boundaries to this experience. It is an open and endless cosmic hollowness on which one's sense of positivity would appear to buoy as if it were a freak, a flake in the unfathomable infinitude.

Indeed, no constructive theory of moral or cultural values can logically follow from the ontological foundation of man set forth in this manner. But this does not mean that in the face of such a foundation all human activity in the world would be seen as futile. On the contrary, a well-knit humanistic ethics could be formulated only from the assumption that man—that is, the source of all meaningfulness in existence—is an emergence from Nothing. The world and man are so related to each other that while the former contains man and subjects him to its laws, man perpetually transcends the world to realise his primordial basis. We figure in the world as aliens, outsiders, sinners, because we have lost our transcendental abode. This state of our separation from the original Being (or Nothing) and our constant running beyond the given accounts for our worldly activity.

Man's destiny consists of an indefinable range of possibilities hidden in the womb of time. Every value that an individual chooses to follow or generates anew has a relevance to his dialogue with his destiny. But this destiny is something in which all human beings participate. We are the coheirs of a culture perpetuated by the reality 'Man'. Ambiguity apears to be the very essence of this culture. It should be clear to an interpreter of history that two equally forceful schemes of values have dominated the process of man—one inviting his consciousness toward the transcendental realm, and the other emphasising the need of his commitment to the welfare of his fellowmen. There has never been a complete equilibrium between these two schemes. Man, therefore, has always lived as a tension.

Thus the story of our development over centuries would basically reflect our quest for a self-identity. Man is an ambivalence, an act with opposite inertia, an intentionality directed both toward the world and toward its ontological foundations. It is this ambivalence that is at the core of mankind's discontentedness with itself, its doing and undoing values, its acts of construction and destruction. So far no culture or civilisation has been founded on an absolute and all-embracing system of values, for human consciousness is unable to mirror such a system. When considered from a transcendental level, our decisions therefore are tentative, experimental, hypothetical. And yet it cannot be ignored that by commiting oneself to the total good of mankind, by helping to accelerate mankind's progress toward its ideal, or by participating in the entire human endeavour as such, we respond to the call of the common destiny of all. Man's organised and rationally controlled activity in the world receives its justification from this destiny.

Notes

1. Wittgenstein, Ludwig, *Philosophical Investigations,* G.E.M. Anscombe (trans.), Oxford, Basil Blackwell, 1958, p. ix.
2. Sinari, R., *Reason in Existentialism,* Bombay, Popular Prakashan, 1966, p. 189.
3. For a discussion of how methodogenic problems arise, see Farber, Marvin, *Basic Issues of Philosophy*, New York, Harper Torchbooks, 1968, pp. 82-5.
4. This and the next two paragraphs are taken from my 'Pure Consciousness as the Ontological Assumption in the Śaṅkara Vedānta', *Anviksiki*, Vol. IV, 1 & 2, pp. 37-8.
5. Wittgenstein, Ludwig, *Tractatus Logico Philosophicus*, P. F. Pears and B.F. McGuinness (trans.), London, Routledge & Kegan Paul, 1961, p. 115.
6. Ibid., p. 151.
7. For a treatment of the impact of the Word on the Indian ethos, see Sinari, R., *The Structure of Indian Thought*, Illinois, Charles C. Thomas, 1970, pp. 209-14.
8. *Ṛg Veda*, I. 167. 37.

14

My Quest for the Self

R. K. Tripathi

I am aware that my concept of philosophy and its purpose is different from many others prevalent to-day. A philosophy carries with it a certain conception of philosophy, and a certain conception of philosophy is part of a philosophy, so that no philosophy can be free from a certain conception of philosophy, and no conception of philosophy is independent of a certain philosophy. It is therefore proper that I make my view of philosophy clear at the very outset if only to prepare the reader for what he should, and for what he should not, expect from me. In the process there may incidentally appear also a justification of my view.

I

The term 'philosophy' like the term 'science' is used in a general as well as in a specific sense. In a general sense, philosophy means a view of something such as history, science, religion, art, etc. In this sense probably everybody has a philosophy or a view and there is a philosophy of everything. There is, however, a more specific sense in which probably very few people have a philosophy, that is, philosophy as a deliberate and earnest search for truth for the sake of directing one's life. In this sense philosophy is something indispensable though not for all but only for those who have somehow developed a strong urge for truth. In a certain sense probably every philosophy—empiricism, rationalism, analysis, phenomenology, existentialism, positivism—is a search for truth. All these may also be helpful in directing one's life directly or indirectly in different degrees. But that is not enough; philosophy should not only be necessary but also sufficient. Philosophy or the knowledge of truth should be by itself sufficient to solve the problems of life presumably by solving the central problem of life. In this, the above-mentioned systems seem to fail either because they do not see a central problem of life or because they are not able to solve that problem by knowledge alone. Philosophical knowledge is not like medical knowledge which prescribes remedies for different diseases but cures none; here knowledge itself cures the disease and nothing more is needed as a supplement. This is what distinguishes philosophy from science and religion both. Neither in science nor in religion is knowledge sufficient ; it requires to be supplemented by action in order to be useful. The very nature of philosophic knowledge is different. Philosophy being the search for truth has necessarily an evaluational and critical attitude but science is dogmatically committed to sense-experience, whereas religion hangs on faith. Philosophy tries to develop a universal criterion of truth and judges everything in the light of that. Criticism in science is confined to the limits of sense-experience and reasoning in religion is confined to the tenets of faith.

From what has been said above, it should be clear that philosophy is not merely a statement of one's beliefs. Sometime back there appeared a book called *What I Believe* in which every contributor was expected to give his philosophy. I would say that philosophy is not what I naturally believe; it is rather a criticism and evaluation of what I believe. It is rather what I would like to believe. Therefore, a philosopher must not be charged with dishonesty if he propounds a philosophy which is opposed to natural beliefs or which rejects natural beliefs as false. Even in science natural beliefs, such as those regarding the motion of the sun, etc., are not respected. But it is strange that some philosophers consider it their duty merely to explain and justify natural beliefs and swear by what is called common sense. Scientists do not accept natural beliefs unless they cohere with established laws and facts, but philosophers seem to regard them as too sacred to be questioned. Common sense cannot be the indubitable starting point of philosophy; it can be accepted, if at all, only after re-examination. Philosophy is not a reasoned and coherent account of what I believe upon instinct; it is rather what I would like to accept as true after reflection and revaluation.

Some people seem to be rather crazy about novelty in philosophy. Old philosophies look like tattered clothes to them and they

want a new philosophy with every change. This attitude is not
even scientific, much less philosophical; it confuses philosophy,
with art and literature. Truth, whether in philosophy or elsewhere,
does not become less true because of age. The value of philosophy
does not lie in its novelty as it does in art and literature, but
in the element of truth that it contains. If truth has already been
discovered, it would be mere vanity to have an exercise in self-
effort for novelty. Not that new philosophies or new ways of discovering truth are not possible, but that is not merely for the sake
of novelty. My object is not to have a philosophy of my own but
to discover truth even if it has already been discovered by somebody
else.

My view of philosophy is therefore governed to a certain extent by what I consider to be the value of philosophy. For me
there are only two kinds of values—empirical and trans-empirical
or spiritual. Obviously philosophy, in the specific sense and not
in the general sense, does not and cannot serve any empirical end.
None of our worldly pursuits would suffer in the absence of philosophy; nay, they may even be hampered by philosophy. So philosophy is either utterly useless or it has some trans-empirical value.
A passion for the search of truth is by no means a worldly passion.
Philosophy can be justified and appreciated only when there is
a passion for truth. One may ask: how does this uncommon
or rather non-natural passion for truth which makes the philosopher indifferent to worldly pursuits arise ?

The philosopher is concerned with the problem of truth not
because he is abnormally curious about the nature of things or the
origin of the world, but because the problem of truth is, to use a
modern phrase, for him an existential problem. He finds on reflection that not only his happiness or unhappiness but all his values
depend on beliefs or what he considers to be true. If so, is it not
worthwhile re-examining what is unconsciously taken to be true ?
The problem becomes more pressing when we find that while we
all aspire for permanent and infinite happiness, the world around
us on which our happiness depends is anything but permanent.
So either permanent happiness is not attainable or the world we
take to be true is not the true world. Philosophy has to ascertain
for itself the truth of the situation.

II

For me the centre of my universe is my self. The world around me is relevant to me and I pay attention to it because of my self. The self is primary and the world is secondary. So I can say that all my problems are problems of my self: all of them arise only to the extent my self is involved or concerned. Not only personal problems but all problems—social, economic, political, national and international problems, and even natural calamities—are reducible to the problem of self. They have a meaning for me only if my self is somehow involved in them and not otherwise. But how is it that I get involved in all or some of them? It is through what I consider to be myself and mine (my body, my family, my reputation, my security, my aspirations, my society, my country) that I get involved. The world does not have and cannot have any hold on me if and when I consider nothing as mine. Nobody can catch me and nothing can affect me except through something which I consider mine. My misery as well as my happiness are both traceable to something which is mine. The most primary and basic thing which I consider mine, and to which I owe my identity, is my body: everything else which is mine is derived from its relation to the body. So the most basic problem for me is: am I this body which seems to be at the root of all problems?

The problem of philosophy therefore arises for me as a reflection on my destiny as the body and its fortunes. It becomes most acute when I become aware of the universality and inevitability of death. Ordinary persons worry about life but to the philosopher death seems to make life meaningless. In this regard the existentialists' emphasis on the fact of death is appreciable. The problem concerning death is primary and all other problems, such as those concerning creation, nature of reality etc., are secondary, because it is through the problem of death or self that I get interested in other problems. I would not care for any other problem if it did not centre round the problem of my self. Philosophy is therefore a search for the true self. The experience of sleep and the inevitability of death force me to ask the question, 'Am I nothing?' This is my encounter with nothingness.

The fact of death poses the problem in two ways. Firstly every thinking man has to ask the question: Is death the end of life or existence? If there is nothing after death, can life have any meaning?

In the face of inescapable utter annihilation, is it possible to take interest in anything of life? Secondly, there is the problem of voluntary death or suicide. If death must come, is it not better the sooner it does? Why should I continue to live? Is it for animal enjoyment? Is it for cultural pursuits? Is it for moral attainments? What can be the end for which life, even for a moment beyond the present, can be justified? This is an inescapable question to any reflective individual. If we come to think of it, there seems to be nothing which can justify our life apart from an unconscious urge to live. Even the most miserable creatures, both men and animals, like to drag on and resist death. But one who seeks the meaning of life cannot be content merely with this natural urge to live. One is forced to examine the values which seem to give direction and impetus to life, and then it appears that there is nothing which can be an ultimate justification for life. The game of life does not seem to be worth the candle. Not until such a moment has come in one's life, not until there has arisen the urge to end life because of its worthlessness, can there be any seriousness or earnestness about the search for the true nature of self because our belief concerning the nature of our self unconsciously affects life and gives direction to it. We have to examine our beliefs if only to find out whether there is anything in life to sustain us in the boredom, the loneliness and the dread of which the existentialists speak.

If one does not have any of these intense experiences, philosophy will be a mere pastime. But for one on whom the misery of life has stamped itself, philosophy will be a necessity. The question of meaning or worth can arise only in the context of the experience of meaninglessness. In this sense philosophy is essentially personal and existential. It is not something meant for all, much less for those in whom the problem has not arisen. But for the awareness of this problem philosophy would appear to be sheer madness. It is this problem that forces one either to accept some philosophy or to invent one. Philosophy can be universal only to the extent that the above problem is universal or can at least be universally appreciated. The unconscious passion for life is so strong that we do not ordinarily even raise the problem of its worthlessness and much less try to solve it. Philosophy seems to be not only useless and unnecessary but even a positive nuisance to those who would not like to be disturbed in their zeal for life or, if at all, would like to have a philosophy consistent with or conducive to their zeal. Any-

way, our point is that it is the consciousness of death as nothing
else that focusses our attention on the question concerning the nature of our self and the meaning of life.

III

If I am only the body then death is my inevitable end and along
with that the end of everything. But if I am something other than
the body, it has to be found out. So how to go about that? One
way is to go out alone like Buddha who made a singular effort in history to find out the end of life all by himself: he could not find anyone whom he could accept as his guide. The other way is to accept
some guide or authority. We have probably only one Buddha so
far in history; most of us depend on authority. All of us depend
on expert advice in various spheres of life such as medicine, law,
education, etc. But it is strange that we demur to accept any
authority concerning the most important problem of life, namely,
the nature of self and the goal of life. Is it because in other spheres
the results are verifiable? Obviously the question of verifiability
arises after acceptance and not before. If we regard *a priori* something as unverifiable, then we have a closed mind and not an open
one. Is it because there are differences of opinion that we do not
accept authority in philosophy? But differences of opinion cannot
be completely ruled out in other spheres also and yet we seek advice. Why do we insist on self-reliance or independence of thought
in philosophy? Is it because we are too sure of the competence of
thought? Or is it because we are not able to swallow what the
experts say? If we are sure of the unaided competence of thought,
then it only shows that we are ignorant of the limits of thought
which ought to be obvious to any student of philosophy. If, however, we are not able to accept what an authority says, the fault
may well be with us rather than with the authority. To blame the
authority, and not ourselves, is nothing short of declaring ourselves
as the measure of everything. We want to have our own way.
This is egoity or lack of humility or receptivity. We are presump-
tuous; we are not capable of self-analysis and self-criticism.

The case of Buddha must not be quoted to show that if Buddha
could succeed everyone can. For one thing, Buddha was an
extraordinary individual, unique and singular, so much so that he is

even regarded as an incarnation of God. For another, even in the case of Buddha, one cannot hold that he did not have any help or suggestion from anywhere. He was born in a society which had traditions. If it were not so, he could not even have the initial sense of direction. He could not even leave hearth and home and go out in search. After all, from where did he get the impulse for renunciation? It is impossible to start in a vacuum. The protagonists of the independence of thought stumble and bleed but do not give in. The rationalist does not care to see the conflicts *a priori* thinking produces, the empiricist does not bother about the scepticism and uncertainty to which empiricism leads, the existentialist, even though he sees darkness about himself, does not like to have guidance, and the positivist does not even see the darkness except in the sphere of language. What is most essential for the seeker of truth is to see that he does not suffer from prejudices and passions, that he knows his limitations and is not too stubborn to welcome help if it comes from somewhere. One who is seized with the problem of life would behave like a drowning man who would catch even at a straw to save himself. After realising the emptiness of wordly pursuits, Spinoza was so restless that he says: 'I saw myself in the midst of a very great peril and obliged to seek a remedy, however uncertain, with all my energy; like a sick man seized with a deadly disease, who sees death straight before him if he does not find some remedy, is forced to seek it, however uncertain, with all his remaining strength, for in that is all his hope placed.'

But the difficulty, it may be urged, is how to choose the right guide. This is like putting the cart before the horse. The rightness or otherwise of the guide can be ascertained only after choosing. This difficulty is there in all spheres. In our wordly pursuits, we do not sit idle; rather we throw in our lot with someone or the other. Why cannot we show the same strength of faith in the sphere of spiritual search? Is it because we lack the capacity to believe? If so, it is necessary to have some self-searching to find out what precisely stands in our way of accepting or believing. It will be found that there is always some obsession or the other which obstructs our surrender to the guide regarding the unknown. Humility coupled with detachment is necessary in every sphere of search. This is my conviction and so I attach great importance to the role of a teacher or scripture in our search for truth. To me this is not dog-

matism but a necessity felt after critical reflection, a necessity
for anyone who wants to reach the unknown. Nor does it mean
a complete suppression of reason, because the teaching has to be
grasped in an intelligent and coherent way which is the work of
reason. Reason cannot give content but it can certainly give coherence and consistency. The enquiry really begins after listening
and does not end with it. *Manana* must follow *śravaṇa*. *Manana*
is necessary for the sake of meeting difficulties against the teaching
by examining rival possibilities; it is also necessary for interpreting
the teaching in such a manner that apparent contradictions disappear. This is because the language about the unconditioned or
the transcendent cannot be straight and literal by the very nature
of the case, as it was originally meant not for the transcendent but
for empirical life (*vyavahāra*). Philosophy may begin with faith
but does not end with it; here faith serves the ends of knowledge
and not the ends of action as it does in religion and other spheres.
If the teaching is about something that cannot be experienced
here and now, then there can be mere faith. But if it is concerning
something which can be experienced here and now, then what is
the sense in not accepting and trying? This may appear to be
something of a gamble. But are we not even otherwise gambling
with life, and walking in darkness? If we do have adventures
in other spheres, why cannot we do so here?

Concerning the method of philosophy therefore my view is that
rationalism is empty even as empiricism is impotent. If the senses
cannot reach the transcendent, neither can pure reason do so.
Reason can at best guess and speculate, but it cannot categorically
assert that the transcendent is there or that it can be known or that
it can be known in this or that way. That the transcendent is, that
it can be known and that it can be known in a certain way—all this
can be known only from the *śruti* or the teacher. The saints and
sages of the world are at once the corroborators of *śruti* well as
the followers and teachers.

IV

Having pointed out the importance of the teacher or *śruti* as
indispensable, let us now see how far we can go independently
in answering the question regarding the nature of self posed by

the fact of death. If I am merely the body then there is an end of the whole matter. But what else can I be other than the body? Not only my life but also my thoughts and ideas seem to go along with the body. Is there some unknown substance which is left over after the death of the body? Even if there be, what is that to me? It is as good as nothing to me. Shall we then say that there is nothing left after death?

Let us pause and look at an experience which is like death, namely, the experience of sleep. There is perfect similarity between sleep and death except that I am aware of waking from sleep but not of waking from death. But if we can wake up from sleep, why cannot we wake up from death? It may be said that in sleep the body and breath are there but not in death. But does consciousness depend on the body and its functions? If so, it ought to be there even in sleep when the body and the breath are there. Is there any consciousness in sleep as well? Apparently there seems to be no consciousness in sleep. Consciousness seems to come and go. Is it produced and destroyed? I am convinced that consciousness cannot be a product, much less of the body and its functions. No causal relation concerning consciousness has been traced and none can be traced. It is true that consciousness manifests itself only when the body and the brain function or are in order even as electricity manifests itself only through some medium, but it does not follow that consciousness or electricity depends on that medium. A medium must not be confused with a cause. It is more sensible to say that the body (as an object) is in consciousness than to say that consciousness is in the body, because consciousness has no physical dimensions and cannot therefore be anywhere in the body. In fact, the body itself is merely a matter of an unconscious belief. Our belief in the body is not based on any knowledge, because all cognitive functions such as perception, etc., are not prior to, but posterior to our explicit or implicit belief in the body and so this belief cannot be a cognitive belief. And belief in the external world is dependent on the belief in the body. So all our so-called knowledge is based on the primordial belief in the body, which is unconscious.

Locke held that consciousness is a function of the soul-substance, a function which stops in sleep. He wanted to deny that consciousness is a quality of the soul as Descartes held, because in that case the quality (consciousness) would be there in sleep

also. Some Indian thinkers also regard consciousness as a quality.
Whether consciousness is a quality or a function is not the real
problem. The real issue is whether consciousness (not its manifestations) can be dependent on anything other than consciousness.
My answer is that consciousness cannot be in any way related to
anything by its very nature. Our thoughts and ideas may be
related but they are only forms of consciousness, or rather conditioned forms of consciousness, and not consciousness as such.
But can there be or is there any such thing as consciousness as such ?

It is unfortunate that even today the importance of sleep-
experience for philosophy is not appreciated in the West. If we
probe into the experience of sleep, three very important facts
seem to emerge. First, we may ask: do I exist in sleep or not?
It is obvious that if I did not exist in sleep, it could not be my
sleep; in that case how could I own it as my experience? I have
to admit that 'I' was there in sleep also. But do I know my
existence in sleep? I do not know anything in sleep. How can
I know my existence? This means that though I do not know my
existence in sleep yet I exist. In other words I can exist without my
knowledge of it; my existence is independent of my knowledge
of it. After death my existence is not known but I may be there even
without knowing it. The possibility is not ruled out.

The second question that may be asked is: if I am there in
sleep, in what form am I there? Was I there merely as a breathing
body without any consciousness? If there were no consciousness,
sleep could not be even called an experience; it would be just a
state. But sleep is an experience and my experience, an experience
of utter ignorance. That is why I am able to recollect and say
that I slept well and I did not know anything. If sleep is an
experience it must be in some consciousness; it must be experienced,
otherwise it cannot be recollected. But surely there is no
determinate consciousness, no particular thought or idea, otherwise
there would have been self-consciousness also and not sleep.
Consciousness in sleep must therefore be formless, indeterminate
and undifferentiated, a fact which explains the absence of self-
consciousness. So sleep-experience or rather an analysis of it
shows that there can be such a thing as pure, formless consciousness,
consciousness independent of any content. We cannot say that
there can be a content independent of all consciousness: there
will be self-contradiction the moment we say it. There may be a

content (rope) independent of a particular knower but it cannot be said to be independent of all consciousness. Even when the rope is not known (in the state of illusion), it is known as unknown. Or else how could we say that the rope was there but I did not know it ? So there is consciousness to which everything is a content, but consciousness itself is not a content any time. That is what is meant by its independence and its self-luminosity. Consciousness is self-evident, that is, evident without being a content. Consciousness can be contentless or pure. This pure contentless conscious ness can neither be negated nor can it be dark and dependent on any knowledge. It cannot be negated because it is not a content, and only a content can be negated. It cannot be dark and dependent on any other knowledge because it is not a content but is self-luminous (unconditionally immediate).

Finally, there is one more aspect of sleep-experience to which attention may be drawn. Sleep-experience, apart from showing that I can be there without my knowing it, and that I am there in the form of pure consciousness, further shows that I can be happy without possessing any object, without possessing even the body. Ordinarily we believe that we derive all happiness from objects and through the body and that if we are deprived of the body and its objects we will be deprived of all sources of happiness. But we find that in sleep we are neither able to use the body nor do we enjoy any object; our deprivation is complete and we do not have the consciousness of owning anything, and yet we feel happiness in sleep. It is a positive experience, not merely a state of *akāma* but of *āptakāma*: we do not miss anything in sleep. This shows that not only my existence, not only my consciousness, but also my happiness can be independent of objects. It is only an illusion to think that we can get happiness only from objects, even as it is an illusion to think that my existence and consciousness depend on my body. The real source of happiness is the self itself; the body and the objects only cloud that happiness and only prevent the bliss of the self from fully and permanently manifesting itself. If we eliminate what is variable, namely, the waking experience and the dream experience, there remains my pure self which is pervasive in all three states, constant in its joy, its existence and its consciousness. If this is my real self, then death loses its sting and my problem is solved.

Awareness of myself as constant being, pure consciousness

and unmixed bliss solves not only the problem of death but also the problem of other selves and creation. Pure consciousness can neither be created nor divided. There can be no real creation nor can there be a real plurality of selves. All plurality is traceable to the non-self and all creation is of the non-self. My fear of other selves or fear of nature (non-self) is baseless like my fear of death. I should have complete fearlessness (*abhayam*). I am infinite, indivisible, eternal and absolute, but not as an *I* but as the true self symbolised by the I.

This is as far as reflection can go. I have reflected on sleep-experience which is like death which poses for me the problem concerning my self and its destiny. But it is to be noticed that all through I have used the expression 'can be', that is, the self can be pure consciousness, can exist without my knowing and can be happy without any object. So the next question is: what is the surety that it is so or that it can be so realised? It is here that *śruti* or the teacher comes in. It is *śruti* that assures us that it is really so, and that the self can be realised and that there is a certain way of doing it. There can be no rational or empirical guarantee or demonstration of all that. It may be further pointed out that the pure self is not a pure hypothesis for two reasons. First, it has been discovered by an analysis of experience, and is not a product of imagination. Second, it can be realised here and now if only the proper steps are taken. The self is in our possession but not its realisation. We have experience only of determinate consciousness but our aim is to realise that indeterminate consciousness which is my real self, which is hidden but not non-existent. All that is necessary is knowledge or discovery.

V

So philosophy for me is essentially a self-sufficient spiritual discipline (*jñāna-mārga*). It is neither an adventure of reason nor is it merely subsidiary to the path of devotion (*bhakti-mārga*). It is an independent discipline in which knowledge is not only necessary but also sufficient. After the attainment of the knowledge of the true self, nothing else need be done; because that knowledge consumes all conflicts and dissolves all doubts, desires and difficulties. In the *bhakti* path knowledge is necessary but not sufficient; it has to be supplemented by *bhakti* or love. So also in Yoga. But I do recognise *bhakti* as also a *mārga*. Pātañjala Yoga is a kind of *jñāna-mārga* while *niṣkāma karma* Yoga is a kind of *bhakti-mārga*. *Jñāna* and *bhakti* are the two basic *mārgas*. As a *mārga* or path, one may differ from the other though in either case the end may be the same peace and tranquillity.

In the *jñāna-mārga*, the attitude is critical and negative. It is the attitude of *doṣadarśana* (seeing evil in everything), of regarding everything as suffering, of rejecting everything as false. The spirit of renunciation is basic and indispensable here in philosophy. Since philosophy traces all troubles to *avidyā*, knowledge is sufficient here. In the *bhakti* path our trouble is said to be due to misplaced love. So long as we love the transitory and the finite our happiness cannot be permanent and infinite, because the nature of our happiness depends on what we love. In the *bhakti-mārga*, the attitude is more positive. There is withdrawal here also but that is only for changing the direction of love to God. In fact there is even a return to the world in the *bhakti* path. God being all goodness (*maṅgala-maya*), His creation cannot be anything but good so there can be no *doṣadarśana* (seeing evil in everything). If in *jñāna-mārga* the conflict is resolved by renouncing everything as evil, in the *bhakti* path it is resolved by accepting everything as good, as a gift from the Beloved who is also all goodness. Even suffering is good for the *bhakta*, as there is only goodness in the world. This is the advaita of the *bhakti-mārga*, removing all duality of good and evil by referring everything to God who is all goodness. Whether everything is rejected as evil or everything is accepted as good, in either case we are beyond all duality and tension.

But while the two *mārgas* are different, they are also related. If *bhakti* needs knowledge, *jñāna* too has to begin with *bhakti* or devotion to the teacher. In fact we may go further and say that *bhakti* is necessary in every spiritual discipline, even in those in which God is not explicitly accepted. In Jainism and Buddhism, at least *bhakti* to the teacher is necessary. *Bhakti* creates receptivity and is a sign of earnestness which is necessary everywhere. *Bhakti* is necessary not only before knowledge but also after that. If the mind is all the time attuned to the transcendent unity then there is no problem. But if and when it comes to a lower plane where there is difference and plurality, it is *bhakti* alone that can give spiritual nourishment and nutrition to the mind; one can engage in nothing else. One likes to hear only of God and talk only of God. So for me there is no conflict betwen *bhakti* and *jñāna*.

15
Logic and Reality

R. R. VERMA

This paper contains one argument and one suggestion. The argument, given in the first section, is to the effect that logical laws cannot legitimately be regarded as analytic.[1] The suggestion is that there is some kind of connection between logic and reality.[2] What kind of connection this is, is explored in the second section. The remarks in this section are mainly based on observations of elementary logic, although it is hoped that they are of sufficient generality to be extendable to higher logic too. The plausibility of these remarks will depend not so much on proofs as on their utility in satisfactorily solving the much discussed riddle of the relationship between logic and reality.

I

The question whether logical laws are analytic or not, as well as its rival answers, are too well known to need any exposition. Now-a-days, when the logical positivistic theory of logical laws still enjoys a massive support to the extent of making it almost uncontroversial, the claim of the non-analyticity of logical laws may seem outdated. But it seems that both the parties to this issue, claiming analyticity or syntheticity for logical laws, have been confused on some points, after removing which many of their arguments lose their point.

The major confusion in this respect has been between two different concepts or varieties of analyticity: structural or formal and epistemological. In fact, this distinction is never drawn by either disputant. But if we carefully look into the definitions of analyticity accepted by both the parties, we will find that they do not specify the same single concept, but two subtly different concepts. As a structural property, 'analyticity' signifies a certain conceptual relationship, a certain form or arrangement of terms in a proposition. By itself, no propositional structure signifies any modality or truth-value of a propositon. That is, no specific structure, by itself, justifies any proposition's modality or truth-value; the question 'why should a proposition of a certain form always have a certain particular modality or truth-value?' can always be raised significantly. This means that the question of a sentence's structure can be decided independently of the question of its justification. Likewise, no particular form of a sentence connotes anything regarding its cognitive richness, factuality, etc., because these latter questions concern the subject matter of a sentence, whereas the form concerns only arrangements and interconnections between terms used in a sentence. The epistemological notion of analyticity specifies a certain method of justification, and thus has a reference to the truth-value or modality of the proposition to which it is to be applied. In this case, analyticity may imply some feature regarding factuality and cognitive richness, etc.

Definitions of analyticity in terms of self-contradictory denial (when 'self-contradiction' itself is explained by some formal properties only), having the same form as that of a logical law and the like, present only structural notions of analyticity. So, a sentence's satisfying them does not guarantee that the other connotations, which are usually indiscriminately associated with analyticity, will also be applied to that sentence. Logical laws are analytic in the formal sense because they have the structure they have, because their denials are self-contradictory (in the formal sense of contradiction), and because they contain no descriptive term essentially. But unless one is obliterating the above-mentioned distinction, this admission does not commit one to accepting other positivistic characterisations (e.g., non-factuality, triviality, linguistic conventionality, etc.) of logical laws. Actually it is analyticity in the second sense (epistemological) which is given utmost importance in issues like the present one. And the supposed victory of positivistic analytic theory lies in showing that logical laws are analytic in *this* sense. But it seems that all attempts to show this have only failed. The standard definition of analyticity in an epistemological sense says that a sentence is analytic if it is true solely by virtue of logic. Clearly, calling a sentence analytic in this sense is assuming the truth of logical laws, and so logical laws themselves cannot be analytic in the same sense. Because calling logical laws analytic in this sense will mean that they are true by virtue of themselves,[3] which is the same as saying that they are 'self-evident'—a notion despised by logical positivists and analytic philosophers in general, and to avoid which was the main aim of the analytic theory of logical laws.

Now, the main reason for calling the logical laws non-factual has been their assumed analyticity, and if the foregoing points have been correct it will be clear that only the epistemological analyticity can ensure non-factuality. In fact, the only significant sense in which non-factuality may be necessarily correlated with analyticity is where epistemological analyticity is defined. But since logical laws (at least the most fundamental ones) cannot be epistemologically analytic, the strongest reason (perhaps the only one available in the current literature) for maintaining complete irrelevance between logic and reality will lose its point.

II

To come now to a positive account of logical laws. It seems that logical laws can be regarded as governing or introducing some logical operations. If it is kept in mind that an implicit definition is no sure mark of analyticity (or, rather, that it is controversial whether implicit definitions are themselves analytic or are a source of the analyticity of some other propositions), then we may also say that logical laws implicitly define some logical operations. A logical law 'introduces' or 'governs' a logical constant or operation in a way very much similar to that in which a theory introduces its concepts, with the difference that the rules of interpretation give theoretical constructs operational meanings, which is not the case with logical constants or operations.

Very generally and roughly speaking, logical operations are certain ways of handling and constructing concepts and sentences. They may be of various types. Those introduced by the so-called 'laws of thought' (henceforth to be called 'basic logical laws') are of a different sort from those governed by the other logical laws. The former are not directly governed or introduced by the non-basic logical laws, but they are throughout used in them in the manner indicated or prescribed by the basic logical laws. Thus, the basic logical laws present a skeleton or framework within which the rest of the logical system moves.[4] According to the hypothesis being offered here, the logical operations of non-basic laws concern some interconnections of concepts or sentences, having more indirect connections with reality. But the basic laws govern the operations which are in the relation of co-determination and correlation with the system of truth-values to be accepted and followed in the logical system. The basic laws of traditional logic, for example, determine the two-valued system of truth-values, the values being 'truth' and 'falsity'. Similar laws of another system will determine another truth-value system with different truth-values.[5] In every case, the system will have some laws determining the system of truth-values which the whole system will be adopting. And it is these laws which will be most basic in the system.

Now, ascribing a truth-value to a sentence (at least to an empirical one) is connecting it in some way or the other with reality, whatever that truth-value may be. If we say that the sentence 'x is red' is true, we mean to say that the concept of redness correctly applies to x. If, instead of some truth-value of the two-valued system, we ascribe a truth-value of some other system to the sentence 'x is red', then the metalinguistic sentence ascribing that truth-value will be interpreted differently. Or, rather, with the adoption of the new value-system, our ways of formulating the very object language sentences will change. Then the fact which we wish to describe by the sentence 'x is red' will be described by a different sort of sentence, although the terms 'x' and 'red' will basically be the same. This means that every truth-value system determines certain ways of using concepts for reality. Thus, we may say that the basic logical operations which are here regarded as being co-determinants and correlatives of a system of truth-values, are certain ways of dealing with reality, or of applying the existing concepts to reality. Somewhat loosely speaking, we may say that they determine the fundamental ways of our commitment to reality. In this sense the operations of non-basic laws may be regarded as belonging to a higher order than those of basic laws, and therefore the former are far more removed from reality than the latter are.

To explain the point let us refer to a distinction made elsewhere.[6] This is the distinction of 'a concept-as-such' ('initial' or 'unoperated concept') and 'a concept on which some logical operation has been applied' ('modified' or 'operated concept'). A logical operation on a concept may indirectly determine another concept on which again some logical operation may be applied. This is one way of complicating concepts. For example, the concept 'red', when in no way applied to any object (neither affirmed nor denied, for example), is unoperated. In conceptual analyses, reflections, etc., we usually have only unoperated concepts, because there we do not apply them to reality in any manner; we only scrutinise their form or content. But as logical operations can be applied to a concept any number of times, an operated concept may in its turn be treated like an unoperated concept. And so, by divesting it of its applicative claim,[7] it also can be made an object of reflection as an unoperated concept is. Thus, 'non-redness' may be made an object of conceptual reflection without raising any question of its correlation with reality.

The direct result of operating upon a concept by a basic logical operation is a proposition. In fact, every proposition seems to need at least one operated concept of this variety. Every proposition has one or the other truth-value, no matter in which system of truth-values one treats it. And if the previous points have any plausibility, a truth-value can be assigned to a proposition only if some basic logical operation is incorporated in it. To put the point in another way, the basic logical operations are, in a sense, relational because they always need something else besides the concepts on which they are to be applied. More precisely, when such an operation is used on a concept, it is used *for* something. When we affirm the concept 'red', we affirm it *of* something, say x, and the result is the proposition 'x is red'. The same is the case for denial. In every sentence we say something by one or the other *sort* of affirmation or denial. These ways of affirmation and denial are logical operations of the variety under consideration. So, without any logical operation, we cannot have a proposition 'p', but only what is representable as 'that p', which may perhaps be treated not as a proposition but as a complicated concept.

Within the framework of the foregoing proposals, it seems that the two fundamental logical operations governed by the basic logical laws of the traditional two-valued logic are unqualified affirmation and denial, or unqualified position and negation (henceforth to be called simply affirmation and denial, or position and negation). Positing or negating a concept of something is, in a way, connecting that concept with that thing. Whenever we talk of reality, we use concepts, and talking of reality consists in applying those concepts to it in certain ways. Affirmation and denial, as determined in the traditional system, are the fundamental ways of doing this if we follow this system. Other laws introduce operations of a different variety. For example, laws of *modus ponens* and disjunctive syllogism partially determine the nature and function of the connectives 'implication' and 'disjunction' respectively. The substitution rules or the rules of equivalence specify some principles of interchangeability between certain forms of sentences or co-implications between them. In all these cases what is directly determined is some relationship between certain types of sentences, which is something different from what the basic laws determine. Yet, even these non-basic laws function within the framework sketched by the basic laws in the sense that they assume that any sentences to be brought under the relationships specified by them as well as the propositions or sentences resulting from these relationship are to be treated in accordance with the basic logical laws. The truth-values correlated with 'affirmation' and 'denial' are traditional 'truth' and 'falsity'. The basic laws specify their relationship and present this dyad as an exclusive and exhaustive value-system for all propositions. So, if we comply with these laws, our questions about a proposition's truth-value, and our decisions about them, will have to be in terms of truth and falsity alone. The non-basic laws of the traditional system assume that every proposition put under them will have either of the two truth-values—'true' or 'false'. The rule of *modus tollens*, for example, says that for any two propositions p and q, if it is true that p implies q, and q is false, then p also is false. This rule will obviously be interpreted in a different way if we are not using the values of truth and falsity, but some other system of truth-values. Likewise, the law of double negation is interpreted in the traditional system as saying that the proposition 'p is true' is equivalent to the proposition 'it is false that p is false'. Using 'p_T' for 'p is true' and 'p_F' for 'p is false', it is representable as '$p_T \equiv P_{FF}$'. But suppose that we use a three-valued system of 'determinate truth' (D_T), 'determinate falsity' (D_F) and, indeterminate truth' (I_T). Then just replacing 'false' by 'definitely false' and 'true' by 'definitely true' in the rule will yield something false, viz., '$P_D \equiv P_{DF\ DF}$'.

Now, as has already been opined, the basic logical operations are some fundamental and most general ways of using our concepts (the so-called descriptive part of our language) to deal with reality, of applying concepts on reality, or of describing or representing reality in a propositional, cognitive form. In determining such operations, basic logical laws determine the most fundamental ways of conceiving and understanding anything. And in doing this, they present the most fundamental and most general perspectives of viewing reality. They provide us with the general patterns in which we can sensibly formulate questions and answers about anything. If we use the traditional system of logic, the possible categories, with respect to the concept of redness for example, by which we can conceive or describe an object, will be only two: being red (non-non-red or red-posited), and not being red (non-red or red-negated). The possible propositions will similarly be of only two forms: 'x is red' and 'x is not red'. Possible questions also will have only two forms—'Is x red?' and 'Is x not red?' —which can have corresponding answers in the propositional forms just cited. In general, traditional logic leaves only two alternatives or perspectives to think of any object x—'x as-*is*-of-a-sort' and 'x as *is not*-of-a-sort'. Any other alternative is impossible to adopt; it is just out of the question in this system. In some other system the position might be different. The previously mentioned three-valued logic leaves three alternatives to think of any object. In the above-mentioned example, the three categories will be: 'definitely red', 'definitely non-red' and 'indefinitely red'.

It is in this sense that a logical system seems to be determining the most comprehensive and general categorisation of reality, perspectives of viewing reality, or forms of understanding anything. This system of categorisation or perspectives is so general as to provide a bare outline in which our whole thinking may move. That is why the principles governing and introducing it seem to be completely trivial and also absolutely irrelevant to reality. What usually seems to be informative and relevant to reality is what can be an answer to a sensibly framed question, and thus complies with the conditions of sensible answers, without itself being about these conditions. That is, whatever strikes us as informative and concerned with reality, presupposes some framework of sensible questioning or answering, thinking or understanding. And, thus, it goes further than that framework itself. Consequently, what specifies this very framework does not strike us as having anything to do with reality.

But, really, it seems as though logical laws (basic ones) are not as unconcerned with reality as they are usually taken to be. They are, of course, not concerned with reality in the manner advocated by the rationalist metaphysicians. If the previous remarks have any credibility, it is clear that logical laws do not describe or record any features of reality, however general they may be. That is why it seems correct to say that a logical law can never be falsified by any fact, that it can only be made inapplicable, if at all. That is, there are no recalcitrant facts for logical laws in the ordinary sense. But nor are they completely conventional or arbitrary. For their acceptance, their plausibility, a consideration of reality is relevant. What type of reality we are presented with, what type of situations we have to deal with, does affect our choice of a logical system. For example, if we have to deal with a border-line case for a vague predicate, the law of excluded middle, on ordinary interpretation, may become inapplicable, and the previously mentioned three-valued logic may prove to be more useful. True, that the direct concern of a logical law even in these cases is not the nature of fact itself (for example, the colour shade of an individual x, when the vague predicate in question is a colour predicate and the border-line case is x). It may be said that its direct concern is the relation between the available concepts and reality (here, facts of x-type). But as one relatum of this relation is reality, it cannot be completely irrelevant and unaccountable for logical laws. Had there been no possibility of the type of facts which we call boundary-line facts, a change in our logical system would have been needless. Of course, another part of the same story will be that had there been no vague predicates (or concepts), a change in the logical system would not have been required. But vagueness of a concept itself is a matter of its relationship with reality. So, in the second part of the story, we are not escaping reference to reality. Moreover, these two parts are the two alternatives of avoiding change in our logical system. Why, as a rule, only the second alternative should be taken into account while judging the plausibility of a logical system, is not clear. A choice of this rule can either be a pragmatically better or an arbitrary decision, which does not seem to affect the theoretical relevance between logic and reality.

Notes

1. This view, which puts the author in basic opposition to the logical positivists, is elaborately argued in 'Logic and Ontology', *The Visva Bharati Journal of Philosophy*, August 71, V, No. 2.

2. 'Logic and Ontology' contained a query also, as to whether logic and ontology may not be viewed as touching each other at their cores, doing almost the same job of 'introducing' or defining the notion of 'being' and then independently building up their huge, otherwise very much different, systems. This query, put as a suggestion, was very much in sympathy with Quine's view that, as reflected in their theories of quantification, the two-valued logic and the intuitionistic constructivists' logic present two different concepts of existence (W.V. Quine, *Philosophy of Logic*, Prentice-Hall, 1970, pp. 87-9). Now, the author's agreements with Quine have weakened and differences widened, and the above-mentioned suggestion also has become more questionable. Yet the author is inclined to think that there is some kind of connection between logic and reality.

3. This sort of argument is given by Arthur Pap also in his *Semantics and Necessary Truth*. But he does not draw the distinction drawn here, and thus the conflict between the two equally legitimate convictions, that the logical laws are analytic, and that they are not analytic, leaves one no less confused.

4. This point is exemplified on the following pages.

5. Henceforth the impression that the author agrees with the covnentionalists in accepting genuine alternatives to a two-valued system might be given. But in fact there is no total agreement with them on this point. In 'Vagueness and the Principle of Excluded Middle' (*Mind*, January 1970) the author has argued that there is nothing like *the* law of excluded middle; there can be *a* law of excluded middle. That is, the usually accepted law of excluded middle is actually ambiguous, and its subtly different interpretations are never clearly recognised. On one interpretation (narrower) it can have genuine alternatives; on the other (wider) interpretation the possibility of its having alternatives does not seem to be genuine. These remarks can be generalised so as to be applicable to all the basic laws. In the remaining part of the paper whenever reference to the law of excluded middle or two-valued logic is made, it is the narrower interpretation which is intended.

6. 'Vagueness and the Principle of Excluded Middle', *Mind*, January 1970.

7. 'Applicative claim' means a claim of some sort of application to or relation with some object.

Notes on Contributors

S.S. Barlingay is Professor and Head of the Department of Philosophy, Poona University. Educated at Nagpur and Oxford, Dr. Barlingay was Reader in the Department of Philosophy, Delhi University, for many years and was a Professor at Zagreb University (1962–64). Besides having published a large number of articles, Dr. Barlingay has three books to his credit including *Modern Introduction to Indian Logic*.

Kalidas Bhattacharya is retired Professor of Philosophy, residing at Visva-Bharati University. He began his academic career as a Lecturer in Vidyasagar College, Calcutta, after which he taught in Calcutta University and was Professor of Indian Philosophy at Sanskrit College, Calcutta. He joined the Centre of Advanced Study in Philosophy, Visva-Bharati University, in 1957, was its Director for many years and has also served as Vice-Chancellor of the University (1966–70). Dr. Bhattacharya has written a large number of books including *Alternative Standpoints in Philosophy*, *Object*, *Content and Relation*, *Philosophy*, *Logic and Language* and *Presupposition of Science and Philosophy*.

Sibajiban Bhattacharya is Senior Professor in the Department of Philosophy, Burdwan University. Dr. Bhattacharya has been a Professor at the Centre of Advanced Study in Philosophy, Visva-Bharati University, and Professor and Head of the Department of Philosophy, Burdwan University. He has also been a Visiting Fellow at the Indian Institute of Advanced Study, Simla (1974–75).

C.T.K. Chari is Honorary Professor in the Department of Philosophy and Psychology, Madras Christian College. Dr. Chari has had a wide and varied career and has been Principal Miller Endowment Lecturer, Avinashilingam Chettiar Endowment Lecturer and Indian Philosophical Congress Endowment Lecturer. He has written and edited a large number of books—including *Philosophy in the Mid-Century, Philosophy, Religion and the Coming World Civilization, Modern Logic: Its Relevance to Philosophy, Time in Science and Philosophy* and *The Concept of Mind*—besides having contributed articles to many journals throughout the world.

Margaret Chatterji is Reader in the Department of Philosophy, Delhi University. She read Modern Greats at Oxford University where she was an Exhibitioner at Somerville College. Dr. Chatterji has written three books so far—*Our Knowledge of Other Selves, Philosophical Enquiries* and *The Existentialist Outlook*—and has edited *Contemporary Indian Philosophy*. She has also published poetry.

Debiprasad Chattopadhyaya is Minister of Commerce, Government of India. Educated at Calcutta and London, Dr. Chattopadhyaya was Reader in Philosophy, Jadavpur University, and has previously written *Individuals and Societies: A Methodological Enquiry* and *Societies and Cultures*.

N.K. Devaraja is Senior Professor in the Department of Philosophy, Banaras Hindu University. Educated at Banaras, Allahabad and Lucknow universities, Dr. Devaraja joined Lucknow University as a Lecturer, later being promoted to Assistant Professor. He then moved to Banaras Hindu University as Sayaji Rao Gaekwad Professor of Indian Civilization and Culture later serving as the Director of the Centre of Advanced Study in Philosophy there. Dr. Devaraja visited the USA on a UNESCO Grant for Regional Cultural Studies and was General President of the Indian Philosophical Congress (1972) and a UGC Fellow (1972–73). Besides over 40 articles, Dr. Devaraja has written a large number of books including *An Introduction to Śaṅkara's Theory of Knowledge, The Philosophy of Culture, The Mind and Spirit of India* and *Hinduism and the Modern Age*.

G. Misra is Senior Professor and Head, Department of Philosophy, Utkal University. Educated at Patna and London, Dr. Misra started his teaching career as a Lecturer under the Government of Orissa. He was Principal of a Degree College in Orissa till he joined Utkal University as a Professor and Head of the Department of Philosophy. Dr. Misra was General President of the Indian Philosophical Congress (1971) and is Executive President of the All Orissa Philosophy Association. He edits *Bharati* and has written *Analytical Studies in Indian Philosophical Problems* and *Fundamentals of Deductive Logic*.

J.N. Mohanty is Chairman of the Department of Philosophy, Graduate Faculty, New School for Social Research, New York, and Director of the Husserl Archives there. Educated at Cuttack, Calcutta and Gottingen, Dr. Mohanty has variously been Lecturer in Philosophy, Calcutta University, Associate Professor of Indian Philosophy, Sanskrit College, Calcutta, Vivekananda Professor of Philosophy, Burdwan University, Acharya B.N. Seal Professor of Mental and Moral Science, Calcutta University, and George Lynn Cross Professor of Philosophy, University of Oklahoma. He has published five books so far including *Edmund Husserl's Theory of Meaning, Phenomenology and Ontology* and *The Concept of Intentionality*.

Rajendra Prasad is Professor of Philosophy in the Department of Humanities and Social Sciences, IIT, Kanpur. He was a Member of the Indian Delegation to the International Institute of Philosophy (1959), General President of the Indian Philosophical Association (1969) and General President of the Akhil Bharatiya Darsana Parisad (1970). He has contributed a number of papers to various journals and coedited *Proceedings of the International Institute of Philosophy, Bhagawan Das Commemoration Volume* and *Marathi Encyclopaedia of Philosophy*. He is the editor of *Indian Review of Philosophy*.

N.S.S. Raman is Professor of Philosophy and Head of the Department of Philosophy, Banaras Hindu University. Educated at Mysore, Rajasthan, Glasgow and Mainz, he started his teaching career as a Lecturer in Government Mahendra College, Patiala. He then joined the Punjab University as a Lecturer later becoming Reader and was visiting Professor at the University of Mainz (1965). He has previously written a number of articles and a book on Karl Jaspers in German.

Santosh Sengupta is ex-Director of the Centre of Advanced Study in Philosophy, and present Head of the Department of Philosophy, Visva-Bharati University. He obtained his M.A. from Calcutta University and his Ph.D. from London University. Dr. Sengupta is a Member of the American Philosophical Association, and has been a Visiting Professor in the USA (1965–66 and 1971–72). He has published *An Enquiry into the Existence of God, Good Freewill and God, Transcendence, Mystery and Maya* and *Belief, Faith and Knowledge.*

Ramakant Sinari is Professor of Philosophy and Head of the Department of Humanities and Social Sciences, IIT, Bombay. As a Fulbright Scholar, Dr. Sinari did research at the University of Pennsylvania and the State University of New York. He has been Visiting Professor at Elmira College, USA, and has taught at Ruia and SIES Colleges, Bombay University. Dr. Sinari has published two books—*Reason in Existentialism* and *The Structure of Indian Thought*—besides having contributed a large number of research papers to various journals.

R.K. Tripathi is Professor of Philosophy at Banaras Hindu University. Dr. Tripathi has had a wide and varied teaching career. He has been Fellow of the Indian Institute of Philosophy, Amalner, Professor and Head of the Department of Philosophy, K.R. Degree College, Lecturer, Reader and then Professor in the Department of Philosophy, Banaras Hindu University, Professor of Philosophy at Kashi Vidyapith, and Visiting Professor of Philosophy, Brock University, Canada. He has previously published *Spinoza in the Light of Vedanta* and *Problems of Philosophy and Religion.*

R.R. Verma is a Professor in the Department of Philosophy, Lucknow University. She was previously Lecturer and then Reader in the Department. Dr. Verma was a Commonwealth Academic Staff Fellow at the University of Oxford (1973–74) and represented the Indian Humanist Union at the Sixth Congress of the International Humanist and Ethical Union (Amsterdam, 1974).

Index